PEOPLING THE PAMPA

Creole type: man of the people.   Selected by an Argentine.   (From
R. Levillier's "Orígenes argentinos", Buenos Aires, 1912.)

AMERICAN GEOGRAPHICAL SOCIETY
RESEARCH SERIES NO. 16
W. L. G. JOERG, *Editor*

PEOPLING
THE ARGENTINE PAMPA

BY

MARK JEFFERSON

SECOND PRINTING

AMERICAN GEOGRAPHICAL SOCIETY
BROADWAY AT 156TH STREET
NEW YORK
1930

COPYRIGHT, 1926
BY
THE AMERICAN GEOGRAPHICAL SOCIETY
OF NEW YORK

COMMONWEALTH PRESS
WORCESTER, MASS.

CONTENTS

LIST OF ILLUSTRATIONS

PREFACE

These pages were written as a result of a journey made in 1918 on behalf of the American Geographical Society to study modern European colonization in Chile, the Argentine Republic, and Brazil. The report on Chile has already appeared in this series (Recent Colonization in Chile, *Amer. Geogr. Soc. Research Series No. 6*, 1921; with a related study: The Rainfall of Chile, *Research Series No. 7*, 1921) and that on Brazil in the Society's journal (Pictures from Southern Brazil, *Geographical Review*, Vol. 16, 1926, pp. 521–547).

The background of the Argentine study is some familiarity with the Creole life of the interior acquired during a residence there before the immigrants reached Córdoba or Tucumán cities in any numbers, from January, 1884, to November, 1889, the first three years in Córdoba as computer, third and second astronomer in the National Observatory, and the last three as assistant manager and treasurer of the sugar *ingenio* La Providencia near the city of Tucumán. Whatever changes the Argentine interior had at that time experienced from the old-Creole ways had come, not from foreigners immigrant to America, but from the impressions made on Creoles in their visits to Europe.

I had a certain intimacy with two or three delightful Creole families and some familiarity with the language and customs of the country. I have spoken in the text of the contrasts of those times and the present. Whatever characterization I have been able to make of the aspects and effects of newer immigration must rest mainly on that earlier acquaintance with the country; and it is a characterization, a picture that I have tried to draw—a picture of a vigorous infant agricultural society born in the midst of an ancient cattle culture.

There are two great works on the Argentine Republic as a whole: Pierre Denis' "La République Argentine: La mise en valeur du pays", Paris, 1920, and E. W. Schmidt's "Die agrarische Exportwirtschaft Argentiniens: Ihre Enwicklung und Bedeutung", Jena, 1920. From both I have drawn repeatedly as I have needed to shed light on the physiographic or economic conditions of the country.

All references to money, except where otherwise specified, are to Argentine paper currency (m/n, *moneda nacional*), the peso of which is established at 44 per cent of the value of the gold peso (paper peso when at par, 42.45 cents in United States currency; gold peso, 96.48 cents).

The manuscript was completed in March, 1924; through editorial changes some later publications have been taken into account.

Ypsilanti, Michigan, November, 1926

CHAPTER I

THE HISTORICAL AND GEOGRAPHICAL SETTING

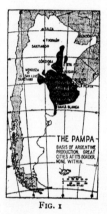

FIG. 1

EUROPEAN capitals have long known the Argentine as the spendthrift of the world. If an American can be made to pay nine francs for a peach, an Argentine, asked nine, will give ten. A billion dollars' worth of goods the Argentine Republic exported in 1920, mainly cattle products and grain.[1] The Argentines do almost half the business of the continent though the other South Americans outnumber them fully seven to one. But where did they get so much money to spend?

This is the land to which so many immigrants have thronged in the last half century that fully half the inhabitants now have new European blood. Herein the Argentine Republic is distinguished from the rest of Spanish America. Elsewhere immigration has been feeble. Elsewhere the people who count are all Creoles, of a very different character from the immigrants. What are these Creoles like? What is the relation of the newcomer in the Argentine Republic to the Creole? And what changes are to come in Argentine society as the Creoles are further outnumbered?

[1] SOUTH AMERICAN COMMERCE IN 1920*
(in United States money)

	Argentine Republic	Rest of South America
Exports	$947,000,000	$1,086,000,000
Imports	$846,000,000	$885,000,000
Number of people	8,000,000	56,000,000

*Calculated from *Statistical Abstract of the United States for 1921*, Bureau of Foreign and Domestic Commerce, Washington, 1922, Table 488, pp. 910–911; *for 1922*, Table 460, pp. 730–731; *Statesman's Year-Book for 1922*, London, 1922.

All through Argentine history the Buenos Aires men[2] have been in contrast to the men of the interior; the Pampa, destined to tillage, against the irrigated valleys that indent the border of the arid Andes. The history has been two-fold. The Argentine Republic has two Fourth's of July, the Twenty-fifth of May and the Ninth of July (veinticinco de mayo and nueve de julio). On the twenty-fifth of May, 1810, the Creoles of Buenos Aires compelled the Spanish city council to relinquish the government to them, the natives. On the ninth of July, 1816, the deputies of the Creole provinces, assembled in the far interior at Tucumán, declared the United Provinces of South America independent of Spain.

INDEPENDENCE AT BUENOS AIRES

The event of 1810 in Buenos Aires was not a revolution. It was hardly a revolt against Spain, for at the moment Spain had ceased to exist as an independent country. Napoleon had overrun it, captured its king, made him abdicate, and put his own brother on the throne. But it was an uprising of the Spanish Creoles, born in Buenos Aires, mostly of pure Spanish blood, against the Spaniards of Spain.

Birth in the New World made these men Creoles. Spanish practice made them ineligible to any public office. For Spanish-born men have always been clear in their minds that the air of the New World made even their own offspring, born out of Spain, of less capacity than native Spaniards. Naturally no love was lost between Creoles and Spaniards, and inevitably the Spaniards had to lose in the contest, since they formed a steadily diminishing percentage of the population.

Four years earlier the Buenos Aires Creoles had inherited from Spain the effects of a war with Great Britain. That was in 1806. Of course the Porteños had no quarrel with the British. Indeed, they were indebted to them as useful smugglers who brought them European wares and took their wool

[2] Porteños, portmen, as contrasted with the uplanders, Arribeños, who are, separately, Cordobeses, Mendocinos, Catamarqueños, Tucumanos, Salteños, and Santiagueños, according to their home provinces.

and hides in exchange in spite of Spanish prohibition. At any rate, Spain having declared war, General Charles Beresford in 1806 landed a small British army that quickly took possession of the town. The few Spanish troops ran away or surrendered before fighting began. Sobremonte, the Spanish viceroy, could do nothing to help and went away to Córdoba to raise militia for the defense. The British were masters of the city before he was well outside. Any revolt against the invader had to be made by the citizens themselves, and, though late to start, they presently made a revolt so effective that the English had to surrender the city to the Creoles on August 12. They had held it 46 days. A few days later the people of Buenos Aires compelled the Spanish *cabildo* to depose Sobremonte and appoint in his place as viceroy Liniers, the man who had led this reconquest. Usually, of course, viceroys were appointed by the Spanish sovereign, but the sovereign was far away, and Liniers had certainly saved Buenos Aires to Spain. Besides, Liniers was no Creole but a Frenchman, for thirty years in the service of Spain. The king confirmed the appointment in 1808 and made Liniers a field marshall.

The episode of the Reconquest is the pride of the Argentines. School children are well drilled in it—the recapture by its civilian inhabitants of a peaceful city which had been invaded by an enemy at a time when the mother country proved powerless to protect it. The event confirmed the Creoles of Buenos Aires in the consciousness of their native worth. Undoubtedly it stimulated them to insist in 1810 that the Spaniards of the town hand the power over to a new governing body of Creoles.

The Twenty-fifth of May signifies the first victory of Creoles over Spaniards in America. They were, you will notice, Porteño Creoles at the Atlantic border of the Pampa.

INDEPENDENCE IN THE INTERIOR

The declaration of independence of 1816 at upland Tucumán commemorates the close of a six years' struggle with Spain which followed on the events of 1810. The strength of Spain

was in Bolivia (then called Upper Peru) because the precious
silver mines were there, and along that border the struggle
raged. Thus it was at Tucumán, which snuggles under the
last outlier of the Eastern Andes, the 17,000-foot Sierra de
Aconquija, 700 miles from Buenos Aires, that there came
together delegates from Bolivia and every Argentine province,
except Santa Fe and the mesopotamian Entre Ríos and Corrientes, and voted that the "United Provinces of South
America wish to break the rude bonds that used to bind them
to the king of Spain, recover their rights, invest themselves
with the high character of a free and independent nation, having in fact and right full and ample power to give their government the form that justice may demand."

This Ninth of July announced the close of the Spanish
régime in South America. It is characteristic of the civilization of the far interior Creoles that three days later the Congress of Tucumán listened sympathetically to a motion to give
the government of the new nation the form of "a limited
monarchy under the dynasty of the Incas." It did not so vote,
and Buenos Aires derided the plan; but a little later the
patriot general Belgrano, who had held off the Spanish forces
in the northwest with a long series of little victories and costly
defeats that mainly served well the patriot cause, publicly
proclaimed to the army and to the people of Bolivia the restoration of Inca rule!

"The [South] American revolution . . . ," says Mitre,[3]
"was not only an insurrection of the Spanish-American colonies
against their mother country but principally of the Creole race
against the Spanish race. The Creole race, which called itself
American, in its hatred confused the old *conquistadores* with
the oppressors and exploiters of the country in colonial times
and, in throwing off all allegiance, threw off allegiance to the
Spanish blood that flowed in its veins and, in making common
cause with the aborigines, made their old grievances its own,

[3] Bartolomé Mitre: Historia de Belgrano y de la independencia argentina (2
vols., Buenos Aires, 1887), Vol. 2, p. 418.

as if it were itself descended directly from the monarchs and caciques who were tyrannizing over the New World before the Spaniards came. This sentiment was more pronounced in countries where native and mixed population prevailed, as in Mexico or Peru. In the United Provinces of the River Plate and in Chile, where the mass of the population in which power rested was made up of Creoles, this sentiment, the product of reasoning in the educated classes, had some currency among the people too."

That any Creoles thought through the consequences of reverting to the rule of the barbarous Incas is unlikely. The thing was inconceivable, quite as much for the upland Creoles as for Buenos Aires men. Very likely the most that was hoped of the scheme was to win a continuance of Indian and half-breed support against the Spaniards. Up there the full-blooded Indians and half-breeds had been of great help to the revolution. They made up the inhabitants of the little republics (*republiquetas*) of eastern Bolivia which annoyed the Spaniards by gnatlike outbreaks, always repressed but forever renewed.

CREOLES AND THE PROPORTION OF INDIAN BLOOD

The Creoles of the northwest had a good deal of Indian blood, for here we are at the very edge of the Conquest, that amazing exploit which flashed Spanish power over the whole upland of the Central Andes in a few brief years. The many children of the *conquistadores* had Indian mothers. Almost no women came from Spain in those early days. The hardships were too great, and the room in the ships was wanted for fighting men. So it came to pass that about the purest Spanish descent possible among the Creoles of the interior acknowledged this Indian great-grandmother in the family. That was the minimum of native blood. It is a far cry back to those days. The Indian women of later days have been no princesses, for the Indians of the Conquest, unless lifted into the dominant class by union with Spaniards, were all depressed

into a servile caste, degraded and despised. The presence of
this despised caste had been and is today the great curse of
Latin America. No advantage of cheap laborers and servants
can compensate for the social and moral disaster of the widespread presence of millions of lower-class women whose unchastity is assumed. You may assume with that the general
unchastity of boys of all classes from their teens and a too
common disregard of marital ties by most classes of men. These
Indian and half-breed women do not appear to be unhappy.
They are ignorant, and no work is open to them but household
service. If they could be given a taste of a decent standard
of life and occupations that would enable them to support
themselves at that standard, it would be the most-to-be-
desired step in progress for both sexes and all classes in the
continent. What a glorious opportunity for the Creole women
of the upper class who have been brought up behind moral
bars which are visibly exemplified by the iron gratings at their
windows and whose personal lives are above reproach! But
they are unaccustomed to initiate movements of any sort.

Descent from the post-Conquest Indians is no matter to
boast of. The Creole who mentions his Indian blood does not
mean post-Conquest Indians. *Mestizo* (half-breed) is the
word commonly applied by the Creoles to the cross between
whites and modern Indians. I never heard anyone apply it to
himself. All the Creole crossing with high-caste Indians was
of the Andine countries of the Conquest. Ingenieros asserts[4]
that at the end of the colonial epoch the "Creoles of Ecuador
were almost aboriginals, and the Creoles of Uruguay were
almost Europeans."

A Spanish traveler of 1795 estimates the proportion of
people of Indian blood in the Argentine Republic as 36 per
cent near the sea, 67 in Córdoba Province, 74 in Tucumán, and
95 at Jujuy on the Bolivian border.[5] Conversational usage
appears to me to make social distinctions between the words

[4] José Ingenieros: Sociología argentina, Buenos Aires, 1918, p. 43.
[5] Roberto Levillier: Orígenes argentinos: La formación de un gran pueblo,
Paris and Buenos Aires, 1912, pp. 115–116.

FIG. 4 (above)—Women of predominantly Indian blood called *chinas* (masc. *chino*), belonging to the servant class, carrying water in Standard Oil tins at the hydrant, outskirts of Córdoba.

FIG. 5 (below)—Family of *chinos* in the mountains of Córdoba at Cruz del Eje. Such ranchos as this, with walls of unbaked bricks and roof of thatch, are the ordinary homes of the poor.

Fig. 2 (left).—Dr. Lucas Allende of Córdoba, lawyer and gentleman. Creole of the old Creoles, of a family dating back to the Peruvian conquest. Of limited means and refusing political influence, he was highly honored even by those who could not use him.

Fig. 3 (right).—Don Eusebio Agüero, Creole business man of old-time Córdoba. Having amassed a moderate fortune by assiduity and attention to details, he enjoyed the esteem of all who knew him. Foreigners especially pointed to him as a Creole whose word was enough.

rather than racial ones, the *mestizos* and Indians making up a proletariat. Its members are called *chinos* (Figs. 4 and 5), the word *mestizo* being distinctly bookish. There is indeed no prejudice against color in South America but much against class. Talent might conceivably raise an Indian to any position in society, but it is not likely to. Actually the richer, better-dressed classes of natives count as Creoles. Below them are half-breeds (*chinos*) and Indians. The most distinctive mark of caste in this *chino* class is its acceptance of inferiority, a trait familiar enough in the peasants of many parts of Europe but a continual surprise to a North American. These people believe, or appear to believe, that they are of less account than others!

BUENOS AIRES CREOLE AT HEART

Buenos Aires so dominates everything in the republic today that it is difficult for the visitor to realize the existence of an older Argentine culture of the interior provinces that really controls the national life and thought even in the capital city. The interior is Creole at the surface as well as at heart. But Buenos Aires is European on the surface and proud of it. It is rather loath to admit that it is really Creole at heart; and the visitor who knows only Buenos Aires may fail to perceive some of the mainsprings of national feeling and action. The Porteños carry their desire to be regarded as European to the extreme of self-consciousness—most perceptibly, of course, in matters of external manners and dress.

An illustration of this shyness of anything that might be called native customs is in the use of the yerba mate, Paraguayan tea, a remarkable beverage widely used in the country.[6] Neither chocolate, tea, nor coffee has its good qualities. This is not merely the opinion of the Creole masses but of many foreign observers who have lived in the country long enough to give it a fair trial. Without any injurious effect

[6] A. B. Martinez and Maurice Lewandowski: The Argentine in the Twentieth Century, transl. by Bernard Miall from the French of the 3rd edit., New York, [1915], pp. 197–198.

on stomach or nerves, it stimulates and refreshes. It has no intoxicating effect whatever and is very cheap. After a hard day's ride in heat and dust nothing can equal the restorative power of a gourd of mate. In the army it is regarded as indispensable. But the open use of mate has been relegated to the lower classes by the unpleasant custom of passing from mouth to mouth the gourd and tube through which it is sucked. The powdered leaf and twigs of the yerba are placed in a small gourd (*mate*) and boiling water poured on. It is immediately ready for drinking and is sucked through a silver tube with a perforated ball on the end, which serves to strain it. Boiling water is added again and again to the same grounds. Daireaux[7] thinks the fifth infusion has the best flavor; and this may be the reason why when it is prepared and served in a cup like tea it finds little acceptance. In better Creole families the promiscuous use of the same *bombilla* (tube) is doubtless avoided. Most Porteños would give you the impression that mate drinking is unknown in Buenos Aires. As a matter of fact it is consumed in quantities. You can buy yerba and the gourds in which it is prepared everywhere, but the use is concealed and hidden by those who have any pretense to style or fashion. Among the lower classes the promiscuous use of the same gourd and *bombilla* is not objected to. With them its popularity lasts and increases, as the growing consumption of yerba attests. It may be called the Creole beverage.

Interior Argentines Came by Way of the Pacific

Unlike the interior Creoles the Porteños came by way of the Atlantic. The route by which Mendoza, Córdoba, and Tucumán had been settled, over the Andes from the Pacific, was an impossible one. The *conquistadores* rather specialized in doing impossible things. The Spanish government long attempted to make the Andine route the only access to the

[7] Émile Daireaux: La vie et les moeurs à la Plata (2 vols., Paris, 1888), Vol. 2, p. 400.

country, completely forbidding the direct Atlantic voyage from Spain. If the people of Buenos Aires had hides to sell they were supposed to carry them overland to Lima, ship them to Panamá, take them across the isthmus, and ship them again to Spain! Barrels of Spanish wine they were welcome to bring back by the same route if they could. Smuggling was inevitable. Smuggling meant bringing goods by the Atlantic to Buenos Aires and taking Creole hides and wool in exchange. Dutch and English smugglers throve. To Buenos Aires men that was simply business; it was no smuggling in their eyes. Later a few Spanish ships—no foreign ones—were allowed to make direct journeys between the River Plate and Spain. But the permission of the inefficient Spanish government was of little importance in comparison with the city's need of foreign wares. What it amounted to in the end was that Spanish ships paid duty on the wares they brought and the foreigners brought theirs in free. Proof is that the duties amounted to but a million pesos a year till Cisneros (1810) was compelled by the *estancieros* to open the port to foreigners, when they leaped at once to five millions!

Not merely did unauthorized, i. e. non-Spanish, ships frequent Buenos Aires, but many of the forbidden foreigners settled in the city. This is evidenced by the abundant foreign names in Buenos Aires families, though foreign or even Spanish immigration was strictly forbidden. Moreover, the physical type of the Porteño is itself much to the point. The Creole of Buenos Aires is taller and less swarthy than the uplander. The men of the interior are noticeably small and dark. Before the epoch of the new immigration, while Indian raids on the Pampa made travel dangerous between Buenos Aires and the interior, the upper classes of the interior intermarried to so great an extent as to affect their physique. A Creole of Córdoba in 1884 had to carry his hat in his hand on the frequented streets at the hour when people were abroad, as he was constantly bowing to some relative. There the names were almost exclusively Spanish.

In Buenos Aires fourteen of the twenty wards had a census taken in 1810 when the whole city had 45,000 inhabitants. It showed 1570 Spaniards, 198 Portuguese, 124 English, 61 Italians, 13 French, and 292 unclassified Europeans—in all 5 per cent of the people foreign.[8] The large representation of Englishmen in comparison with present figures[9] was a result of the frequent visits of English ships. There was little chance of the foreigner of the laboring class getting into Buenos Aires in those days. Like all stupid governments the Spaniards were never easy in their consciences except when they were saying no.

THE PAMPA

The Pampa lies between Buenos Aires and the mountains of Córdoba (see Fig. 1). It extends on a very gentle grade from the sea to the Andes, about 700 miles. Actually rising three or four feet to a mile, it looks perfectly flat (Fig. 6). Its material is a fine compacted dust; the geologist calls it loess. In the cliffs forming the walls of gullies it is often seen 50 or 60 feet deep without a single pebble, as in the *barranca* of the Paraná in Figure 20. It was undoubtedly brought into place by the wind and in the drier western parts still moves freely. Every summer thunderstorm in the open country about Córdoba begins with a wind squall that sweeps enormous quantities of dust into the air until the rain begins. At such times the sun is completely hidden in the cloud of dust, and you cannot see the head of the horse on which you ride. A famous "dust storm" was that of January 12, 1894, with the wind at 88 miles an hour.[10] Figure 1 shows the Pampa as a solid black area.[11] Beyond the border of that area northward

[8] J. A. Alsina: La inmigración europea en la República Argentina, 3rd edit., Buenos Aires, 1898, p. 16. The 1914 census showed 49 per cent foreign (Tercer censo nacional, 1914, Vol. 2: Población, Buenos Aires, 1916, p. 3).

[9] 9195 out of a total population of 1,575,814 (*ibid.*, Vol. 2, p. 148), i. e. 0.6 per cent as against 3 per cent in 1810.

[10] W. G. Davis: Climate of the Argentine Republic, Dept. of Agric., Buenos Aires, 1910, p. 46.

[11] The boundary of the Pampa on Figs. 1 and 8 and Pl. I is after Pierre Denis: La République Argentine: La mise en valeur du pays, Paris, 1920, Pl. 1 and pp. 160–162 (Engl. transl., London and New York, 1922, Map I and pp. 162–163).

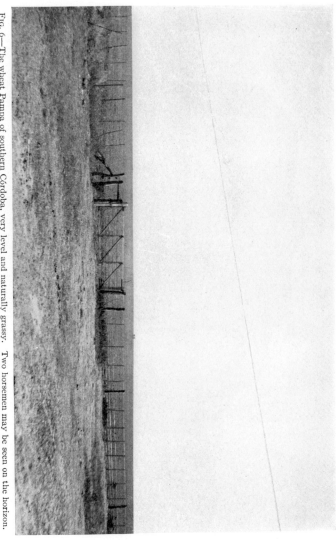

FIG. 6—The wheat Pampa of southern Córdoba, very level and naturally grassy. Two horsemen may be seen on the horizon.

Fig. 7—The *monte* in northern Córdoba. This is the sort of scrub, rising to occasional low trees, that surrounds the Pampa. Between the bushes and trees there is much bare ground, with a very thin wiry grass.

and southward, but still more westward, comes the *monte*—
scrub of smaller *chañar* bushes and occasional larger algarrobo
trees, very well shown in Figure 7 from northern Córdoba.
This *monte* comes in as the land gets drier westward along a belt
having from 18 inches of annual rainfall near Bahía Blanca to
30 in northern Santiago del Estero Province (Fig. 37). It
consists of drought-resisting shrubs and trees with little leaf,
tough bark, and abundant spines. Between them the ground
shows bare for feet at a stretch and is baked hard and firm by
the sun. Much of the same bare ground prevails in the Sierra
de Córdoba, whose southern end and the Sierra de San Luis,
southwest of it, are bare unmitigated dirt and rock, like the
Eastern Andes of Mendoza Province, a vast reservoir from
which the winds draw freely. Why the algarrobo, quebracho,
and *caldén*, all trees, should grow on the drier ground and not
on the grassy, moister pampa is not easy to see, especially as
they also occur along the moist river valleys. Darwin suggested that the violent winds might prevent the growth of
trees on the Pampa, but the eucalyptus is found to do excel-
lently everywhere without watering.

The two tongues of *monte* along the Tercero and Quinto have
now suffered, of course, from man's need of firewood. Souiyer
de Souillac noted this along the Carcarañá near the boundary
of Santa Fe in 1784. "Both shores are always covered with
algarrobos, willows, and *chañar* shrubs."[12] The same author
says the heights around Córdoba were at that time crowned
with dense old groves, but these, according to my own observations, had given place to *chañar* thickets in 1884. Now the
irrigation works from the dam at Córdoba (Fig. 9) have made
it possible to grow sizable willows there. Figure 8, which indicates every stream of running water, shows how scarce
streams are on the northern Pampa. The slopes of the Sierra
de Córdoba in the northwest shed a great number of brooks
toward the plain, usually to be absorbed within a mile or two.
The larger streams along the eastern front are called First,

[12] R. J. Cárcano: Historia de los medios de communicación y transporte en
República Argentina (2 vols., Buenos Aires, 1883), Vol. 2, p. 94.

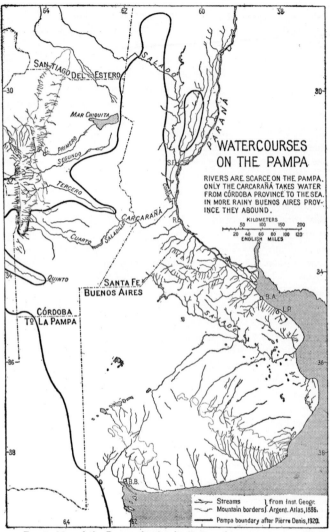

Fig. 8—Map of the Pampa showing its limits and its watercourses. Scale, 1:9,200,000.

Second, etc.—in Spanish, Primero, Segundo, Tercero, Cuarto, and Quinto—of which only the Tercero and, in flood times, the Cuarto, united with the Carcarañá, flow into the Paraná at the same point where the Coronda sheds some of the waters of the Salado. In the southeast, where the rainfall is upwards of 35 inches (Fig. 37), running streams are more frequent. On the rest of the Pampa they are quite unknown, as the water sinks into the almost level soil without running off. In Santa Fe Province wells find abundant water at 30 to 60 feet, often tasting strongly of salts but healthful. At San Francisco, where the salt taste of the water is called an "*enormidad*," cistern water is used. Artesian waters are met in the western part of the province on the railway line between Rosario and Córdoba.

Although the numbered streams from the Sierra de Córdoba flow into more humid country as they go eastward they all diminish in volume downstream. The Primero and Segundo flow—when they have water enough—into the Mar Chiquita, which is strongly salt, as if their waters did not sink into the ground but evaporated into the air. The Río Cuarto does the same thing in the lagoon in its lower middle course, the stream that seems to continue its course to the Carcarañá being stagnant and salt tasting, as indicated by its name, Saladillo. The waters of the Salado at Santa Fe are "good," which means not too salt to drink. The old route from Peru by Córdoba to the Río Tercero and the Carcarañá to Buenos Aires was fixed by occurrence of water all along the way. The northern, streamless Pampa of Santa Fe is preëminently colonist ground, because it was less valuable for cattle than the better-watered Pampa of Buenos Aires and so might be given to the foreigners.[13]

[13] Although Buenos Aires Province occupies the bulk of the Pampa as outlined on the maps, Figs. 1 and 8, that province is not discussed in detail in the present book. That is because its dominant system of land tenure is in the form of *latifundia* devoted mainly to cattle raising and there has hence been little true agricultural colonization in the form of small farms owned by those who work them. What little colonization there has been of this type is dealt with in the chapter on land laws and settlement in Buenos Aires Province in Karl Kaerger: Landwirtschaft und Kolonisation im Spanischen Amerika (2 vols., Leipzig, 1901), Vol. 1, pp. 460–526.

If you had turned your eyes westward from the outskirts of Buenos Aires about a hundred years ago you would have seen "immediately back of the city a broad level steppe that was enlivened by innumerable herds of cattle and horses. In the immediate neighborhood were some little truck and vegetable farms which were mostly managed by less well-to-do Spaniards with the help of negro slaves. Farther back were enormous horse and cattle ranches belonging to Spanish land owners. But the number of these ranches diminished with the distance from the Port. Soon we should come to the end of them, and the land would become a barren steppe swept over by wild Indian tribes who were hostile to the Spaniards. If you went still farther across this solitude to the north and west you would stumble rather suddenly on new zones of culture. A number of provincial cities had grown out of the already mentioned military and trading stations, Córdoba, Tucumán, Mendoza, etc., with a Spanish population that was strongly permeated with Indian blood. Their villages had a Spanish-colonial aspect in contrast to the Spanish-European aspect of the Port. . . . The connection with Buenos Aires was relatively slight. Trade, which the Indians made dangerous and only possible under armed escort if directed toward Buenos Aires, went mainly to Peru."[14]

On the greenish-brown expanses of the untilled Pampa the horizon is as level as that of the sea and disappointingly near (Fig. 6). Here and there are patches of brilliant red flowers clinging close to the soil, farther on there is a stretch of silvery grass bowing and changing slightly in color with every puff of wind. But when you have crossed 700 miles of these plains and are drawing into the Province of Mendoza the scene becomes dismal and dusty. Here is bare, dry sand thinly grown with stunted thorn bushes, with occasional miserable hovels unfit for men—nothing else. The Andes are a great relief to the eye on this journey. My first glimpse of them was on an

[14] Georg Hiller: Einwanderung und Einwanderungspolitik in Argentinien, Berlin, 1912, pp. 9-10.

FIG. 9—The dam at San Roque in the mountains of Córdoba, built about 1886, making possible the irrigation of the heights above the city of Córdoba. In consequence land rose in value from 400 to 8000 pesos a square league (about 46,700 acres) before water flowed in the ditches.

Fig. 10—In the Andes, on the Chilean side of the Iglesia Pass between Mendoza and Santiago. Up here at 10,000 feet it is treeless. The zigzag mule track shows in the foreground; for the most part it is passable for carriages.

early February morning in 1886, with the sun shining across the plain on the thin line of snow ridge between Aconcagua and Tupungato. It was southern midsummer. Doubtless the snow lay deep on all the Central Cordillera, but we could see nothing of that. For in front of the Andes at Mendoza stands the 7000-foot Paramillo of Uspallata, a dreary wall of mud-colored slopes masking the splendor behind. If you were high above on the crest of the Paramillo you would see the central ranges beautifully displayed, their broad snowfields ribbed by black rock ridges, but that view calls for a painful climb. From the plains snow is glimpsed only on the peaks of Tupungato and Aconcagua, loftiest peaks of the American continents, but here tiny and pale with height and distance. The scene is a desert one, though the train runs into Mendoza along an avenue of trees, and irrigated trees line each street. The cobblestone pavement (Fig. 11), the low adobe houses, at that time still uncoated with stucco, the bare deserted plaza are very depressing. Every green field is rigidly framed in desert, the same desert that climbs up the face and over the crest of the Paramillo.

Mendoza and San Juan

Mendoza and its northern neighbor San Juan are the oldest Argentine cities, founded in 1561 and 1562 at the eastern foot of the Andes by expeditions across the lofty, barren range from Chile. They formed part of the Chilean province of Cuyo till 1776. The lowest pass here is 12,500 feet above the sea, but it is an easy one. In 1886 it required four days of mule travel and might easily have been crossed in a buggy except for the first few hours on the Chilean side (Fig. 10). The main obstacle to travel was the necessity of carrying food, as there is no plant life throughout the last three days' travel from Chile except the useless cactus.

The rainfall at Mendoza averages 8 inches a year, at San Juan 2 (Fig. 37). That is desert rainfall and must have seemed very little in comparison with 20 at Valparaiso and 15 at

Santiago. But to the eastward of the range it is even less.
Life in San Juan and Mendoza Provinces can be maintained
only by irrigation, and the water sources are meager. Over
95 per cent of these provinces are desert and must always remain desert. Sarmiento, born and reared in San Juan, writing
about 1840 called them agricultural provinces.[15] This is still
true. In the few places where there is water enough for irrigation a few people till the soil. The valley of San Juan lies
between its mountain ridges exactly like a Chilean valley.
The likeness is enhanced by the lines of poplars and willows
along the irrigation ditches. The people still look Chilean
with their carved wooden stirrups and heavy leather protection for the leg when riding through scrub. Chilean, too, is
the general use of the poncho even in the city and the red
flag that indicates the meat shop.[16] Very few cattle are
raised. The main products are wine and alfalfa seed, which
is a local specialty. The old-time native wine is still produced
here, sweet and heavy in alcohol, an object of contempt to the
European wine makers of Mendoza, who are highly up-to-date.
But as their market is the interior of the republic, which likes
these wines, they are obliged to imitate them. Most of the
vineyards, however, are growing "French" grapes, and the
wine is shipped as Mendoza wine.

Work in San Juan is carried on by old-fashioned peon labor
on patriarchal estates which have not been touched by immigration. In 1913 Victor Bonvicini established 180 Spanish
families on a colony 8 miles southeast of the city made available by draining 6000 hectares of swamp land which he sold
them at $200 paper a hectare, one-sixth down, the rest in
five annual payments with 6 per cent interest.[17] Scarcity of

[15] [D. F. Sarmiento:] Vida de Facundo Quiroga i aspecto físico, costumbres i
hábitos de la República Arjentina, 2nd edit., Santiago de Chile, 1851, pp. 14–15
(English translation by Mrs. Horace Mann under the title "Life in the Argentine
Republic in the Days of the Tyrants," New York, 1868, p. 13). The first edition
appeared in 1845.

[16] Notes of Dr. Alfred Coester, who accompanied the writer on his 1918 trip.
Dr. Coester was at the time teacher of Spanish at the Commercial High School,
Brooklyn, N. Y. He is now professor of Spanish at Leland Stanford, Jr., University.

[17] Data from the Bonvicini office, San Juan.

Fig. 11—A Mendoza street in 1918. Formerly the cobble paving extended entirely across the street. This is in the arid region. The trees are only kept alive by an almost continuous flow of water in the gutter.

Fig. 12—The Italianized Plaza San Martín at Mendoza in 1918. By incessant labor it has been made minutely ornate. Nothing could be less Creole.

Fig. 13—The old-Creole Plaza of Córdoba in 1884. Very bare, its cherished adornment being the evening promenaders. Maintained with a minimum of effort.

land with water will not allow much expansion of such colonization. In early days the Pampa served only to raise half-
wild cattle and was exclusively pastoral, but there were no
wild horses or cattle in San Juan or Mendoza.

It is interesting to have Darwin's picture of Mendoza as it
appeared to him in 1835 after a journey across the barren
Andes from Chile. "The country was beautifully cultivated
and resembled Chile. This neighbourhood is celebrated for
its fruit; and certainly nothing could appear more flourishing
than the vineyards and the orchards of figs, peaches, and olives.
We bought watermelons nearly twice as large as a man's head,
most deliciously cool and well flavoured, for a halfpenny apiece;
and for the value of threepence, half a wheelbarrowful of
peaches. The cultivated and enclosed part of this province is
very small; there is little more than that which we passed
between Luxan and the Capital. The land, as in Chile, owes
its fertility entirely to artificial irrigation. . . . The inhabitants say 'it is good to live in, but very bad to grow rich in' ".[18]

To the eastward of Mendoza no mountains barred the way
to the Atlantic, but the 700-mile distance, first across the
waterless *travesía* to San Luis and then the broad, Indian-
infested Pampa thence to Buenos Aires, was an effective obstacle. It was easier to climb up two miles into the air on the
mountain trail to Chile. Chilean intercourse with these
provinces continues even now, though the eastern pathway
has been opened up. The Mendoza Creoles are Chileans
who were adopted into the Argentine family in 1776 when
Cuyo ceased to be Chilean. The law and the census of course
treat modern Chileans in Cuyo as foreigners, but, unlike the
European immigrant, they represent the old-Creole culture
of the interior provinces, though the old times have passed
away. San Juan and San Luis have grown, but Mendoza has
expanded enormously by the coming of the European immigrant, who now abounds and has brought a new conception

[18] Charles Darwin: Journal of Researches into the Natural History and Geology
of the Countries Visited During the Voyage of H. M. S. 'Beagle' Round the World,
London, 2nd edit., 1886 impression, p. 330.

of labor with him.[19] The old order persisted there as long as the Pampa persisted as a barrier.

When General Roca drove the Indians off the Pampa in 1876, when the railroads at once began to spread across it, reaching Mendoza in 1885, when the wines of Mendoza and San Juan began to find a market in eastern provinces, then and not till then the French and, after them, the Italians came to Mendoza to elaborate those wines. The three Argentine censuses of 1869, 1895, and 1914 disclose very clearly that there were rather more Chileans in San Juan and Mendoza Provinces in 1869 than now, though total population has grown more than threefold.[20] The 500 Europeans of 1869 had become 14,000 in 1895 and 90,000 in 1914. From one-half of one per cent they have increased to 23 per cent. In 1869 Europeans were a curiosity; in 1914 they have become the most significant quarter of the population economically though not socially. Yet they have brought about an economic situation that has transformed life extraordinarily for classes who do not recognize them socially.

TUCUMÁN AND ITS SUGAR INDUSTRY

Immediately after the settlement of Mendoza from Chile the Spaniards, overrunning Bolivia in search of the precious

[19] GROWTH OF CUYO CITIES
Population in thousands

Year	Mendoza	San Juan	San Luis
1869*	8	8	4
1895†	28	10	10
1914†	59	17	15

*Primer censo de la República Argentina, 1869, Buenos Aires, 1872, p. li.
† Tercer censo nacional, 1914, Vol. 1: Antecedentes y comentarios, Buenos Aires, 1916, p. 116.

[20] POPULATION OF SAN JUAN AND MENDOZA PROVINCES

	Thousands of Individuals			Percentages	
Year	Total	Chileans	Europeans	Chileans	Europeans
1869*	126	8	0.5	6.3	0.4
1895†	200	7	14.0	3.5	7.0
1914‡	397	7	90.4	1.8	22.8

*Primer censo de la República Argentina, 1869, Buenos Aires, 1872, pp. 636–637.
† Segundo censo de la República Argentina, 1895, Vol. 2: Población, Buenos Aires, 1898, pp. clxii and clxiv.
‡ Tercer censo nacional, 1914, Vol. 2: Población, Buenos Aires, 1916, pp. 314–315 and 323–324.

metals, began to descend from the tableland into the north-western valleys among the Andes of what is now the Argentine Republic. Tucumán they settled in 1565; Córdoba, first called Córdoba del Tucumán, in 1573, when Mendoza was twelve years old. They had come by way of Panamá and Peru, crossing the whole width of the Andes to their eastern border. Tucumán and Córdoba lie at about 1500 feet above the level of the sea. From these towns stretch off to the eastward the broad gentle slopes of loess whose humid eastern border is the Pampa. The typical northern upland provinces are Jujuy, Salta, Tucumán, Catamarca, La Rioja. Here the Bolivians play the same rôle as the Chileans in Mendoza.[21] Almost all of them are found in Jujuy and Salta, next to the Bolivian border. Their race and culture type is indistinguishable from that of the Argentine Arribeños. The Europeans in 1869 were but 500. They had become nearly 13,000 in 1895 and 39,000 by 1914. From a fraction of one per cent of the population they have become 5 per cent—still a very small proportion in comparison with the 23 per cent of Europeans in Mendoza and San Juan. The northwest is still strongly old-Creole, even now that the Pampa is crossed by a network of rails.

At Tucumán the aspect of the Andes is one of great charm. The eastern chain of the Cordillera terminates in this province in the lofty ridge of Aconquija, 17,000 feet above the sea. It rises abruptly from the plain, unmasked by foothills or outer ranges. The rainfall here is 38 inches a year (Fig. 37), so the whole lower slope of the mountain is clad with a luxuriant subtropical forest of lance, cebil, cedar, walnut, and laurel, so

[21] POPULATION OF THE FIVE NORTHERN UPLAND PROVINCES

Year	Thousands of Individuals			Percentages		
	Total	Bolivians	Europeans	Uplanders in the Republic	Bolivians in Uplands	Europeans in Uplands
1869*	367	5.8	0.5	21.1	1.6	0.14
1895†	543	6.9	12.9	11.2	1.26	2.6
1914‡	731	17.1	39.3	9.3	2.3	5.4

* Primer censo, *loc. cit.*

† Segundo censo, *loc. cit.*

‡ Tercer censo, Vol. 2, pp. 302–303, 329–330, 334–335, 343–344, and p. 350.

dense that only its outer edge can be penetrated. Below lie
the canefields and east of them is a carpet of greensward, lovely
and velvety to the eye but useless for pasture.[22] Let us some
evening look from a housetop on the border of the canefields
toward one of the sugar estates that lie for eighty miles along
the skirt of the range. It is the fine season in Tucumán.
Already the scent of orange blossoms is in the air. The lanes
outside are lined with orange trees, and across the straw-col-
ored canefields the eye is arrested by patches of pink peach
blossoms just short of the forest's edge. In the expanse of
forest tops, too, you catch glimpses of lighter hues than the
green of the old-year foliage. Most of the trees are evergreen, but the tint freshens as spring draws on. High above
the forest line are grassy slopes reaching up to the black ridges
of rock and the snowfields.[23] At this hour the noises of the day
are ceasing. The last *carretas* are creaking lazily away down
the lanes, leaving their load of gold and purple canes beside
the cane conveyor of the factory. You hear distinctly each
armful of heavy canes flung down on the boards of the conveyor. The factory glitters with the many lamps. The night
shift has begun work, for the hundred-day *zafra* (sugar-mak-
ing campaign) of the cane country allows no pause from mid-
May to late August. It is an all too short period to realize on
the costly investment of improved machinery between unripe
canes in May and frost-soured juice in late August or
September.

The writer had intimate knowledge of one of these establishments from 1886 to 1889, when the sugar industry was hardly
ten years old. The company had title by grant of 1717 from
the Spanish king to a singular strip of land, a narrow ribbon
on the north bank of a little river, from fixed boundaries on

[22] This is no cattle country. Good beef must be brought from Córdoba, the
native meat being lean and tasteless.

[23] As the winter is the dry season here, there is very little snow by the end of
winter. One of the finest sights of the province may be had after a summer thunderstorm has crashed and raged its hour or two of furious violence, when the clouds
lift in the west and reveal the whole upper third of the range blanketed in an un-
broken sheet of white.

the plain, where access is easy, "to the eternal snows on the hills," the southern boundary being the river and the northern a line always 1200 yards distant from the river in a north-south direction. On account of the dense forest the surveys have never extended more than fifteen miles from the factory. The snow appears to lie ten or twelve miles farther on. Canefields and factory occupy about a mile and a half at the eastern end of the strip. Three or four miles back begins the forest, thinned at the edge by the cutting out of the best firewood—lance and cebil—but soon too thickset with trunks and the mat of parasitic growths to allow passage. Lines for surveyors must be cleared out with the ax. In the forest the river almost always has water, but on the plain during the dry months it soon runs out in a bed of sand.

The owners of the *ingenio* were a half dozen Córdoba men, all Creoles, who had accumulated modest fortunes in commerce. The place had cost them several hundred thousand dollars, in large part for machinery made by the Fives-Lille Company in France—elaborate apparatus for making white centrifugal sugar and for distilling alcohol.

The enterprise was purely national and Creole. Among the higher employees were five Europeans and one North American. In harvest time the factory used two hundred hands, with perhaps fifty more through the year in the forest, cutting wood and working in the canefields. The canefields of the establishment were leased to concessionaries who were supplied with money as they needed it for their work at 6 per cent interest. They delivered the cane as it ripened, receiving interest on the value of their deliveries until settlement was made at the end of the harvest. In addition to this cane from its own lands the establishment bought a considerable quantity outside. As the small cane growers outside were too far from other *ingenios* to sell their cane elsewhere, all through the three years the price paid them was three Bolivian cents an *arroba*, though the price of sugar varied from eight to twelve cents a pound. (The Argentine Republic, like other Latin

American states, has adopted the metric system and has a dollar of its own. Even in the northern provinces Bolivian dollars are never seen and have not been seen—outside a money changer's office—this many a year, and if they were offered to a cane grower in payment of his produce he would doubtless refuse them, but the *arroba* and the Bolivian dollar, *boliviano*, are nevertheless the old customary units in the North like all the things of Peru, so the weigher at the scales, which indicate kilograms only, must reduce them to *arrobas* of 11.485 kilograms each and figure that each 57⅛ cents of the Argentine dollar he pays with go to each *boliviano* of the value.) The cane was not supposed to be paid for till the end of the harvest, but of course the growers came for advances as soon as they had made any considerable deliveries, and such advances were usually made, since the establishments were Creole and treated their neighbors with friendliness rather than a banker's close adherence to terms.

CREOLE LABOR

Even today there is no European labor in the sugar factories. Europeans ask too high a wage and generally do better for themselves elsewhere. The help is typically Creole—a kind of laborer who did not develop the country and could never have developed it. On the contrary the country has developed him. The French geographer Vidal de la Blache has protested vehemently against the concept that man is the creature of his environment. The Arctic did not create the Eskimo nor England the Englishman. Nature—the environment—he says, offers man varied opportunities. Actual societies depend for their form on the extent to which men have perceived and acted on these opportunities. When the *conquistadores* or the Incas before them founded San Juan and Mendoza they reacted to opportunity. They put available water on the available—because treeless—land. They tilled it and drew life from it—by proxy, truly, for the Indian, to whose labor they had won the title in battle, did the work.

However, there was no wealth in that. It needed imagination and the instinct of the agriculturist, both of which the Spaniard lacked, to see that the Pampa held treasures surpassing all the mines of precious metals in the world. On the Pampa nature offers a vast field for agriculture and a vaster field for grazing. In the earliest Spanish days escaped cattle and horses found abundant grasses to satisfy their hunger all the year, for no winter snow covers the ground. There they multiplied. It is inaccurate to say that the Spaniard peopled the Pampa with these countless herds, yet they were Spanish horses and cattle taking advantage of the virgin plains of a new world.

The Gaucho

Presently Creole and Spaniard discovered the new opportunity that nature thrust upon them, and took advantage of it. In the good old days on the Pampa, in the days before the immigrant came, the gaucho was developed almost wholly by his environment; he was not a herdsman who cared for cattle, not a breeder who improved their race, not a careful owner who counted his herds and saw to their sustenance, but a hunter of horses and cows who lived on an abundance that nature came very near thrusting in his hands. The animals cared for themselves. His occupation was the chase; his prey, the half-wild cattle. He reacted to the environment truly. When they tell you today that the gaucho is extinct they are thinking of him in his high state as master of horse and cattle hunting, the man who needed only a knife and a rope and the Pampa to provide himself with horses, cattle, clothing, and food. There is no need for such prowess now nor has there been since steamers and railroads brought laboring men to the Pampa. In his quintessence the gaucho has long disappeared. Adepts in his arts were few as adepts always are, but gauchos of a sort appeared on the Pampa as soon as it was peopled with animals, and they still are found there. The Argentine Creole in the mass (frontispiece), as he existed apart from the ruling class of the cities, was the gaucho.

Sarmiento has drawn the old-time picture.[24] With none of the means of civilization and progress that depend on gatherings of men in numerous communities, this gaucho had taken on habits of his own. Toil he left to his women folk, to keep a wretched house, cook food, shear sheep, milk cows, make cheese, and weave the coarse stuffs of his clothing; all fell on them. He would not work. At most some men deigned to raise a little maize for the family food. Bread and wheat were not in common use, but meat was consumed in enormous quantities. Tiny boys got their exercise and trained themselves for manhood dexterity by throwing *bolas* and *lazo*, making hens, goats, and calves their constant victims in an unwearied pursuit. As soon as they got on horseback, which was as soon as they could walk to the horse, they went on errands; or rather, an errand served them as pretext to mount. The gaucho, man and boy alike, got up in the morning and mounted his horse as inevitably as a city man washes his face and knots his necktie. It was the habitual beginning of his day. Then he considered where to go! To grow, to ride better, to mount and dismount from a running horse, to throw his animal, to tame a wild one, to venture at a gallop across the roughest ground was to delight in the consciousness of his powers.

Darwin observed their skill in Uruguay in 1832. "The Gauchos are well known to be perfect riders; the idea of being thrown, let the horse do what it likes, never enters their heads. Their criterion of a good rider is a man who can manage an untamed colt, or who, if his horse falls, alights on his own feet, or can perform other such exploits. I have heard of a man betting that he would throw his horse down twenty times, and that nineteen times he would not fall himself. I recollect seeing a Gaucho riding a very stubborn horse, which three times successively reared so high as to fall backwards with great violence. The man judged with uncommon coolness the proper moment for slipping off, not an instant before or after the right time; and as soon as the horse got up, the

[24] *op. cit.*, 1851 edit., pp. 23–24; Engl. transl. p. 20.

man jumped on his back. . . . The Gaucho never appears to exert any muscular force. I was one day watching a good rider, as we were galloping along at a rapid pace, and thought to myself, 'surely if the horse starts, you appear so careless on your seat, you must fall.' At this moment, a male ostrich sprang from its nest right beneath the horse's nose; the young colt bounded on one side like a stag; but as for the man, all that could be said was, that he started and took fright with his horse."[25] Young manhood brought an independence, a freedom, a self-reliance that the world finds it hard to equal. The Pampa was free, cattle and horses were free, almost as free as water and light and air. The poor gaucho was richer than the wealthy of other lands. Nowhere in the world has there been known such a wealth of horses and cattle. About 1914 there were about as many horses in the Argentine Republic as there were people.[26] The Falkland Islands and the Northern Territory of Australia had proportionately as many or more, but no other country. In the United States there were 5 persons for every horse. France, Germany, and Britain had 3 or 4; Montana, the Dakotas and the near-by parts of Canada, Alberta, and Saskatchewan, well over one horse to a person, but Buenos Aires and Santa Fe Provinces had 1½ or 2. Corrientes, between the Uruguay and Paraná Rivers, had 2.7. In early days animals probably bore a still higher ratio to the scanty population. Cattle were still more numerous than horses in the Argentine, numbering 3 per capita; the Pampa provinces had 4 or 5 and Corrientes 12. A few of our Western states attained 3 or 4, but the greater part of the United States had only 3 heads of cattle to five persons.

[25] Darwin, *op. cit.*, pp. 152–153.

[26] The figures for horses and cattle on which the statements in this passage are based may be found in the following sources: *International Yearbook of Agricultural Statistics for 1923*, Inst. Internat. d'Agric., Rome, 1924, Tables 97 and 100 on pp. 178–181 and 186–189 (by countries and dependencies); Tercer censo nacional, 1914, Vol. 6: Censo ganadero, Buenos Aires, 1917, pp. 39–42 and 155–158 (by Argentine provinces); Fourteenth Census of the United States, 1920, Vol. 5: Agriculture, Washington, 1922, Table 81 on p. 629 (by states of the United States); Sixth Census of Canada, 1921, Vol. 4: Agriculture, Ottawa, 1924, Table LXXI on p. lxxxvii (by Canadian provinces).

A poor peon applied for work on horseback, driving his little troop of "animals" before him. He felt disgraced, "no better than a gringo," if he had not at least fourteen horses of his own. These he expected to pasture on his employer's land and usually could up to the seventies or eighties of the last century. It was a long task to fence the Pampa and make it clear to the gaucho that pasture was private property. Far from aspiring to be like the men of the cities, the gaucho disdained city dwellers, city tasks, city clothes, and city manners. The contrast was extraordinary. Something of it survives today. The cities affect the latest, most punctilious of European fashions; the country is elemental in its reduction of human life to simplest terms. This independent, self-reliant man is no home-maker. His children are always dirty and ragged and live in the midst of swarming dogs. While the women work, the men lie stretched on the soil in absolute inaction. Disorder and dirt are everywhere. His house is a most wretched hut of wattle or sun-dried bricks with thin and leaky thatch above and almost no furniture. The rich man owned land and animals but lived little better. Darwin was put up one night in 1834 at the house of a rich landed proprietor. "After witnessing the rude wealth displayed in the number of cattle, men, and horses, Don Juan's miserable house was quite curious. The floor consisted of hardened mud, and the windows were without glass; the sitting room boasted only of a few of the roughest chairs and stools, with a couple of tables. The supper, although several strangers were present, consisted of two huge piles, one of roast beef, the other of boiled, with some pieces of pumpkin; besides this latter there was no other vegetable, and not even a morsel of bread. . . . Yet this man was the owner of several square miles of land, of which nearly every acre would produce corn and, with a little trouble, all the common vegetables."[27] Such wretchedness "was disappearing" in 1840, but it was still to be seen among the lower classes in 1885 and it was still at hand in 1918—the

[27] Darwin, *op. cit.*, p. 44.

terms accepted by many a poor immigrant in his penurious struggle towards a first capital. This gaucho was the common type of Argentine. We can even show his picture. Córdoba Province had eight of him to a single city dweller in Sarmiento's day and still has five or six.[28] Of one-story houses that the census calls "*adobe-paja*," which I take to mean "*ranchos*" of adobe with slightly thatched roof, 266,977 were enumerated in 1895, these even then constituting 28 per cent of all the houses in Buenos Aires Province and from 80 to 90 per cent in the Andine states. Houses of this type were 71 per cent of all the houses in the Province of Córdoba in 1895.[29] In 1914 they are not reported, though seen everywhere.

We have mentioned that Sarmiento, born in San Juan, calls Mendoza and San Juan agricultural provinces. In others pasturage abounds, but raising cattle was, for a long time, not the occupation of the people so much as their means of subsistence. They have carried their own physical and mental adaptation to a life of subsistence on cattle to a high degree of completeness. Darwin visited an army outpost near Bahía Blanca in 1832. "What a life of misery these men appear to us to lead! . . . The little hovel, built of thistle-stalks, in which they slept, neither kept out the wind or rain; indeed in the latter case the only effect the roof had, was to condense it into larger drops. They had nothing to eat excepting what they could catch, such as ostriches, deer, armadillos, etc., and their only fuel was the dry stalks of a small plant, somewhat resembling an aloe. The sole luxury which these men enjoyed was smoking the little paper cigars, and sucking maté."[30]

General Arent,[31] a Prussian officer who went out to train the Argentine army in 1910, regards the gaucho as superior

---

[28] Sarmiento, *op. cit.* According to the 1914 census the total population of the province was 735,472; the rural male population, 221,779; the percentage of males over 15 years, 30 per cent of the total population (Tercer censo nacional, Vol. 2, p. 279, and Vol. 3, pp. 114–116).

[29] Segundo censo de la República Argentina, 1895, Vol. 3: Censos complementarios, Buenos Aires, 1898, p. 22.

[30] Darwin, *op. cit.*, p. 112.

[31] Alfred Arent: Argentinien, ein Land der Zukunft: Jubiläumsschrift zur Hundertjahrsfeier der Begründung der Republik Argentinien, Leipzig-Naunhof, 1910, p. 164.

to the material of any European cavalry, so well is he accustomed to the life of an army in campaign and so expert is he with horses. Arent, however, has nothing but impatience with his officers and the upper-class Creoles generally. The gaucho is careless and heedless of his stock, brutal and wasteful in his handling of them. On this point Darwin relates[32] the following episode. "One day, riding in the Pampas with a very respectable 'Estanciero,' my horse, being tired, lagged behind. The man often shouted to me to spur him. When I remonstrated that it was a pity, for the horse was quite exhausted, he cried out, 'Why not—never mind—spur him—it is *my* horse.' I had then some difficulty in making him comprehend that it was for the horse's sake, and not on his account, that I did not choose to use my spurs. He exclaimed, with a look of great surprise, 'Ah, Don Carlos, que cosa!' It was clear that such an idea had never before entered his head." To the art of caring for and breeding cattle the gaucho never contributed anything. Cattle abounded, horses abounded, grass was superabundant. His business was not cattle breeding but cattle hunting. A man starting on a journey would drive a dozen horses before him, shifting his *recado* from a tired one to a fresh one as he went. For pasture he paid nothing; they pastured as they went. Stealing horses was a crime, and there were some criminals, some who even killed a cow for food and carried off her skin. To borrow a horse without the owner's knowledge was no crime. You turned the animal loose, and it went back. To kill a cow for needed food was accepted as proper, but it was good form to see that the owner got the skin. Before the railroad and steamships put the Pampa in touch with Europe the hides were the main marketable part of the herd. Men ate enormous quantities of meat and, like Eskimos, demonstrated that life may be satisfactorily maintained on a straight meat diet.

But the population was widely disseminated. There were no schools or arts. The sons of well-to-do families grew to

[32] Darwin, *op. cit.*, p. 152.

manhood without learning to read; but they had a prodigious
sense of individual importance. Sarmiento says: "The Argentines of whatever class they may be, civilized or ignorant,
have a high sense of their worth as natives. . . . How much
must have contributed to the independence of a part of America the arrogance of these Argentine gauchos, who have never
seen anything under the sun better than they, neither learned
men nor powerful men. The European is for them the lowest
of all because he cannot resist the sudden leap of a horse."[33]
The gauchos roared with laughter, says Darwin,[34] at his attempt to throw the *bolas* with the result of catching the horse
on which he was riding by the hind legs. Yet Darwin was well
thought of by the gauchos because of his compass, his matches,
his ability to distinguish poisonous snakes, and uncanny knowledge of insects. Again, Sarmiento: "The life of the Pampa
developed in the gaucho every physical faculty but none of
those of the intelligence. . . . He is strong, proud, energetic.
Without any education or sense of the need of it . . . he is
happy in the midst of his poverty and his privations, which
do not exist for him. . . . The gaucho does not work. Food
and clothing he finds prepared in his house. Both are provided by his cattle if he is owner, by the house of his patron or
relative if he possesses nothing. The care called for by the
cattle is reduced to races and pleasure trips. The branding,
which is like the harvest of the husbandman, is the festival
he looks forward to with joy, for there in the presence of all
the men for twenty leagues around he will display his almost
unbelievable dexterity."[35] Strongly thrown into relief by the
gaucho's deep sense of independence and personal worth was
his ingrained courtesy and sense of hospitality. His desire to
shine in all competitions has been called childish, but it did
not prevent him from recognizing that the other man had
claims to be heard. If he was without property he accommo-

[33] Author's translation from Sarmiento, *op. cit.*, 1851 edit., p. 25 (in Mrs. Mann's Engl. transl. the passage is on p. 21).

[34] Darwin, *op. cit.*, p. 45.

[35] *op. cit.*, 1851 edit., pp. 26–27 (in Mrs. Mann's Engl. transl., pp. 22–23).

dated himself to serve a patron who afforded him the opportunity to acquire animals and gave him pasturage in return for moderate services. The authority of the patron he has always accepted without reserve, and in return he looked to him for protection from government officials, whom he did not understand, and for care for himself and family in sickness and in misfortune.

The man unwilling to accept this position was the outlaw, a *gaucho malo*, long since extinct. In the first half of the nineteenth century he could easily coexist alongside the loosely organized society. Authority, judicial as well as police, was always vested in the local authorities, the *comandante de campaña*, now the *jefe político*, who arrested, fined, imprisoned, and perhaps executed an offender without reference to law. In the isolation of the open, thinly peopled plains, before the railway, this was necessary. Today it causes resentment in European laborers to see a police officer arrest two men for exchanging blows in a café and fine them or send them to jail in default of fine with no reference to judge or complaint by either party. The gauchos were never self-governing but always subject to central authority, with their patron for protector of civil rights. The immigrant without patron seems to have no such opportunity to express himself politically as comes to him so readily in the United States.

As to the gaucho's sense of hospitality Darwin has this to say: "As he [my host] had been very obliging—not only providing me with food, but lending me his private horses—I wanted to make him some remuneration. I asked my guide whether I might do so, but he told me certainly not; that the only answer I should receive, probably would be, 'We have meat for the dogs in our country, and therefore do not grudge it to a Christian.' . . . It was only the high sense of hospitality, which every traveller is bound to acknowledge as nearly universal throughout these provinces."[36] Speaking of Chile, Darwin says that there are much more strongly marked

[36] Darwin, *op. cit.*, p. 113.

FIG. 14—Hardwood of Santiago del Estero in the old-time oxcart made entirely of wood. The crooked wood is characteristic of the *monte*. It is hard and makes excellent fuel. This wood is an important product of Santiago.

FIG. 15—The Río Dulce and *monte* near Santiago del Estero. The river brings water from the mountain border in Tucumán. As it goes farther south toward the Mar Chiquita depression (see Fig. 8) it becomes too salt to drink and therefore takes the name Saladillo. This photograph was taken during the dry season, in May, whose average rainfall is 0.6 inch out of a year's total of 19 inches (see Fig. 37).

gradations in social position there than in the Argentine and that, as a result of the more uneven distribution of wealth, there exists among the guasos of Chile, who correspond to the gauchos of the Pampa, a feeling of inequality unknown to the latter. "A traveller does not meet here [in Chile] that unbounded hospitality which refuses all payment, but yet is so kindly offered that no scruples can be raised in accepting it. Almost every house in Chile will receive you for the night, but a trifle is expected to be given in the morning; even a rich man will accept two or three shillings. The Gaucho, although he may be a cut-throat, is a gentleman. . . . The Guaso does not by any means consider every man his equal; and I was quite surprised that my companions did not like to eat at the same time as myself."[37]

The *capataz* (foreman), says Sarmiento, "needs a will of iron for his task, a character resolute to the pitch of rashness to restrain the audacity and turbulence of these land freebooters whom he has to muster and rule in the desert courses. At the least sign of insubordination, the *capataz* seizes his iron whip handle and deals to the insolent blows that cause wounds and bruises. If resistance continues, rather than appeal to pistols he leaps from his horse, knife in hand, and quickly reëstablishes his authority by the superior skill he shows in handling it."[38] The Argentine peon of today is most peaceable and patient. His morals are no better than those of the upper classes, and he is addicted to drunkenness, which is practically unknown in the upper class. He still retains aversion to all labor except on a horse. He might be called peon, a word that came from Spain when it meant "man on foot," but he was on horseback, and that was exactly what the Spanish word for gentleman[39] had originally meant. There is no question that the possession of the horse, conferring a mastery of distances and a wide familiarity with places and peo-

[37] *ibid.*, p. 258.
[38] Author's translation from Sarmiento, *op. cit.*, 1851 edit., p. 10 (in Mrs. Mann's Engl. transl., p. 9).
[39] *Caballero*, from *caballo*, horse.

ples, enormously enhanced the sense of dignity of the Argentine gaucho and immensely increased his enjoyment of life.[40] This was perceived at once by the Italian immigrant who was presently to appear on the Pampa as it began to be fenced and the gaucho began to disappear. Almost invariably the Italian newcomer in the Argentine Republic developed two ambitions: first, to own a horse, which was easily done with the savings of a few weeks, and, second, to become adept in its use; and that he never was. His awkward postures on horseback are the constant delight of the Creole horseman.

FACTORY LABOR IN TUCUMÁN

This personal satisfaction of the Creole laboring class with the work of the cattle ranch, together with the abundance of meat, their chief food, combined to make them content with a nominal wage. The working class in this horse-and-cattle-raising society was ill suited for factory work. They had no conception of fixed, steady manual labor in one spot, but they were the material the Creole *ingenio* owners were familiar with and had to use. They are still the main resort of the *ingenios* for the hundred days of the *zafra*. Much the greater part of them came from the semi-arid province Santiago del Estero, which lies next east of Tucumán, and Quichua Indian blood is strongly visible in their faces (Fig. 16). Yet almost all their names were familiar Castilian ones, like Juan Acevedo, José Ruiz, Juan de la Cruz Castro, Pedro Díaz, Segundo Martínez, Juan Balmaceda, and Clímaco Moyano. The capable foreman of the lumber gang was invariably referred to as Indian and answered to the un-Castilian name Manuel Chanampa. I fancy he may have come from the Chaco. The peon class in Santiago found a poor but easy sustenance in the fruit of the algarrobo tree, about equivalent to an inferior bean; but by autumn the algarrobo had become scarce, and the three months of irksome toil in the sugar factories were an escape from starvation. Labor was required of the

[40] Paul Walle: L'Argentine telle qu'elle est, Paris, [1912], p. 115.

FIG. 16—Santiago Indian workers on the sugar establishment La Providencia near Tucumán in 1887. The man at the rear of the cart is wearing the old *chiripá* for trousers—just a folded blanket.

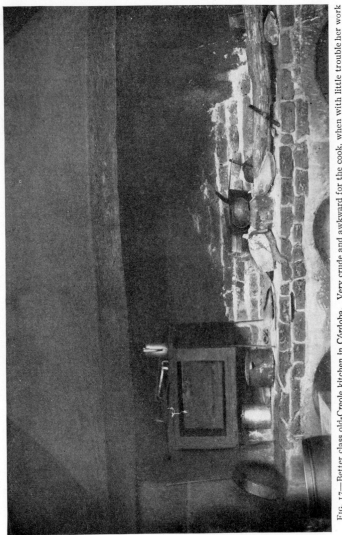

FIG. 17—Better class old-Creole kitchen in Córdoba. Very crude and awkward for the cook, when with little trouble her work could have been made easier. Typical of Creole institutions.

working class by law, with the highly moral preamble that "idleness conduces inevitably to one or another form of vice, as one may see in the alarming extent of vice and idleness side by side in every part of our country. To avoid this be it enacted that every citizen who cannot show proof of employment or life-sustaining occupation shall be treated as a tramp, i.e. made to labor on the public works." Men of the laboring class were obliged to possess an authorized contract with their patron which specified the terms of employment, the law furthermore obliging the men to repay any advances that had been made by working them out. The improvidence of the peon was against him. He always received an advance when he was hired and spent nearly all he earned; he never got out of debt till the end of the harvest. But in spite of a common opinion to the contrary he was not enslaved. One man in the factory in question managed once to owe as much as $155, and $50 or $60 were common debts, but generally speaking the men earned a good deal more than was advanced to them. Rarely did a man fail to carry money home. The brevity of the *zafra* suited their disinclination for steady work very well.

The wages paid at that date (1888) were $18.50 a month, Argentine paper currency, for single men and $20 for married. Housing of a rude sort was provided, and also meals under house management at a charge against a man's account of $6 a month. Women who wanted to cook were given credit with a butcher who was under contract with the house to supply beef at two cents a pound, heads and hearts being charged double and all other cuts alike. A few other supplies like salt and flour were dealt out to the women on fixed dates, and settlement was made with them every month, the house paying them $6 for the board of one man and charging it against his wages. At mid-month each man was given a dollar or two "for cigarettes" and at a month's end from $5 to $10 as needed, the house inquiring rather closely as to the needs. Some of the women cooks who took on a good many boarders made more money than their husbands. All these persons were called in a loose way Indians, but they spoke Spanish. A few of the older women, especially when excited, could speak only Quichua.

The hiring of the men was handled by agents who always reminded me of slave dealers. They visited each *ingenio* before the harvest, inquiring its needs, and then tried to collect the men at Santiago, making advances of $25 to $50 to each and registering his engagement before a police commissary, after which it was their task to get the men to us without loss of numbers. Unmarried men were liable to jump their engagement and disappear; then the police were asked to bring them back.

A peon named José Ruiz, with an advance of $8, was missing the morning after an agent had brought him to our establishment and transferred his account to us. A tracker—an individual whose reputed ability to read on hard and dusty ground the record of everything that has traveled over it for days makes Sherlock Holmes's exploits seem simple—was sent after him and quickly brought him back. Ruiz was reprimanded in scathing language that dwelt on the baseness of his ingratitude and, without the intervention of any public authority, was confined by his feet in the factory stocks all day, given fifty lashes on the bare back at dusk, and left all night again in the stocks. Next morning he was put to work under guard of a foreman armed with a whip. Probably the lashes were very painful, but I fancy the exposure in the stocks was harder to bear. The stocks were in the middle of the factory ground floor, where considerable numbers of men were always passing, and none of them seemed to pass him without words of derision. Their attitude seemed to be that he wasn't a "good sport," wasn't taking his work as he had taken his advance. If they had any sympathy for him they allowed no sign of it to show. As far as Ruiz's work was concerned it would have been cheaper to let him go. He never earned any wages paid him.

Such punishments did not belong to the patriarchial institutions of Creole days but grew out of the attempt to apply them to modern manufacturing. He was the last man whipped in that establishment and the next-to-last man put in the stocks. Public sentiment strongly disapproved such measures. The patron class was violent in moments of passion but not cruel enough to use such methods of obliging men to work. In 1888 the establishments were forbidden to use other coercive measures than confinement in a strong room, and this only for a limited time. The only persistent cause of difficulty with the men was drunkenness. The middle- and upper-class Creole uses wine and liquor but, with rarest exceptions, in great moderation only. The peon, on the other hand, is much inclined to drunkenness. There were plenty of exceptions; and, thanks to the free-air life and abundant food of these men, there was nothing to be seen in the least comparable to the soddenness of such British cities as Liverpool or Glasgow; but when drunk the peon would fight and had to be disarmed and confined. For this the command of any person in authority sufficed, so great was their docility, as illustrated by the following case.

One night the director of the establishment was recounting the excellent service one of the foremen had given him for two years. He was able to reward him with a small cane concession to cultivate for his own profit, and it was a great satisfaction to have the men see the advantage of intelligent service. Within two hours the foreman in question came down the road crazy with drink, brandishing a long cutlass, his poncho wrapped about his left arm, while he kept two mounted policemen busy warding off his blows and guiding him toward the factory. To the chief he surrendered his weapon, sobbing violently, and was placed in the stocks the whole day, a far different example to the men than had been intended. Next day the stocks were removed.

Creole institutions assumed that the privileged upper class would use its superior intelligence and resources to care for the peon in all emergencies. This the peon might claim as a right. The mistress on a large estate had the health of a great number of families in her hands. This care was a religious obligation. In the factory no patroness was assumed to be present. The care of the men became a matter of business. A sick man could not work, and so he presented himself at the office if able to be up and stated his complaint, and the bookkeeper or the superior official would supply ipecac, castor oil, epsom salts, camphorated oil, or other simple remedies; quinine was used almost constantly. These remedies were administered on the spot, and the offer of them had occasionally the effect of persuading the man that perhaps he might as well go to work. If he did not work he was not paid unless he had met with an obvious accident in the service. On the other hand if he chose he could accumulate many days of overtime every month, for in many out-of-door tasks like woodcutting a day's work was a measured amount. In the factory the hours of labor were twelve a week day—eighteen on Sundays, to change the night and day gangs. The only holidays during the *zafra* were on the occasion of breakdowns or once a month a half-day pause to clean out pumps and vats. Hardly any of the men could read or write, nor were any schools provided for them or their numerous children. They had few wants and were not unhappy. Generally their working power was much inferior to that of a European laborer, and their standard of living was below even the lowly one of the Italian immigrant.

CHANGED FACTORY CONDITIONS TODAY

In 1918 the same factory was found in idleness on a drizzly Sunday, the explanation being that it was election day. That is a great change. There had been no echoes of election in Tucumán *ingenios* in the eighties. Much new machinery and enlargements of the factory attested many profitable years. A branch track from the railroad ran into the yard of the establishment with a power crane to lift the bundles of cane from the flat cars into the conductor. The men were of the same type, still Santiago men, but a good many of them had now settled permanently about the factory. Wages were higher, and labor-saving machines suggested economies in numbers employed. But the old type of labor persisted.

Out in the canefields, however, there were novelties. Great blocks of gigantic canes attested the introduction of the drought-resisting "Java 36" that has resulted from the experiments of the Tucumán Experiment Station. In Tucumán sugar is an old industry, but the first factories were small and crude, producing a very poor dark sugar. Until 1872 wooden *trapiches* (rollers to crush the canes) were mostly used.

The Argentine Sugar Industry[41]

The first modern factories were introduced soon after the first railway connected Tucumán with Córdoba in 1876. They were extraordinarily productive at first, often returning their capital in a single season. In 1888 an import tax of 9 cents gold a kilogram was placed on foreign sugar, and the price was 25 cents paper per kilogram. At the then premium on gold of 153 that amounts to about 16 cents gold, but in a paper-money country paper prices in the interior are always higher than their gold equivalent. The country was not producing enough for its own needs. In 1890 the production was 41,000 metric tons, and another 30,000 tons were imported. Even in the eighties profits of 30 per cent were common, and the Creole managements were wont to celebrate a successful harvest by declaring a thirteenth month's pay to all hands employed. By 1896 production had been increased to 136,000

[41] This account is based mainly on the author's recollections and notes of 1886-1889. Some use has been made of Emilio Lahitte: Consideraciones sobre el censo de la industria azucarera, in Tercer censo nacional, Vol. 7: Censo de las industrias. Buenos Aires, 1917, pp. 539-566; of the section entitled "La industria azucarera" in Emilio Lahitte: Informes y estudios de la Dirección de Economía Rural y Estadística, Vol. 1, 2nd edit., Minist. de Agric., Buenos Aires, 1916, pp. 87-198; and the section on sugar cane (pp. 418-423) in C. D. Girola: Cultivation of Plants for Industrial Purposes in the Argentine Republic, Agricultural and Pastoral Census of the Nation in 1908, Vol. 3: Monographs, Buenos Aires, 1909, pp. 393-438.

tons, which was more than the market could absorb. Two thousand tons were imported, probably on earlier order, but were not needed. No more sugar was brought into the country from outside till 1906. Meanwhile the serious agricultural depression of 1896 in Europe, verging on disaster, had led to a premium on exportation. From 1897 to 1901 an internal tax of $30,000,000 was collected from the manufacturers and $18,000,000 repaid them in export premiums; but this was stopped in 1906, since which time competition has been free. The country can now supply itself and could make much more sugar; but it cannot normally compete with foreign sugar abroad on account of the cost, or rather the inefficiency, of peon labor. The crop varies from year to year to an extraordinary degree, the production of 1914 being four times that of 1917, a year of drought and frost.[42] The government has always aided the *ingenio* owners in every way, but the Argentine people have always paid dearly for their sugar. The real importance of the sugar industry has been in its contributions to the development of railways, three additional lines reaching Tucumán by 1892 and making the marketing of every product of the province feasible. It has been estimated that two-thirds of the freights of the northern railroads are derived directly or indirectly from the sugar industry. The Experiment Station and the Provincial government have encouraged the planting of fruit and peanuts as well as cane, diversifying

[42] ARGENTINE SUGAR PRODUCTION, 1858–1923*

(in thousands of short tons of 2000 English pounds)

1858	0.75	1896	185	1903	160	1910	164	1917	97
1876	3	1897	123	1904	143	1911	199	1918	138
1880	9	1898	81	1905	153	1912	162	1919	328
1884	27	1899	103	1906	131	1913	304	1920	231
1891	51	1900	128	1907	125	1914	370	1921	211
1894	94	1901	151	1908	178	1915	165	1922	238
1895	146	1902	146	1909	140	1916	93	1923	282

* 1858–1884 from Lahitte, *op. cit.*, pp. 117, 91, and 105 (Tucumán Province only); 1891–1894 from Girola, *op. cit.*, p. 421; 1895–1923 from *Yearbooks of the U. S. Dept. of Agric.*, Washington: *for 1899*, p. 781; *for 1903*, p. 652; *for 1907*, p. 686; *for 1911*, p. 603, *for 1914*, p. 603; *for 1920*, p. 684; *for 1923*, p. 851; *for 1924*, p. 807. The amounts are probably some approximation to the facts but they are not to be relied on closely, especially the earlier ones.

the business of agriculture in the province, with results that are already apparent.

Neither the grapes of Mendoza nor the sugar of Tucumán have contributed to the peopling of the Argentine Pampa. The special interest of the Tucumán development is in its native labor under Creole social conditions, very different from those introduced by the immigrant on the Pampa.

CHAPTER II

IMMIGRATION AND POLITICAL CONDITIONS

How did the immigration that peopled the Pampa take its course? What effect did political conditions in the Republic

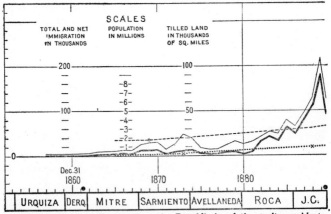

Fig. 18—The growth of the Argentine Republic in relation to its presidents. (Abbreviations: Derq. for Derqui, J. C. for Juárez Celmán, Pel. for Pellegrini, S. P., 1892–1895, for Luis Sáenz Peña, Qui. for Quintana, F. Alco. for Figueroa Alcorta, S. P. for Roque Sáenz Peña, d. l. P. for de la Plaza.)

The curves for total and net immigration are based on pp. 32, 30–31, and 52 of the source cited below in footnote 5 and on the communication referred to in the Appendix, Table I; those for tilled land and population on the following publications:

have on this stream of prospective settlers? How many of those who came stayed in the country, and in what measure did they contribute to the extension of its agriculture?

These questions are answered in the diagram above (Fig. 18). Three things stand out in it: that the last seventy years—the presidential epoch—have been the period of growth of population by immigration and of opening up land to cultivation, for all the values were near zero in the fifties; that immigration to the Republic had a great increase during and immediately after each of the two terms as president of General Julio A. Roca, reaching pronounced peaks in 1889 (219,000) and 1906 (253,000); that it took a still sharper drop after each of these peaks, in the panic of 1891 and during the World War, becoming less than the emigration at each of these periods and making the country lose population.

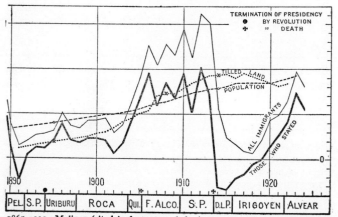

1865-1909, Molinas (cited in footnote 1, below), p. 144; 1910-1917, *Estadística Agrícola* (see footnote 8), *1910* to *1917-18*; 1920-1923, *Annuaire International de Statistique Agricole* (see footnote 9), *1909-1921*, pp. 6 and 24; *1923*, p. 65; *1924-25*, p. 74. For each of the years 1899 to 1909 Molinas' tilled land figures for the next year were used (Molinas 1900 = diagram 1899, etc.) in order to insure uniformity with the system employed in *Estadística Agrícola*.

LITTLE IMMIGRATION AT FIRST

From the independence of 1810 to 1854, when Urquiza became president, the Argentine Confederation grew very little: there was no immigration of significance and nothing like general agriculture. This is expressed in the diagram by the fact that all the lines start near the bottom at the left. The first census of the population was taken in 1869, and there have been two others, 1895 and 1914. In 1865 there were 373 square miles of tilled land[1] in the republic—an eighth of an acre per capita. How small that is one best realizes on learning that European countries have from about one third of an acre in Great Britain to more than two in Denmark.[2] There was very little farming done in the country.

In our own country, by opening up our wonderful Western domain, we have been rapidly increasing the land under cultivation from 177,000 square miles in 1850 to 786,000 at the present time (1920). There has been but moderate change in the number of acres per capita, increasing from 4.9 in 1850 to 5.7 in 1880 and 1890, to diminish since to the present value 4.8.[3] But in the period that has since elapsed (1865 to 1914) the Argentine Republic has increased its cultivated area 255 fold and is cultivating over 60 times as great an area per capita—from an eighth of an acre to 7.7 acres per capita.[4]

The immigration of 1857 was 5000 persons:[5] in 1810 there was probably hardly any immigration. As a matter of fact Buenos Aires city is known to have received only 700 foreigners in the forty years from 1770 to 1810.[6] Before independence there was practically no immigration, because the Spaniards did not allow it. Even natives of Spain had to get a difficult special license to come to America. We have seen (p. 011) that there were occasional exceptions. They never were numerous. At independence, immigration was at once proclaimed to be the great and pressing need of the country; but it did not come for nearly fifty years, because those were years of anarchy and tyranny. The Spanish habit of exclud-

[1] F. T. Molinas: La colonización argentina y las industrias agropecuarias, Buenos Aires, [1910], p. 144. The acreage per capita is calculated from the population in 1865 as given in Molinas, *loc. cit.*

[2] Same reference as in footnote 9, below.

[3] Fourteenth Census of the United States, 1920, Vol. 5: Agriculture, General Report, Washington, 1922, Table 3 on p. 32.

[4] Cultivated area in 1914: 24,586,642 hectares (60,755,000 acres); population in 1914: 7,885,237 (Tercer censo nacional, 1914, Vol. 5: Explotaciones agropecuarias, Buenos Aires, 1919, p. xiii, and *ibid.*, Vol. 2: Población, 1916, p. 109).

[5] Resumen estadístico del movimiento migratorio en la República Argentina, años 1857–1924, Direcc. Gen. de Inmigración, Buenos Aires, 1925, p. 32.

[6] Georg Hiller: Einwanderung und Einwanderungspolitik in Argentinien, Berlin, 1912, p. 9.

ing Creoles from any share in government had kept them unfit to govern. The patriots who governed the United States under the Revolution and under the Constitution had usually governed first under England. Government was no novelty to them, but the men who undertook to guide the first steps of the new-born Argentine Confederation were mere theorists at governing, men full of excellent schemes which did not work. They wanted immigration and did not know how to get it. And they were city Creoles. Behind them were the Pampa and the upland provinces; in both, the gaucho.

AGRICULTURE DEVELOPED ONLY AS RESULT OF LATER LARGE IMMIGRATION

The thing that was fundamental in the gaucho character was his familiar use of horses and cows. He might be poor or he might be rich; he might be white or he might have a considerable strain of Indian blood; he might be subservient to a patron or he might enforce homage as a landowner or even as an outlaw—a *gaucho malo*—but he could not very well live much in town. His interests were dead set against town interests. Agriculture was a town affair carried on in those days in the outskirts of the cities, as is market gardening— the intensest form of all agriculture—the world over. Those 373 square miles of tilled land are proof of it. Now that 4,700,-000 immigrants have come, there are nearly 100,000 square miles of cultivated land.[7] And these immigrants brought it under tillage. See how the allowance of tilled land per capita of the population[8] has increased through the last half century.

	1865	1873	1888	1895	1900	1905	1910	1914
Acres per capita	0.13	0.7	1.9	3.0	3.7	5.6	7.0	7.7

[7] As in footnote 4 above, 60,755,000 acres, or 95,000 square miles in 1914. Total immigration to 1914, inclusive, 4,660,549 (Resumen estadístico, pp. 3 and 32). The *net* immigration, i.e. immigration minus emigration, was for the same period 2,640,648 (*ibid.*, pp. 3 and 31).

[8] Ratios from 1865 to 1905 inclusive calculated from tilled land and population figures in Molinas, *op. cit.*, p. 144, in doing which the population figures for 1900 and 1905 were correlated respectively with the tilled land figures for 1901 and 1906 for the reason mentioned in the caption of Fig. 18 ; ratio for 1910 from *Estadística Agrícola* (published by Direcc. Gen. de Econ. Rural y Estadís., Minist. de Agric., Buenos Aires), *1910-11*, p. 9; ratio for 1914 from data cited above in footnote 4.

This looks large beside 0.9 in Italy and Germany, 1.5 in France, 1.7 in Russia, 2.0 in Rumania, and 2.2 in Denmark, though 4.8 in the United States and 6.0 in Canada are more like Argentine figures.[9] There is a great difference in the extent to which these countries concern themselves with agriculture, to say nothing of some difficulty in deciding what is agricultural land. Of some 18,500,000 acres that New Zealand calls cultivated land 16,500,000 are in grass.[10] There may be some question of the extent of cultivation involved in maintaining that grass. At one time in Texas all land that had wire fence around it was called improved, which with us is supposed to mean cultivated. So in the Argentine Republic much grazing land is planted to wheat for four or five years as a preparation for reseeding it to alfalfa. Are the enumerators careful to deduct it from the cultivated land when it is again seeded to alfalfa and returned to grazing? Still, I think the figures are approximately good. The United States has had steadier values for the same period, the acres of improved land in farms per capita there being:[11]

	1850	1860	1870	1880	1890	1900	1910	1920
Acres per capita	4.9	5.2	4.9	5.7	5.7	5.5	5.2	4.8

But with us people have tilled the land from the beginning. We did not emerge upon agriculture from a stage of hunting wild cattle. Texas, which may be more fairly compared with the Argentine, especially as it was so long Spanish, has a present per capita acreage of agricultural land similar to the Argentine. But Texas shows about the same beginnings as the rest of the United States:[12]

	1850	1860	1870	1880	1890	1900	1910	1920
Acres per capita	3.0	4.4	3.6	7.9	9.3	6.4	7.0	6.7

[9] Ratios calculated from: *Annuaire International de Statistique Agricole, 1915 et 1916*, Inst. Internatl. d'Agric., Rome, 1917, Table 3 (Repartition de la superficie productive), pp. 14–15, and Table 1, pp. 2–3.

[10] *Statesman's Year-Book for 1925*, London, 1925, p. 413.

[11] Fourteenth Census of the United States, 1920, Vol. 5: Agriculture, General Report, Washington, 1922, Table 3 on p. 32.

[12] Acreage of improved land in: Fourteenth Census of the United States, 1920; Vol. 6, Part II: Agriculture, Southern States, Washington, 1922, Table 2 on p. 655, population, *ibid.*, Vol. 1: Population, Table 8 on pp. 20–21.

Texas might well have been expected to have a cattle-hunting period like the Argentine when plowed land was almost non-existent, but the figures do not let us believe it. However, the great agricultural states of North and South Dakota, taken as a unit, show most surprising figures:[13]

	1860	1870	1880	1890	1900	1910	1920
Acres per capita	0.4	3.1	8.5	21.5	29.0	31.3	33.3

The two states had more than 19 acres per capita in cereals alone in 1919 and show a high use of the land.[14]   The Territory La Pampa, which the Argentines call their Far West, in 1914 had 26 acres in cereals to each inhabitant, 44 acres of cultivated land, though 15 acres of this, in alfalfa, is very likely really pastoral land.[15]

In every case, however, the amount of Argentine tilled land in 1865 turns out to be extremely small. It appears that nowhere in the world is there a land that has been colonized from Europe for three hundred years and still had to wait the arrival of newer Europeans to begin any effective use of its soil.

Rosas' Contribution In Breaking Power of Gaucho Chieftains

The independence of the gaucho, especially when he owned land, made him slow to accept the authority of the town theorists in the place of the Spanish authorities whom he had helped so materially to overthrow. Rather he tended to gather power into his own hands and to seek to extend it. Each such gaucho if forceful tended to become one of the *caudillos*, or petty chieftains, who loomed so large in the period of anarchy that followed the Revolution.

[13] Acreage of improved land in 1860 and 1870 in: Ninth Census of the United States, 1870, Vol. 3, Washington, 1872, pp. 86 and 81; from 1880 to 1920 inclusive in: Fourteenth Census of the United States, 1920, Vol. 6, Part I: Agriculture, Northern States, Washington, 1922, Table 2 on p. 617 (N.D.) and Table 2 on p. 645 (S.D.); population, reference as in preceding footnote.

[14] Cereal acreage, Fourteenth Census, Vol. 6, Part I, Table 32 on p. 623 (N.D.) and Table 32 on p. 651 (S.D.); population, reference as in footnote 12, above.

[15] Cereal, alfalfa, and cultivated acreage in: Tercer censo nacional, 1914, Vol. 5: Explotaciones agropecuarias, Buenos Aires, 1919, p. xiii; population, *ibid.*, Vol. 2: Población, Buenos Aires, 1916, p. 109.

It was the great contribution of Rosas to the Republic, selfish and bloodthirsty tyrant though he was, that he so completely broke up and destroyed the power of the numerous *caudillos* who infested the country. His epoch (1830–1852) was one when country was put above city, anarchy above law, barbaric force above civilized society, and—since civilization appeared to come from Europe—all Creole things above the things of Europe. It was an epoch when thousands of decent citizens could save their lives only by flight and exile. As a logical part of this program immigration was forbidden and all intercourse with foreigners discouraged.

How Roca Brought Prosperity

Quite as striking as the prevention of immigration by the epoch of anarchy was its stimulation half a century later in the two terms of General Roca, who completed Rosas' campaigns of the thirties against the Indians in western Buenos Aires Province by their destruction or capture in 1870, finally opening up the Pampa to the railroad that was to make its wide occupation possible. It is the irony of history that Rosas, idol of all the most brutal elements of Creole barbarism, came from cultured Buenos Aires, and Roca, the support and stabilizer of civilization on the Pampa, came from the old-Creole province of Tucumán.

Before Roca the greatest immigration in any year was 48,000 in 1873 (Fig. 18). His first term began with 27,000 and raised it to 81,000, and two years after the end of the administration (1889) the first high point of 219,000 was reached. His second term began with an annual immigration of 67,000 in 1898 and saw it rise to 126,000 in 1904. In another two years the second high point was reached, 253,000. This latter wave of immigration continued with minor fluctuations until the World War, rising to a maximum of 323,000 in 1912. The two waves are seen from the diagram to comprise together the mass of the modern immigration to the country.

Are we going too far in associating the greater part of the remaking of the Argentine by immigration with General Roca? Was it not perhaps chance that it came along in his times? The net immigration to the Republic before Roca first became president was over 173,000.[16] These men were already eagerly at work developing the long neglected treasures of the Argentine soil. Almost every individual of them was in touch with the home country, reporting his progress by sending money back. The remittances spoke more eloquently than any letters. If they were large the distant son was prospering, if they diminished or failed he was faring ill. Ignorant and illiterate as the immigrants have usually been, the clearest word that passed to Europe was not the written word but that spoken by the constant stream of those who went back and the fact of their return. Remittances were balanced against numbers of emigrants returned. Few students realize the importance of the return currents that tend to offset the streams of immigrants even to countries like the United States. There came to the United States in the year ending June 30, 1912, a total of 1,017,155 aliens.[17] This is usually regarded as a million added to our population in that year. But it is also reported[18] that 615,292 aliens left our shores during the same year, the net result being an addition of 401,863 persons. Our government has kept this record only since July 1, 1907. The Argentine government has kept it systematically since 1870. Figure 18 shows the total immigration by an upper thin line and the net immigration by a heavier line. It is certain that the would-be immigrant in Europe estimates very accurately the prosperity of the New World colonies, despite his extreme general ignorance. There was at hand a rich, virgin soil, and it was the clear intention of the Argentine authorities to open it up to the 173,000 im-

[16] Resumen estadístico, p. 3 (1880 included).

[17] *Annual Rept. of the Commissioner General of Immigration for the Fiscal Year Ended June 30, 1925*, Bureau of Immigration, U. S. Dept. of Labor, Washington, 1925, p. 137, Table 48.

[18] *loc. cit.*

migrants who had stayed; these were the "colonists" at work upon it. What was needed to send back to Europe the word that should expand the streams of immigrants? Mainly stability—stability in politics, stability in currency, stability in markets. This General Roca gave them. His two six-year terms were without revolution, and that cannot be said of any other administration up to that of Roque Sáenz Peña in 1911. Roca was strong in command of his army, and under him the country was assured of peace. That is of immense significance.

You are trying to establish a farm with inadequate resources in a foreign land, whose very language you do not well understand. An officer comes along with his squad to commandeer your horses, your grain, or your own service. What can you do? You are helpless. Immigration is at once checked at the source in distant Europe. But suddenly General Roca takes office, and you have peace and security. You work long hours and your family works and the harvest comes and you remit and Europe knows that all is well. Then the immigrant stream begins to swell. There is no propaganda for immigration like the prosperity of the immigrant. Roca gave them peace and security that meant prosperity. And the peace and security that Roca brought lasted beyond Roca's day. A black dot occurs on the diagram (Fig. 18) every time that a revolution has overthrown a president. What a pity a good president like Roca couldn't continue! The constitution allowed him six years, and he could not succeed himself. He and Juárez Celmán had married sisters. Juárez Celmán became president; there was good hope and peace continued and there were good harvests and the word went back to Europe. Always large remittances and few returning emigrants. The immigrant stream flowed stronger and stronger—till revolution came. Look again at that diagram and see the peace of Roca delineated in that peak of the late eighties. How few returned, how close the heavy line to the thin! But in the next decade of panics and revolutions the wide gap between those lines shows us returning throngs to discourage emigra-

FIG. 19—General Julio A. Roca, twice president and twice precursor
of a peak of Argentine prosperity.   (From a contemporary print.)

tion from Europe until other days, till Roca comes again and brings peace—and immigrants!

Roca brought a great improvement in finance, too. If a dotted line had been put on Figure 18 to tell how many centavos in gold the paper peso was worth at any time it, too, would have shown a peak in Roca's times. Four centavos it was, sometimes three in the earlier days. You paid a paper peso to have your shoes polished in Buenos Aires. In 1883 under Roca the country was put on a gold basis, and the paper peso was worth a hundred centavos in gold. This value lasted only through 1884 and then began to decline. At the end of Roca's term it was at ninety-three centavos. Not so bad if you think of what went before. But it was enough to set back immigration a little, though not much. Harvests were abundant, public order was perfect, business was good. There was much wonder at the time, much discussion how the peso could fall in the face of so much prosperity. It seems likely now that with all the prosperity of the day the government was spending and borrowing in excess of its powers to pay, except with the printing press. It is striking how the immigrants came in spite of the fall of the peso—the rise of the premium on gold, as it is called in the language of the exchanges. But Juárez Celmán was not a strong man. He could not maintain peace, nor could his successors. When Roca came back again the paper peso was fixed, in 1899, at forty-four gold centavos, with machinery for keeping it there; but until then there was revolution after revolution and the net immigration was very small indeed. At the time when things came to a head and Juárez Celmán was put out in 1890, the country lost more people than it gained.

What happened at the time of the World War was entirely different. Business was not good. The market was disrupted; ships were not to be had; and, most serious of all, men were not allowed to leave Europe but were called to the war.

CHAPTER III

ESPERANZA, THE FIRST AGRICULTURAL COLONY

Santa Fe Province to 1850

The modern Argentine immigration before General Roca was strikingly similar to the Chilean immigration of the same period. It began in the Province of Santa Fe, which lies along the west bank of the Paraná River for six hundred miles, beginning 125 miles above Buenos Aires (Fig. 8). The Legend of the Grains of Wheat has it that in 1527 Cabot planted 52 grains of wheat not far from the present city of Santa Fe and three months later harvested 52,000. At the fall of Rosas in 1852 this was frankly cattle country. You might hear it remarked any day that its fertility was wonderful; but it was academic, that faith in its fertility—a bit of *réclame* for the country. It had no significance in Argentine practical life. The land sold readily enough at $10 a square league, which means in our units six and two-thirds acres for a cent,[1] if we admit their money to have been as good as ours. Of course they hadn't the least faith in its agricultural value nor a conception of the overturn that was to come in the generation then beginning.

A number of educated Creoles were familiar with the capacity and industry of the laboring classes of Europe. Everyone knew the hopelessness of developing the country's soil resources with gaucho labor and that the Creole cattle harvesting—it was little more than that—kept the standard of life low, the people poor, and the government poor. Perhaps a few realized that land would be more valuable if agriculture were introduced on the fertile Pampa—the gaucho never dreamed

[1] One square league containing about 6672 acres.

FIG. 20—*Barranca*, or bluff, of the Paraná River at San Lorenzo, a little north of Rosario (see Fig. 21). Forty and fifty feet of water are found near the bluff, and ships used to come close up to it to load. It consists of fine reddish yellow loess, and the river is consequently reddish yellow. The shore opposite is low.

of it. The long frontage of Santa Fe on the deep stream of the Paraná would then make it easy to carry the products of the farms to Buenos Aires.

A short decade was to see colonies of European workers settled on this cheap land and, after a few years of the greatest hardship, establishing forever the superiority—almost the magic—of agriculture here. The border of Santa Fe Province that fronts the Paraná River for so great a distance is mostly low and liable to floods. Only south of the mouth of the Carcarañá River does the bank form the high bluff shown in the photograph (Fig. 20) and on the map of the Paraná River region (Fig. 21). The city of Santa Fe itself is not on the Paraná but four miles west of it across the low flood plain at the point where the Salado River enters it (Fig. 57). Thus the new port of Santa Fe terminates in a four-mile channel across the flats, and the city, unlike Rosario, is somewhat exposed to floods. South of Santa Fe City the strip of swamp land west of the river continues southward (Fig. 21) to the mouth of the Carcarañá, margined on the west by the indefinite channels of the Santa Fe River—which in a manner continues the course of the Salado but appears to derive its water mainly from the Paraná at high stages—by the Coronda lagoon, and by the Coronda River, which joins the Paraná at the mouth of the Carcarañá. Our picture of the bluff was taken at San Lorenzo, about twelve miles north of Rosario. North of Santa Fe the same strip of swampy flood plain continues west of the Paraná channel to the San Javier. The swamp land is a barrier behind which Corrientes and Entre Ríos Provinces always lay secure from the raids of Pampa Indians. An inspector on the ground in 1872 figured[2] that a square league of land at that time would yield, by grazing alone (though he included butter and cheese, which were quite un-Creole), 2062 *bolivianos* and, by the agriculture of that day,

[2] Guillermo Wilcken: Las colonias: Informe sobre el estado actual de las colonias agrícolas de la República Argentina presentado á la Comisión Central de Inmigración, Buenos Aires, 1873, p. 25.

36,000 *bolivianos*, the *boliviano* being then about 55 centavos of the Argentine peso.

THE FOUNDING OF ESPERANZA BY AARON CASTELLANOS

Esperanza, the first of these colonies, is famous in the Argentine for its success, and, partly because it led in the movement, there has grown up a somewhat romantic legend of its beauty, its wealth, and the intelligence and industry of its settlers. Originally taken up by French-speaking and German-speaking Swiss, it has later added a considerable number of Italians, but it is known as the Swiss colony. A president of the Republic visiting the colony on a holiday occasion is reported to have asked a little girl if she was Argentine and got the answer, "No, Suiza de Esperanza" (Swiss of Esperanza), and a charming young lady, to whom the author was presented at a dinner in Córdoba in 1918, was referred to in the same terms.

The founding of Esperanza[3] was entirely due to the imagination, the vision, and the restless activity of an Argentine from the upland province of Salta, Aaron Castellanos, whose portrait is shown in Figure 22. The idyll of those labor-loving farmers compelling the scrubby wilderness to yield luxurious crops and abundance to take the place of penury had its only real existence in the dream of that Salteño Creole. Its symbol was the name that he gave the colony: Esperanza, or Hope. If the dream did not fully materialize in the lives of the colonists, it has become a solid part of the faith of the Argentine people. In 1824 Castellanos was trying to open up navigation on the Bermejo under a contract with the provinces of Salta and Buenos Aires, only to fall into the hands of Lopez, the dictator of Paraguay, who took away his boats and papers and kept him in prison for five years. Next we find him cajoling the Federal government to let him colonize Patagonia,

[3] The present account is based mainly on the works of Wilcken (cited above) and Cervera (cited below, footnote 9) and the statements of settlers and their children at Esperanza.

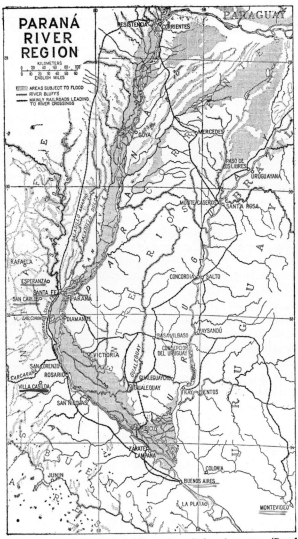

Fig. 21—Map of the Paraná River region. Scale, 1:6,500,000. (Based on the map by Chavanne cited on p. 164.)

The stippled area is liable to flood. Enough railroads are shown to suggest the traffic crossings at Santa Fe–Paraná and at the Ibicuy-Zárate train ferry. The strong bluffs are marked by hachures.

offering to bring European settlers for all the valley bottoms
of the Río Chubut from the Atlantic to the Andes. Then he
turns up in Europe trying to get a railway built from Rosario
to Córdoba by bankers whom he knew how to interest, for he
knew the country and could make them see his visions with
him. He was advised to get people in the Argentine to take
up his projects, which included colonization. As the bankers
perceived, he had no strong friends in the governing class in
the Confederation, and he was to feel the need of them. He
did not in his own country inspire the ready confidence that
he did abroad. His proposition for the railroad was rejected,
only to be undertaken twenty years later at much greater
expense. But he was persistent and in 1853 won over the
provincial legislature of Santa Fe to give him a contract,[4]
ratified a year later by General Urquiza for the Confederation,
to bring over a thousand Swiss families to settle on lands
belonging to the province but quite useless because the Indians
overran them. Castellanos was to bring them in five groups of
two hundred families each. He undertook to select and collect the immigrants from northern Europe, peaceable folk who
understood farming, and bring them to Santa Fe, advancing
them all the necessary expenses of the trip. This outlay he
expected them to repay him in three annual sums, with interest
at 10 per cent. The province was to supply each group of two
hundred families with 7 square leagues (about 46,700 acres)
of land that it had—good land, but perfectly valueless then,
that was bringing no return whatever; it was to build them
huts and supply them with tools, oxen, seed, and supplies at a
total expense of $200 a family, which was to be returned by
them later. The province further agreed to relieve the colonists from all sorts of taxes for the first five years and to ask no
military service from them except within their own concessions. They appear to have understood that they had Indians
to fight, for four hundred of them brought their own rifles.
One gets the impression that they rather looked forward to this.

[4] Wilcken, *op. cit.*, pp. 19–20.

Fig. 22 (left)—Don Aaron Castellanos of Salta, old-Creole founder of Esperanza, the first agricultural colony, in 1852.
Fig. 23 (right)—Don Antonio Hessel. Argentine of German parentage, mayor of Esperanza in 1918, owner of a machine shop.

FIG. 24—House of Simon Grenon, French Swiss colonist of Esperanza, still alive and vigorous on his farm in 1918. He was one of the founders of the colony. His lot was at the border of the settlement; he therefore long used adjacent lands for raising cattle. The house is substantial but quite un-Creole.

Castellanos counted on a considerable return from his undertaking. The colonists were to pay back his advances for transportation. Further, they were to give him a third of each of their first five harvests, and finally the Province of Santa Fe was to grant him 32 square leagues of land, half of it on the banks of the Paraná and half on the banks of the Salado. Just as Castellanos was the only person with vision to perceive the future of agriculture in Santa Fe, it is likely that no one else perceived the immense value of his stipulated returns, at least at first. Santa Fe was used to making large donations of public land. Oroño lists[5] some two hundred square leagues thus given away between 1857 and 1865, including two square leagues (20.8 square miles) to each colonel in the war with Paraguay, with a regular scale for other ranks ending with a quarter square mile for each private soldier.

LOCATING THE IMMIGRANTS

Castellanos gave bonds for the fulfillment of his part and went to Europe. There he was diligent. In June, 1855, he wrote from Paris that his first group of two hundred families— he really brought 208—would sail from Dunkirk that autumn. The letter found the Province of Santa Fe in financial straits, a frequent condition of the old Creole states. Cullen, the governor, and two other citizens loaned $900 to make a beginning of preparations for the colonists, as two-room shanties 15 by 30 feet had to be built for each family and their lots surveyed and marked out before their arrival. It sheds light on the sources of revenue possessed by the province to see that this loan was repaid in December from a sale of sheep from the provincial ranch! One may be sure that the governing authorities, with no money or steady sources of income and a feeble hold on power, were annoyed at the necessity of acting for these colonists, whom they had never seen and whose advantage to them they only half believed in.

[5] Nicasio Oroño: Defensa y reclamación de derechos de las tierras de la Colonia General Oroño, Buenos Aires, 1900, pp. 63–66.

Castellanos asserts that nothing was ready when the colonists arrived in January, 1856, but this was certainly an exaggeration. Lots had been marked out, huts built, and some of the supplies were on hand. But on the day the first of them reached Santa Fe Governor Cullen had to lay aside his civil office to take command of the forces who were starting to drive out invading troops from Buenos Aires! He probably gave imperfect attention to the arriving colonists. Heaven knew they had cost him trouble enough already.

The colony was not located as agreed "on the right bank of the Paraná River and both shores of the Río Salado to the north of the old town of San Javier—to be selected by Castellanos' representative from any land that belonged to the province there." Just as the surveyor was starting out for that point he received word from the Federal authorities not to go. No explanation was given. Wilcken, writing fourteen years afterward, says[6] the original site was "too exposed and accessible to the Indians." But it was certainly no worse in that respect than the site finally occupied eight leagues northwest of Santa Fe city. As it happened this site was among private lands, and this involved another deviation from the contract which was to make trouble for many years.

INITIAL DIFFICULTIES OF THE COLONY

The colonists' lots made up a block of three square leagues of land (31.2 square miles, or 20,000 acres; Fig. 25). The contract called for this and also another four square leagues around it, which were not to be sold but used in common for pasture. This was not provided. It would have been a very narrow strip and hard to get at from the inner lots of the colony, and the idea was not at all in harmony with the idea of a purely agricultural colony. The authorities would have had to buy it, as I surmise they bought the central three leagues. Possibly they saw the futility of the pasture land, and possibly they also saw that there was no difficulty about

[6] Wilcken, *op. cit.*, p. 21.

it for the moment in any case. The land around, though of private ownership, was entirely unused, thanks to the Indians, and the colonists might use as much as they wanted for grazing cattle. Argentines of the old days never begrudged neighbors the use of their grass. There were no fences. Pasture was free, like air and water.

On considering the shortness of money and the troubled politics I think the Santa Fe government made a pretty good showing. This item of the four leagues of communal land, together with every other individual item of the contract between Aaron Castellanos and the provincial government of Santa Fe, even to the kinds and weights of food to be supplied, was adopted bodily from the contract of one year earlier with Dr. Auguste Brougnes,[7] who had promulgated at Buenos Aires the possibilities of European immigration and actually brought a colony to Corrientes, reaching that city exactly a year before the first settlers for Esperanza arrived at Santa Fe. The authorities of Corrientes had nothing ready. Scurrying round for a location, they put the immigrants down in the remote territory of Misiones, the very northeast corner of the republic. The land was not merely unsuitable for the cereals, the money crop that must inevitably support the colonists from the start, but it was the property of private individuals, who soon ousted the colonists. All of Dr. Brougnes's undertakings failed, but the plans of the colony at Esperanza are his, word for word. The failure of the Corrientes government to meet its contract makes the activity of the Santa Fe authorities look very creditable.

The greatest handicap of the Esperanza colony has not yet been mentioned. As attention was called to the proposed colony by the preparations for its reception, the local "peasantry" manifested the most active dissatisfaction with the scheme. "Why do so much for foreigners, who have no claim at all on the country, and nothing of the sort for us, who have made so many sacrifices for the nation for many years?"

[7] F. T. Molinas: La colonización argentina y las industrias agropecuarias, Buenos Aires, [1910], p. 49.

These gaucho peasants were of course the material of revolutions. They were the soldiers used by the *caudillos* in fighting their individual feuds and combined wars as well as in the defense against the Indians. The government needed them every day to maintain itself in power. This sentiment must have greatly discouraged activity in behalf of the colonists. There was no further thought of granting Castellanos his 32 leagues of land—he was indeed on a later day voted 10—, and the agreements about location and common land were certainly broken. The present writer does not think it necessary to go back of the facts stated to find reason for their action in an alleged unreliability of all Creoles. It was unfortunate but not unintelligible.

The colonists arrived, the first company on January 25 and the last of them in May, 1856. Castellanos had apparently filled his part of the contract admirably. They are often called industrious, labor-loving agriculturists. They are surely associated with the beginnings of that agricultural development of the Republic that has since grown to magnificent proportions. They were its pioneers. But Wilcken, who visited Esperanza in 1872 in the course of a tour of inspection of the colonies, says they were ignorant "of every notion of agriculture or tillage of the fields. Very few of them were farmers at all, having been recruited mostly among people without trade or business and of the lowest condition in populous cities."[8] He also states that they had very little zeal for work. Some of them certainly were like that.

WITHDRAWAL OF CASTELLANOS

Castellanos came not only with the colonists of his contract but also brought an agreement on the part of European firms to settle 60,000 colonists in the Chaco. In the then state of the public mind this was not to be thought of. "How do we know that a lot of foreigners like that, all set down in one place, won't claim the region for themselves and turn us out of it?"

[8] Author's translation from Wilcken, *op. cit.*, p. 21.

Castellanos was highly indignant at the breaches of his contract and refused to bring the later sections of his colony or to look after the people at Esperanza. For a while it looked as if the colony would go to pieces, but presently General Urquiza saved it by taking over Castellanos' claims against the colonists, paying him 200,000 *bolivianos* for them. He turned the further care of them over to the Province of Santa Fe. Probably they would have been saved much of the sufferings of the next four years if they could have kept the services of a capable and energetic man like Castellanos, especially on account of his knowledge of the country. But at the beginning Governor Cullen and in 1865 Don Nicasio Oroño, then governor of Santa Fe, gave the settlers their personal attention and were rewarded by their devotion.

Hardships of the First Years

The first four years in the new colony were of very great hardship. The conception that the patron class had of suitable accommodations for workingmen was an exceedingly meager one. The standard of living under the old cattle system had been very low. It was expected that these European workers were different, that they would soon improve their surroundings, but the authorities did not feel called on to give them any better houses than the gauchos lived in. It would have certainly called up a storm of protest if they had. Their adobe houses with roofs of thatch were miserable hovels and doubtless seemed so to the Swiss. Had they been skilled farmers they would probably have liked it less than they did. But there was a certain Swiss Family Robinson air about the adventure that helped them through. Simon Grenon seemed to delight in pointing out the variety of forest and fruit trees that he had on his place (Fig. 24), raised from seed brought out in his pocket, in true Robinson fashion.

The French Ambassador who visited the colony in September, 1856, was loud in denouncing its condition. "The advantages of the climate were more than offset by economic circumstances of quite a different character. To what end cultivate the ground when you cannot get your produce out for lack of roads? Moreover our workingmen cannot live in miserable huts, naked and hungry, with a guitar and a few gulps of *maté*, as the poor native gaucho does. They have other necessities and earn too little to buy objects that are dearer than in France."[9] They had trouble with the rain, which came too late and too much, and they had a visitation of locusts, which do serious damage to narrow strips of Argentine territory almost every year. The ground was covered with scrubby woods such as those shown in Figure 7 from the Province of Córdoba, but very likely the trees were larger in 1856. Each family, in order to obtain title, was bound to clear half of the 83-acre lot[10] which was assigned to it, and after cutting the trees they had great trouble with the roots, which did not rot and made plowing well nigh impossible. The government had to help them with food and seed, to release them from paying back their passage money, and reduce the payment on their harvests from a third to a fourth. The first harvest was the only one that they paid a third of. But the task of establishing new farms in those woods was bound to be a tremendous one even for people familiar with such problems and supported in some comfort at home. No doubt the homesickness of those years was very acute. Nor were they helped much by inner resources. They had no schools for a long time and even refused to send their children to such schools as the state provided for them, so that the first children born at Esperanza grew up unable to read. The Protestants among them, 80 families in 1871, allowed their two ministers to leave rather than support them.[11] There were many sects, and they were disunited and unwilling to help one another. Nature and man

[9] Author's translation from [M. M. Cervera:] Boceto histórico del Dr. Manuel M. Cervera sobre colonización argentina y fundación de Esperanza, Esperanza, 1906, p. 62.

[10] 20 *cuadras cuadradas*, equivalent to 83.4 acres, or 33.74 hectares (Wilcken, *op. cit.*, p. 274; Georg Hiller: Einwanderung und Einwanderungspolitik in Argentinien, Berlin, 1912, p. 19).

[11] Wilcken, *op. cit.*, pp. 8 and 9.

through those years seemed to compete with each other in displaying their worst qualities.

Experience has shown that the thing essential to carry such a colony through its early trials is an energetic leader with knowledge of the country and influential friends in the government. We shall see a notable illustration of this in the protection Don Carlos Casado was able to give the colony Candelaria.

In the practical experience of Esperanza and neighboring colonies the 83-acre lots assigned to each family are too small. The colonists were firmly persuaded that they must let the land "rest" at least one year in three. The contract obliged them to clear only half their land to acquire title, but they seem to have cleared it all and to have wanted two more lots for each family, to keep one in crop, one in pasture, and one always resting. No family at Esperanza had more than one concession; consequently some of those who were capable of it bought cheap land outside in quantity large enough and abandoned their lots with all that went with them. In the two years from 1869 to 1871 the population of the colony decreased by 136 members.[12] There seems to have been no ground for their notion that the soil needed rest. Rotation of crops accomplishes the end more economically. It is a problem of intensity of cultivation in relation to the price of land, two things that cannot be kept apart. European high cultivation goes with dear land: It would not have been economical on the cheap lands of Santa Fe. Farms in the Argentine commonly enough run up to 200 and 300 hectares, but of course their size varies greatly with place and the crop.

The colonists were supposed to be provided with two horses, two oxen, seven cows, and one bull to each family, in all twelve head of stock.[13] By 1869 they had 19½ head to a family,[14] showing the natural tendency to adopt the stock-raising habits of the country, as it required less labor and

[12] ibid., p. 8.
[13] ibid., p. 20.
[14] ibid., pp. 11 and 7.

helped them out of their difficulties. This, of course, involved the use of more land, as it was used less intensively.

POOR MARKETING FACILITIES AND THEIR EFFECT ON THE CHOICE OF CROPS

It had been a terrible handicap to the colony to be set down 24 miles from the navigable waters of the Paraná.[15] It took the first settlers three days to make the journey with their ox teams. In 1864 a 40-vara (115-foot) road was laid out to Santa Fe and a stage service established.[16] That specification of the width of the road is eloquent of Pampa conditions. Road material is entirely wanting on the fine loess of the region. In practice one drove over the Pampa anywhere before fencing was general. Where the rut is worn too deep or a hole has been worn, you turn aside. For this a certain amount of width is the best provision. A 10-meter road causes loud complaint in rainy weather. There is not room enough beside the track to seek out a better road. In 1918 I found that causeways with culverts were being built across the *bañados* in Santa Fe, but that calls for capital not at hand sixty years ago. Freights to Santa Fe in 1871 were a little more than 6 cents a bushel for wheat or maize, with 2 cents a bushel octroi at the gates of the city and a 27-cent toll at the bridge for each round trip of the cart. The water carriage thence to Buenos Aires was 60 cents a hundredweight. The railroad did not connect the colony with Santa Fe till 1883. At times the freight on wheat from Esperanza to Buenos Aires cost a third of the value of the wheat.

[15] Nevertheless Molinas (*op. cit.*, p. 65) asserts that the change was a fortunate one in spite of the difficulties of transportation, because it made possible the large-scale production of wheat, which was to be the mainspring of colonization in the province. The lands along the Paraná, he says, were poor in phosphoric acid and other elements necessary for this plant. Proof of this is seen in the precarious existence led by the eight colonies actually founded on or near its flood plain, mainly on the San Javier (see also, below, p. 86): Santa Rosa, Helvecia, Francesa, San Javier, California, San Martín, Reconquista, and Avellaneda (indicated on Fig. 28 along the San Javier from south to north respectively by the years 61, 65, 67, 67, 66, 87 [on the Saladillo Amargo]; the last two beyond the northern edge of the map in about lat. 29°10′S.)

[16] Cervera, *op. cit.*, p. 71.

These freight charges quickly had their effect on the choice of plants in the colony. The potato crop, for instance, fell off rapidly. In 1871 the potatoes that the artisans and merchants ate in Esperanza were brought in by cart from Santa Fe. In 1868 the colony had produced 4850 *arrobas* (of 25 lbs. each); in 1870, 600 *arrobas;* and in 1871, 360.[17] "Though none of the colonies produces enough potatoes for its own consumption they are known to have a wide and certain sale and sell at 25 cents an *arroba*. They have the advantage of giving two crops a year if the farmer picks the best time to plant and cultivate. But most of the colonists pay no attention to such details. They plant their potatoes and leave them to providence without any weeding or cultivation at all. Both crops are exposed to loss if ripened late, as it is sure to be if cultivation is neglected. The first harvest, in November and December, is attacked by a brown beetle and the second planting by winter frosts. If the potatoes are cultivated, both crops may be made before their enemies appear."[18]

POOR TILLAGE

We shall find it true all through the colonization of the Republic that most of the colonists showed a dislike of work. Is it an echo of gaucho influence? Everyone knows the advantages of a thorough tillage and breaking up of the soil. The best farmers always practiced it, and the good harvests were there to be seen.

Mostly the colonists confined themselves to wheat and maize. As the wheat did better on ground that had first been planted to maize they usually planted new ground to maize but seemed to have the idea that, as they were really meaning to get a crop of wheat out of the ground later, it was not worth while to try to get much of a crop of maize, although it was really about as profitable as wheat. So they plowed superficially and scattered the maize broadcast. Then the weeds so

[17] Wilcken, *op. cit.*, p. 12.
[18] Paraphrased from Wilcken, *op. cit.*, p. 279.

choked the plants while they were young that the harvest
rarely paid the cost of preparing the ground. Not far away,
at the colony California, a small group of Americans were
planting their maize in rows, cultivating it thoroughly and
getting phenomenal crops.[19] The weeds were asserted by the
Esperanza colonists to be evidence that the soil was worn
out by the cultivation of fourteen years. As a matter of fact
the luxuriance of the weeds was the best evidence of the good
quality of the soil. "Even now if the weeds were cut and
burned and the roots plowed up and the ground continuously
tilled there is no doubt the results would amply repay the
labor. There are plenty of good examples to imitate. The
more experienced and skillful colonists never allow the weeds
to grow. As they sink the plowshare deep into the earth they
pull up the weeds by the roots with great ease. This procedure
not merely prevents them from extending their roots deeper
but avoids the absorption they would make of the nourishing
juice of the earth, weakening the crop." I quote this passage
from Wilcken[20] as an example of the criticisms he makes of
the colonists as farmers. Cultivation did not appeal to them.
This was obvious enough in the maize fields in 1918. The
colonists had no notion of tillage. At that date the outlook
was discouraging. The maize crop had been selling mainly
to the Germans, and the English would neither allow the use
of sacks for the crop nor allow it to be shipped. Even in
the experimental plats of the agricultural school the best
corn was hardly comparable to the ordinary run of our American fields.

CLOSING THE COLONISTS' CONTRACTS

In December, 1862, the first titles began to be issued to the
settlers who had now completed their five years of cultivation
of their lots. This gave them definitive ownership of their
83 acres. Such a lot was now worth, unimproved, 600 to 800

[19] Wilcken, *op. cit.*, p. 277.
[20] *ibid.*, p. 277.

bolivianos. This delivery of title, following the good harvests of 1861 and 1862, must have encouraged the colonists to better efforts. They now showed evidence of possessing a higher standard of living than the gauchos about them by improving their houses. In 1861 there were still 437 ranchos and only 33 houses had *azotea* roofs.[21] By 1871 there were only 15 ranchos and 220 houses had *azotea* roofs; besides there were 150 brick houses with roofs of thatch.

The failure of the government to provide the four square leagues of common land outside the colony made trouble for a long series of years. No doubt the colonists were well posted on the terms of their contract. There was no visible occupancy of the private lands around the colony, and the settlers of the outer tiers of lots raised cattle on the lands without paying much attention to the agriculture they were brought to practice. One such, the French Swiss Grenon, is reputed to have made a fortune in this way and added a number of concessions to his original one. He is one of the few original settlers still on the land he first settled. Many of the settlers prospered and retired to the larger cities or engaged in other business there. I was told that none of the sons of the colonists practiced farming, but that statement was a little too sweeping.

As the lands in the colony acquired value when prosperity began to come in its fifth year, the owners of surrounding land sought to take profit by selling out to would-be agriculturists. But possession was strenuously resisted by the colonists of the outer tier, who resorted to acts of violence rather than allow "their communal pasture land" to be taken away from them. This brought them into conflict with the police, and the unpleasantness spread to the inner settlers, who had no advantage or interest in siding with the disorderly element, which alone had been profiting from the grazing land. The state had no power to dispossess legal owners of their land, and any

[21] Cervera, *op. cit.*, p. 70. The *azotea* is a roof of flat tiles barely sloping enough for drainage and strong enough to walk upon; it is used to sit upon on pleasant evenings and even to sleep on in hot weather. But it demands house walls of solid brickwork to sustain it.

damages paid the colony must have been for general account, which would not have been satisfactory to the trouble makers. The outline of the colony on the official map of Santa Fe Province[22] in 1913 shows nearly a square league of undivided land on the north, marked "enlargement of Esperanza," and a group of lots adjoining on the west appears to have been added to the colony, perhaps as compensation for the lacking four leagues of communal land (see Fig. 25).

THE FRENCH-SPEAKING AND GERMAN-SPEAKING SETTLERS

The colony was laid out (Fig. 25) in two groups of 105 lots of 20 square *cuadras* (83.4 acres) each, with 20-meter streets between the lots and a north-south strip 3 *cuadras* (1279 feet) wide between the two groups. The eastern group was assigned to the French-speaking settlers and the western one to those speaking German. The actual division among nationalities, in 1869, was 557 Germans, 928 German and French Swiss, 243 Argentines, 94 French, and 34 Alsatians,[23] the Argentines being mostly the children born in the colony. The division by groups was not absolute. French-speaking settlers were found on both sides and Germans too, and there were intermarriages between the two, which brought about a further intermixture. There does not seem to have been any particular hostility between the two. Even during the World War there was much less than might have been expected. Mayor Hessel began cleaning out the ditches after a flood on the German side and was criticized by the French for it, though it seemed to him the quickest way to get the water to run off. When he came to the French side again he was accused of putting in more time than on the west. However, this was only talk. Citizens had general good feeling for one another and avoided war topics.

[22] Provincia de Santa Fé: Registro gráfico construido con los datos recopilados por la Dirección de Obras Públicas y Geodesía, 1: 250,000, [Santa Fe], 1913. Also edition in 1: 500,000.

[23] Wilcken, *op. cit.*, p. 8.

During the period when imperial Germany was reviving national feeling among the extra-European Germans there had arisen certain troubles with the Creoles and the government, but in this the French had no part. A Creole resident

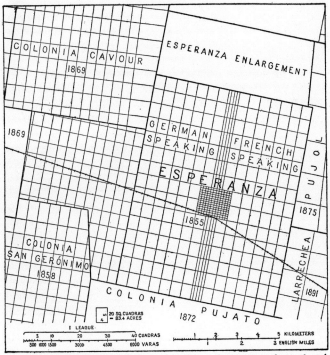

FIG. 25—Plan of Esperanza Colony with a later enlargement on the north and (probably) an enlargement on the west, with neighboring colonies. Scale, 1:172,000. (Based on the map cited in footnote 22.)

in whom I have confidence volunteered the information that the Germans never called themselves Argentines even in the second generation (though I met some who did) and were the only foreigners inclined to be exclusive. All had their clubs, for instance, the Germans among others, and all admitted anyone who was interested to their functions. This the Germans did not do. They had a Club de Canto, he said, an excellent singing club, and, though they were all born Argentines in these days, they celebrated all the national holidays of the German Empire. They also celebrated the Argentine Twenty-fifth of May, as did everyone in town. Some of the faculty of a large normal school in the town went over to the German club, which was near, to hear the music but were denied admittance. The club was only for Germans! Even in the second generation the children of Germans call themselves German. This is practically unknown with Italians and French. The Italians become assimilated very readily. They are delighted to own a horse and wear the poncho and to throw the lasso like a gaucho, but, as has been remarked, they do not become expert in this. As far as I could learn there are no born Germans here in the city. About 1884 some government inspectors were denied admission to a German school, and the police had to use force to get them in. There was some doubt whether the Germans were complying with the law that required the national language, national history, and national geography to be taught in Spanish (*idioma nacional*, the statute calls it). This resistance of the Germans brought a penalty. A city in the Argentine Republic must have at least 8000 inhabitants. Esperanza did not have that number, but, because it was the first agricultural colony and therefore rather a pet with the nation, it was allowed a city charter. That enabled it to elect a mayor, *intendente*, from its own citizens. Otherwise the mayor would have been appointed by the governor of the province. As a penalty for the school episode the city charter was revoked, and the city became a mere municipality. A petition was sent to President Roca to ask his good offices to restore their lost standing, mainly on the ground that they had had it. Roca used his influence with the Congress, and an act was voted reënabling the city. In return the city raised a thousand dollars with which they commissioned a Córdoba artist to paint an excellent full length portrait of General Roca. This now hangs in the assembly hall of the municipality.

THE TOWN OF ESPERANZA

The strip between the two groups of lots was for the town site. If any part of it was sold, it was to be for settlement only, and half the proceeds were to go to the province and half to some public need or improvement for the municipality. It is in the center of this strip that the city of Esperanza stands. It is a neat town of 9000 inhabitants with solidly built brick houses and occasional bars in the windows in good Creole fashion. The Lehmann family, of which the governor of Santa Fe Province is a member, have a two-story house in the main square with a balcony and front ornamentation, with blank walls at the side in city fashion, over a garden thoroughly concealed behind a high wall alongside. This house contains business offices of the Lehmann landed interests in Santa Fe. Vionnet, a storekeeper in Esperanza, has a very attractive *palacete* behind a garden on a side street. So has a wealthy German widow. A Vionnet was one of the original settlers. A considerable number of the colony founders undoubtedly acquired wealth. Some of them have removed to Santa Fe and Buenos Aires. There are many factories and workshops, some of which, by supplying the capital city Santa Fe even today, show the value of the Swiss artisanship introduced by the colony. There are well-smoothed dirt streets (Fig. 26). It was more or less rainy while I was there in June, 1918, and there were four or five inches of mud in the streets, but because of the crowning the water ran off pretty well and there were no deep ruts or holes, although it was not much like the paved streets of a town of that size with us. But the climate was good. Here it was midwinter, and an overcoat was not needed. The grass and the palms in the plaza were beautifully green.

Elsewhere, however, few trees were to be seen except the orange trees in the patios.

THE TOWNSPEOPLE

The complexions of northern Europe are plainly to be seen through the region, even in high places. The governor of the province is named Lehmann, son of a German Swiss who had been a bookkeeper in the colony offices at Esperanza and had made a fortune founding colonies for profit between 1875 and 1885.[24] This bookkeeper had married a Creole lady named Leiva, who now administered the Lehmann properties and was regarded as a woman of force and ability. The governor, thus of German and Creole blood, was a very agreeable young man of distinctly German appearance but Creole manners. I found him very attentive, and he put me in the way of needed information with the same courtesy that the upper-class Creoles always show. He referred for some details to his mother, who lives in the *palacete* at Esperanza. There was a bust of the governor on the mantel made by a young fellow who had been sent to the penitentiary for "some trifle." The likeness was excellent. The governor remarked "I pardoned him out."

At the station platform at Esperanza I noticed that almost all the passengers were of Teutonic light hair and eyes, but I heard only Spanish spoken, even by very German-looking persons. On the outskirts of the town I saw some very peasant-like old Swiss women picking up sticks of firewood who looked as if they must speak German. Perhaps they could, but it was Spanish that they were chattering among themselves. All over town you saw children of the most un-Creole complexions but absolutely Creole of speech. There were some Creole faces, too; I should say a quarter to a third of all in sight—nothing, however, like the overwhelming preponderance of Creoles I had seen in the so-called German parts

[24] See below, pp. 93—94.

FIG. 26—A street in the town of Esperanza. There are few bars on the windows, but most of the houses are of the Creole type. The street is of dirt but well arched and not very muddy. The horse was still, in 1918, the general means of getting about all over the Republic except in large cities.

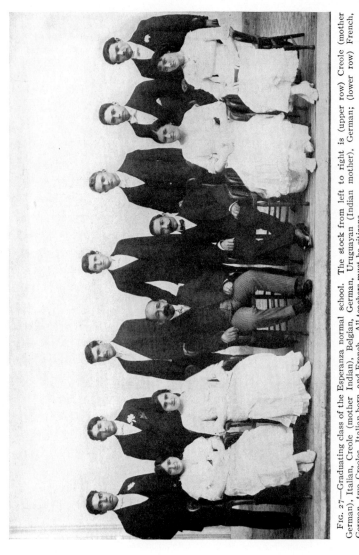

FIG. 27—Graduating class of the Esperanza normal school. The stock from left to right is (upper row) Creole (mother German), Italian, Creole (mother Indian), Belgian, German, Uruguayan (Indian mother), German; (lower row) French, German, two Creoles, Italian born, and French. All teachers must be citizens.

of Chile.[25] Yet no one thinks of calling Santa Fe or any part of it German. Hard looking revealed a house or two that showed something German in its construction, as in the lines of the sloping roof of the house next to the municipal building in the square. But it was not noticeable. The sidewalks of Esperanza were excellent, of broad red tiles, *baldosas*, which the Italians have made abound in the land.

I asked a Tucumán barber at Esperanza if there were many Creoles in town. "Quite a number," he said, "but we are all Creoles. The word means those born in the country, and although the greater part of the people here had foreign parents, they were born here and are Argentines" (see Fig. 27). I referred to the blondness. He admitted that they showed their foreign origin but would not call them foreign at all. Neither should I. The "melting pot" has certainly functioned here effectively.

The mayor of the town was Antonio Hessel (Fig. 23), son of German parents. His mother came in 1857. He keeps a machine shop, occupied in great part with automobile repairs. I noticed that he spoke Low German to the men in the shop. It is not, however, a garage but a *taller mecánico*. Automobiles are not very numerous in small Argentine towns, and horseflesh is still cheap. Mr. Hessel is a very agreeable gentleman of dark hair and skin and an excellent Creole manner. I fancy, however, there are not many Creole mayors in South America who are running machine shops. For one thing, their capacities do not usually lie in that direction.

He told me some items from his mother's voyage to the Argentine that had made a tremendous impression on her, then a child of eleven. A storm had dismasted the ship, the *Barbara*, and washed the captain overboard. The mate, thus left in charge, had never made the voyage to South America and did not know much about navigation. With broken mainmast the voyage was long and slow. In his doubt of the time

[25] Mark Jefferson: Recent Colonization in Chile, *Amer. Geogr. Soc. Research Series No. 6*, New York, 1921.

of arrival he put everybody on short rations, mainly beans. Unexpectedly one day they made Montevideo. As they were half starved, they were given so much to eat that they were all made violently ill and in that condition reached the colony. From Santa Fe she recalled that the children were allowed to ride in an ox-cart for the three-day journey, while the men and women walked alongside.

FURTHER SPREAD OF COLONIES

In the center of the too large public square is a monument with, around its base, high reliefs of the arrival of the colonists— an impressive piece of work. In spite of the hardships endured by the people at Esperanza from 1856 to 1860, in spite of the fact that the colonists cherished for years a bitter resentment at the failure of the government of Santa Fe to provide the four leagues of communal land promised them, and the annoyance felt by the governing officials at this resentment, the colony must be said to have been a success at once. For other colonies followed, slowly at first and then with great rapidity.

The adjoining map (Fig. 28) shows the colonies that began near Santa Fe and spread westward and northward from these (the darkest shade is used for those founded in the fifties and progressively lighter shades for each subsequent decade). In 1869 there were but four towns of a thousand or more people in the whole Province of Santa Fe: Rosario (23,000) and San Lorenzo (1400), both on the high bluff of the river Paraná, and Coronda (1200) and Santa Fe (11,000) just west of the river's flood plain, the river here swinging off to the east (see also Pl. IA). West-northwest of Rosario a belt of colonies is easily distinguished on Figure 28 on both sides of the line of the Central Argentine Railway that leads to Córdoba. Most of the land in the southern part of the province, however, is in large, individual estates. The colonies could

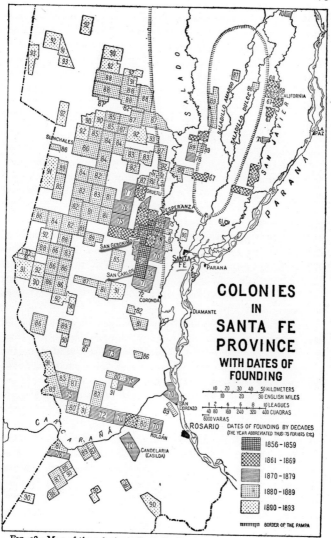

COLONIES
IN
SANTA FE
PROVINCE
WITH DATES OF
FOUNDING

10   20   30   40   50 KILOMETERS
10   20   30 ENGLISH MILES
1   2   4   6   8 10 LEAGUES
40 80   160   240   320   400 CUADRAS
6000 VARAS

DATES OF FOUNDING BY DECADES
(THE YEAR ABBREVIATED THUS:75 FOR 1875 ETC.)

1856 – 1859
1861 – 1869
1870 – 1879
1880 – 1889
1890 – 1893

⊥⊥⊥⊥⊥⊥⊥ BORDER OF THE PAMPA

Fig. 28—Map of the colonies in Sante Fe Province, with the dates of founding.
Scale, 1:3,000,000.   (Based on the map cited on p. 66 in footnote 22; the dates of
founding from publication by Carrasco cited below on p. 100.)

get land at the border of the scrub because the Indians constantly threatened it and made it worthless.

The Part Played by the Immigrant in the Life of the Republic

An important effect of modern colonization in the Argentine Republic, of which we have now had our first glimpse, is the abundance of skilled workmen that have come to the country among the immigrants. It is easily seen everywhere in the contrast of the mason work in old Creole buildings and newer ones. The Spanish masons of the colonial houses built with admirable style and taste but indifferent execution. An example of this work is the old house in Córdoba shown in Figure 29. Their flat surfaces are never flat, their corners and lines are only approximately straight, but there is a simple, pleasing dignity in the general effect. The Spanish workmen were followed by Creoles who were still less skillful and generally had neither taste nor style. The Río Cuarto street in Figure 30 gives an example of their work, not too lasting and lacking in character of any sort. Nowadays the masons are almost wholly Italians. They are good workmen. They build solidly and execute admirable flat surfaces and true corners. They tend to adorn their work with wreaths and garlands that give it a somewhat overtrimmed effect. A good example is the Italianate house from Rosario, Figure 31.

All the common arts are practiced in the Republic today by immigrants and sons of immigrants, making readily accessible facilities and commodities that poorer Creoles of the old times dispensed with (Fig. 17) and the richer ones imported from Europe. Italians, Basques, and Gallegos manufacture butter that is available everywhere. In 1885 there was no café or hotel in the city of Córdoba that supplied it on its table; indeed, there was none for sale in this city of 30,000 people. The older Creoles make slight use of it even now. Formerly

FIG. 29—A Spanish-colonial house in Córdoba in rather severe but pleasing style. If used as a dwelling it would have bars in the windows.

Fig. 30—Creole style of buildings at Río Cuarto, Province of Córdoba.

FIG. 31—Modern house in Rosario—the ornate work of Italian masons, with French half-window *grilles* instead of full Spanish *rejas*. Note the plaster wreaths and festoons.

Fig. 32—Calle Florida, the fashionable street of Buenos Aires. The narrowness of the street is Creole. The tall buildings are modern, and the mason work is Italian. From noon to 1.30 vehicles are excluded and the street is given over to promenaders.

in wealthy families one saw it used on bread with sugar at dessert occasionally. Foreigners who wanted butter in the eighties had it sent up to them from a creamery at one of the colonies on the Central Argentine Railway, at a cost of about 97 cents United States money per pound.

Oranges, lemons, and bananas abound in the northern part of the Republic and were grown there commonly enough in 1885, but at that time they could not be purchased anywhere in the central city of Córdoba. Lemons were at times kept in cafés for use with drinks but not always, for mixed drinks were little used by the Creoles, who made up the whole population. That does not mean that lemons were not appreciated by the people of Córdoba. An American in Tucumán who found a Creole friend polite enough to offer to take a bushel of them with him to another American in Córdoba was astonished to find that they never arrived. The bag alone was delivered! There was no one in those days with the business inclination to have lemons and other fruit shipped to Córdoba and placed on sale. Even the delicious grapes, peaches, and nectarines grown in the gardens of Córdoba were only to be had in private families. They were not on public sale. Now a great variety of fruit, including Oregon apples, is freely sold in all large towns.

Beer is brewed, leather is tanned, wood is wrought into chairs, tables, and house trimmings by immigrant workmen. The upper-class Creoles deny that the immigrants have brought them any European culture. They regard the immigrants, all of them, as rude and ignorant, which is true only in a way. It is also true that the influence of European models in beautifying cities, laying out parks, planning harbors, and building subways in Buenos Aires has not come through immigrants but through the enjoyment by Argentines of repeated foreign journeys; yet the hands that have done these things and mostly the heads that guided them have been foreign. Initiative and wealth rest securely with the Creoles. To participate in them the foreigner must Argentinize his very soul and generally ally himself by a fortunate marriage.[26]

However, if you want a shoe soled, a lock or kettle mended, a bookcase made, a book bound or a pamphlet printed, a roll of film developed or a camera repaired, you will go to an immigrant or the son of an immigrant. The practical arts of civilization are mostly in foreign hands.

The settlement at Esperanza became from the very first a focus of industrial activity. You could get things done there that could not be done in the capital city, Santa Fe. In 1869, 1475 individuals called themselves agriculturists, but 381 gave business or skilled labor as their occupations.[27] The little village at once saw several saw mills and grist mills set up, six blacksmiths' shops, three shoe shops, to say nothing of a number of journeymen cobblers who would come to your house, mend your old shoes, and make you new ones as they do in Poland to this day. Also there was a brick kiln, and probably the bricks were better burned than those the Creoles had been turning out. In addition there were, of course, the necessary butcher shops, bakeries, tailor shops, and a café that had a billiard table. Today we read in the Santa Fe papers the advertisement of Nicolas Schneider, who manufactures agricultural implements at Esperanza, a village of 9000 people! I have already mentioned (p. 71) the mayor's machine shop. Farm implements appeared in the colonies almost from the start. Esperanza, for instance, in 1871, fourteen years after its founding, had 65 "Buckeye" reapers, and San Gerónimo, an adjoining colony, 42.[28] At present most of

[26] It is freely stated at Santa Fe that the immigrant men prefer Creole wives and immigrant women Creole husbands. Probably a foreign air has some attraction. The statistics of Santa Fe Province for the year 1912 (*Anuario de la Direcc. Gen. de Estadist. de la Provincia de Santa Fé, 1912*, Rosario, 1913, table on p. 75) record 5423 foreigners married that year, of whom 4068 married among themselves, while 1074 foreign men married Creole women and 281 foreign women married Creole men. Almost exactly three quarters of the foreigners married foreigners and one quarter Creoles, the men four times as often as the women because of greater opportunity of initiative on the part of the men. But it is clear that the fusion of races is going on rapidly. Some of the "Creoles" of this list of course are wholly foreign in blood but Argentine of birth.

[27] Wilcken, *op. cit.*, p. 7.

[28] *ibid.*, pp. 13 and 31 respectively.

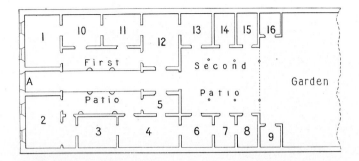

Fig. 33 (above)—Plan of the house of Don Doroteo Olmos, Córdoba, now used as city offices. The rooms are sketched about to scale (40 feet to an inch), and their original use, as indicated by an Argentine engineer, was as follows: A, front door; 1, office of house owner; 2, ladies' reception room; 3, bath room; 4, room of parents; 5 anteroom to 4; 6-8, daughters' rooms; 10, son's room; 11, guest room; 12, dining room; 13-16, kitchen and servants. Carriages drove through to the back. This plan was typical of a well-to-do Creole's house.

Fig. 34 (below)—Street view of the same house in 1918. This was the principal avenue of the city.

FIG. 35 (above)—Plan of a block in Santa Fe city, showing Creole individualism. In six cases houses project beyond the inner sidewalk line, and in one a house projects far into the street, causing the tram tracks to swerve.

FIG. 36 (below)—Photograph of the far-projecting house, No. 171 San Gerónimo Street. In front of the house the sidewalk is 11 inches wide. Sidewalks commonly vary a good deal in width, but this case is exceptional.

the agricultural machinery used in the Republic comes from the United States. A machine like a header and thrasher, a German admits, is too complicated to be built anywhere else. In 1885 Daireau[29] estimated the American part of the agricultural implements in use at 10 per cent, the rest being English, and adds a story of a wonderful French reaper (Vierzon's) which outdid everything else in the Buenos Aires exposition of 1881 and also in actual harvest work, but which the French lacked business capacity to keep on the market.

The demand for these labor-saving machines, which began thus early and has continued with vigor ever since, was due to the forces which drove the colonist to extensive monoculture of wheat. Chief of these was an unlimited market, first at home in a country that had hitherto grown almost none, and later in the Old World, which could not compete as long as Argentine land remained cheap. The agencies that grew up for handling a crop of wheat made it satisfactory to grow and easy to finance. It quickly became an understood business. If a year of drought or discouragement came, it was never forgotten that another year might bring fortune.

It is easy for students of agriculture to point out that a greater variety of farm activities would make for a better rounded life, for greater comfort in life while it was being lived, but their words have always failed to impress the colonist. They proposed strange crops that he did not know how to raise and for which he knew of no local demand. They called for continuous labor throughout the year, telling him it was better to work all the time. Many of the products were for home use, and he thought it less trouble to do without them or buy them at the store. No one was offering him money to set up an all-around farm, while his local dealers were always willing to make advances against a crop of wheat. The conditions of wheat culture are agreeable to the colonist, even if they do not make for his permanent well-being—use of ma-

[29] Émile Daireau: La vie et les moeurs à La Plata (2 vols., Paris, 1888), Vol. 2, p. 347.

chinery, easy credit, certain sale of his crop, and a vast amount
of idleness, to which he was not the less inclined because he
was apt to spend it in drunkenness and other vicious ways.
The widespread use of machinery saved labor in that it enabled
much more work to be accomplished in a given time than could
be done without it, but, as the work was work that previously
had not been done at all, it rather created a need for new labor
to handle the machines and keep them in repair. This could
only be foreign labor.

This is the modern culture that the Republic has acquired—
more significant than Palermo parks or the underground railway of Buenos Aires or the great avenues to be opened up
through that crowded city at vast expense: the widespread
facilitation of the practical modern arts and industries in a
hundred cities, small and large, throughout the country. I
have traveled over great stretches of it when it was a cow
country without milk; now the Spaniards of Galicia have
scattered creameries everywhere. Every city has foreigners
engaged in business, gathering the products of the country for
exportation and supplying the food and tools and clothing of
the people. Commerce has not merely won its materials
through foreign hands but is very largely carried on by foreign
firms, and in its smaller branches by thousands of individual
foreigners.

CHAPTER IV

OTHER EARLY COLONIES IN SANTA FE PROVINCE

SAN GERÓNIMO

San Gerónimo, close southwest of Esperanza, was the second colony to be founded.[1] Castellanos had formed some sort of engagement with a firm named Beck and Herzog in Basel to collect and forward colonists for him. They appear to have been very reliable people. Somehow—perhaps because he did not get word to them promptly enough of his refusal to go on with his contract with the government of Santa Fe Province—they continued to send on Swiss settlers. Thus in 1858 came some more families from Valais, where the people were mostly woodmen and herders. They wanted land at Esperanza, but it was all taken up. Don Enrique Foster, a large landholder, initiated the San Gerónimo colony by offering these families free lots on his land to have them settled there as a defense against the Indians. The Indians made continual trouble. The settlers at Esperanza had constant attacks to meet. The French and the Germans had alternated in the patrol and defense of the colony. Sometimes the night attacks were so savage that they all had to gather at the church in the center of the village. But the losses of the Indians in these raids against village settlements and the slight booty to be gained made agricultural settlement the best defense possible against the marauder.

A number of families accepted Foster's offer and used some money they had brought with them to begin raising cattle. But they did not make a success of this and presently went to raising wheat, for which the demand was constant (all through

[1] Guillermo Wilcken: Las colonias: Informe sobre el estado actual de las colonias agrícolas de la República Argentina presentado á la Comisión Central de Inmigración, Buenos Aires, 1873, pp. 29-34.

this period the Republic was importing wheat and flour for its bread). Then they prospered very quickly. After two years one of the settlers, named Rodemann, offered to go back to Switzerland and get more colonists if the province would pay his expenses. This was done, and he brought another group of twenty or thirty families. Later he took a neighbor over with him on the same errand. No agent, as has already been intimated, enjoyed the confidence of the prospective immigrants so much as did a returned immigrant, and no one was likelier to bring really desirable settlers to the colony. These later colonists appear to have bought their lots, and no help was given to them. In 1872 unimproved lots at San Gerónimo were worth 300 to 400 *bolivianos*, and well-improved ones from 800 to 2000, according largely to the buildings. By that date there were 196 families in the colony, and we may imagine there was little trouble with the Indians. The concessions here too were of 20 *cuadras* (83 acres), but a good many of the more prosperous colonists, those who had saved money and loaned it out at interest, had several concessions each. This colony was supplied with the communal land for pasturage that had been promised Esperanza but not delivered. A village was already established with church and school, enough for half of the children only; but this, we shall find, was doing pretty well. The distance at which many of the colonists necessarily lived from the central village and the usefulness of children on the farms combined with the ignorance of the colonists and their apathy for education to deprive many of the children of all schooling whatsoever. It was not uncommon for children born in the colony to grow up to manhood without learning to write or read. The Province of Santa Fe contributed $30 a month for a teacher in each of the colonies, though he sometimes had to wait six months or a year for his pay and perhaps take it in provincial warrants that could only be collected at a discount of 30 per cent. It is a rather surprising characteristic of the Northern immigration that it brought no zeal for education. It was the Creole landowning, governing class that supplied what interest in education there was. The material of the colonies, however, often profited admirably by the opportunities that were offered.

SAN CARLOS

The arrangement that Castellanos had made, as we have seen (p. 54), called for the collection and forwarding of a series of five groups of two hundred families. When, as a result of the failure of the province to fulfill its part of the compact, he declined to bring any more than the first two hundred families, Beck and Herzog, the Basel firm with whom he had made the arrangements, were so interested that they went on with the work and, in 1859, became the founders of the third colony, San Carlos,[2] the province ceding them 20 square leagues of land for the purpose. Probably the years 1857 and 1858 were the years of bad harvest that made difficult the beginnings at Esperanza. By 1859 the good harvests may have come. At any rate San Carlos prospered, as far as the colonists were concerned, from the very first. For one thing Beck and Herzog put in good administrators and looked after their people. What with the novelty of climate and environment, the strange people, and the relations with the government, occasions were always arising where the colonists needed good advice and guidance. This Beck and Herzog supplied. They got rid of undesirable persons, who sought to make trouble, and the colonists advanced smoothly and rapidly to prosperity. Unfortunately the firm became involved in expenditures so heavy in handling the affair that their career ended in bankruptcy; but the Swiss colonizing company which was formed to continue their undertaking carried it on capably and to the satisfaction of the colonists.

It is to be expected that there will be vicious people, lazy people, average people, industrious people, and exceptional people in any colony. When prosperity comes it comes mainly to the "fortunate" colonists of the last three classes. In-

[2] Wilcken, *op. cit.*, pp. 47–91.

dustry, thrift, and persistence count much more than intellectual quickness or education. A number of modern Italian visitors have commented on the fact that a good many of the immigrants who have attained real wealth have been ignorant and far from quick-witted but always endowed with those three qualities. More brilliant men have usually tried various things but fared less well. The first step toward wealth has invariably been the painful saving of a small capital under conditions of real hardship and privation. Capital has been so scarce in the country that it grew rapidly from these beginnings. They quickly found borrowers among their fellows at 18 per cent. More than that was accounted usurious and discouraged by the better members of the priesthood.

There exists for San Carlos a sketch of the personal history of 21 families.[3] Bautista Goetschi is a fair sample of the prosperous individuals. He was a Swiss farmer who reached the colony in May, 1859, receiving from the administration an advance of 500 *bolivianos*. With him came wife, three sons, and a daughter. Evidently all worked. By 1863 he had repaid the advance and had only one more payment, a third of the coming crop, to make on his land to own it, a concession of 83 acres. He had 63 cows, 9 horses, 36 acres in wheat that would yield him $1000, a smaller field in corn, an orchard of 1000 peach trees, a garden, and his house and buildings in good shape, though the house was the original rancho. It was noted of him that he and his sons were rarely seen in the plaza or public square. They were always at work at home. The sons had learned Spanish, but the father knew none as yet. By 1872 Bautista was growing old but was still an active worker, had been justice of the peace several times, owned several concessions—all fenced, at an expense of 700 or 800

[3] Wilcken, *op. cit.*, pp. 64–77. William Perkins, land agent for the Central Argentine Railway, wrote the first report on individuals in 1863 when commissioned by the government to inspect Esperanza, San Gerónimo, and San Carlos. This report is entitled "The Colonies of Santa Fe: Their Origin, Progress and Present Condition, With General Observations on Emigration to the Argentine Republic," Rosario de Santa Fe, 1864 (published in English and Spanish). Wilcken continues the stories to 1872.

bolivianos each—and a fine grove of all sorts of fruit trees. Though still living in the primitive house he had the materials ready to build a larger and more commodious one. One son was married and in business as a butcher, the two others still working with the father. The daughter had married well. The family fortune was rated about $30,000.

THE ITALIANS OF SAN CARLOS

Two special features of the San Carlos colony were the inclusion of a large number of Italians—Piedmontese, North Italians all—and a considerable number of Argentines. In 1871 there were 1024 Italians, 501 Swiss, 305 Argentines, and 117 French among the 1992 members of the colony.[4] De Amicis[5] tells of their showing him an old Indian woman at San Carlos in 1896 who answered his inquiry about the weather in the Piedmontese dialect of Italian! This must be supposed to be a rather dramatic touch arranged for De Amicis by his Genovese compatriots. Though the number of Italians has enormously multiplied in later days, let no one suppose that any other language than Spanish is needed in the Argentine Republic for travel or business. Some of the older colonists never learn much of the language of the country, as happens in the United States, but the younger generation make it completely theirs and usually forget what their parents taught them of the overseas language. The ignorant Italian peasant brought with him no very clear conception of Italy as a country. His had been a limited village horizon. His acquaintance with government had been with petty officials whom he detested. The Spanish language of his environment was of practical value as soon as he came in contact with Creoles, and he wanted it. A young Italian journalist in Mendoza complains that you find a Creole newspaper in almost every Italian's house, while he could get no readers for the Italian paper that he sought to found on European lines.[6] Among 19,000

---

[4] Wilcken, *op. cit.*, p. 48.
[5] Edmondo de Amicis: In America, Rome, 1897, p. 63.
[6] Vicenzo Vacirca: La Provincia di Mendoza e gli Italiani, Mendoza, 1911, p. 78.

Italians in the Province of Mendoza not 500 subscribed for either of the two great Italian papers published in the country. Many admitted that they had forgotten their Italian.

CREOLE ATTITUDE TOWARD FARMING

There is special interest in the 305 Argentines of San Carlos, too.[7] Rudesindo Acuña, Dionisio Britos, Juan Cane, Mariano Escalante, Pedro Freire, José Gallo, Pablo Novedo, Feliz Olmo, Juan Pons Estevans, Creoles by name and all rated Argentines, owned 28 concessions among them.[8] It does not follow that these are Argentines who became agriculturists. They may not have sowed grain themselves. If the contract required the breaking of a certain area of ground to validate their title they may have hired some one to do it or subrented it. But while it is certain that these things happened, in some cases it has also happened that Argentines have tilled the ground and have done it as a result of the foreign immigration. Agriculture is likely to displace cattle raising in the Republic to a great extent wherever the rainfall is sufficient, and that is so large a part of the territory that agriculture is destined to play the chief rôle in the national economy when the national resources are rationally used. Today the products of agriculture and grazing are of about equal value. But all Creole tendencies are towards cattle raising. Everyone in the country knows something of cattle, and, if it is true that fine stock has brought revolutionary changes in Argentine stock raising, these are changes that interest the Creole and that he readily comes to understand. Probably it is not far amiss to say that he regards cattle as a gentleman's business and agriculture the business of a *gringo*, as white Europeans and North Americans are nicknamed. A small but growing number of Argentines and still more persons with a good deal of Argentine and some

[7] Wilcken, *op. cit.*, p. 48. At Esperanza only foreigners obtained concessions. The 243 Argentines stated above (p. 66) as being in the colony in 1869 were mostly, as there mentioned, the children of the foreign settlers.

[8] From list of San Carlos lot owners, by nationalities, in Wilcken, *op. cit.*, pp. 78–91.

immigrant blood are occupying themselves with agriculture, but the number is distinctly small. The mass of agricultural labor in the Argentine Republic is performed by the immigrant. As a general rule there is no other farm labor in the land.

The word *colono* in Argentine Spanish means simply farmer. Spanish inheritance gives the too large "white-collar" class of Argentines something of a horror of labor that soils the hands. Governor Lehmann of Santa Fe, whose Creole blood from his mother and whose associations in general would tend to give him a Creole point of view, appeared a little insistent, I thought, that his father "had never been a *colono*, only an office employee."

Of course Creoles found occupation in the villages of the colonies as barbers, tailors, and dependents in the shops and cafés, but such men were not probably the owners of the Argentine concessions.

Success of San Carlos

The main products at San Carlos,[9] as at the two earlier colonies, were wheat (in 1871, 180,000 bushels) and maize, with rather negligible quantities of beans, sweet potatoes, barley, and other crops. Farm machines were in universal use in all three colonies, American machines giving best satisfaction, as they still do. The lack of the railroad, while a drawback, was not as serious as at the older colonies, for the market for San Carlos was Rosario or Coronda, and the land between was higher and drier than towards Santa Fe. Peddlers from both towns came through the colony almost every day. There was no running water, but wells reached water in abundance at depths of 18 to 45 feet.

The colonies soon brought very concrete returns to the province for the trouble and expense incurred in founding them. They drove off the Indians for good, they increased the value of all lands, public and private, and they paid a considerable

[9] Wilcken, *op. cit.*, p. 51.

tax to the province after the exempted five years of their
beginning, which was a matter of importance to a government
that had always lacked ready money. Furthermore, they
stimulated business by the founding and developing of minor
industries and supplied large quantities of the wheat that the
country was then importing for food.

Colonies Along the San Javier

Besides these colonies at the northeastern border of the
Pampa a number of others were placed between 1865 and 1871
far to the north of Santa Fe along the San Javier, whose water
is always described as "exquisite," presumably for its crystal
clearness in contrast to the turbid stream of the Paraná. They
are confined to the west bank, where there is the only strip of
land high enough to escape flooding—a limited strip. The
San Javier affords connection with the Paraná at all seasons.
These colonies were (see Fig. 28) Cayastá, Helvecia, Estancia
Grande, Francesa, California, Inglesa, Eloisa, and Alejandra.[10]
There was considerable difference in the way the land was
acquired. It had belonged to the province, and the Indians
were wont to sweep over it, making it well-nigh untenable. The
main path of the Indians was from north to south, as the land
east of the San Javier was low and subject to flood (Fig. 21)
from December to July, when the Paraná is swollen by the
rains of the southern summer. The fortress-colony Alejandra,
which secured the rest from further invasion after 1870, was
just at the northern limit of Figure 28. In the drier season the
San Javier lowlands had value for pasturage.

The American Colony California

The colony California[11] is a touch of home to us. Laws and
edicts in regard to colonization in Chile and the Argentine
Republic contain occasional references to the desirability of
securing immigrants from the United States. To any one

[10] They may be identified on Fig. 28 by their dates of founding from south to
north as follows: 67, 65, 71, 67 (southerly of the two), 66, 68, 68, and 70.
[11] Wilcken, op. cit., pp. 133-136.

acquainted with the wretched conditions of the immigrant's life in South America and the comforts easily acquired in the United States such a thing seems out of the question. Yet it happened. Twelve American families—old-fashioned families, for there were 72 individuals—came to Paraná in 1866, bought a square league of land for 300 *bolivianos*, and divided it into strips of 1000 acres, stretching back from the San Javier fifteen times as far as they had frontage. They were said to come from California, but one wonders if they may not have been ex-Confederates like the members of the Colonia Americana near São Paulo, Brazil. They brought with them money and all sorts of farm machinery, including a threshing machine, which they sold to the Colonia Helvecia on their way, perhaps on account of the difficulty of transporting it. They were, says Wilcken,[12] all experienced farmers and tilled the soil with a thoroughness and care that was unknown in the country. Moreover, each man was carpenter, blacksmith, and mason; so they did not need to call in any mechanics. When one of them had an especially big job on hand he would call in his neighbors at a fixed price of one and a half *bolivianos* a day with board or two *bolivianos* without. In the six years of their existence they had never needed the intervention of courts or police. They were hard workers and great eaters, some astonishment being caused by their three meals a day, beginning with a breakfast at six in the morning, the Argentine custom being to breakfast towards noon and have dinner at night. Although we think of American standards of living as so much higher than Argentine ones that emigration from the United States is unthinkable, these men lived in houses so miserable, affording so little shelter from the cold of winter or the heat of summer, as to cause surprise, especially as they were so capable and so thorough in all their work. The explanation given was that they had been much annoyed by Indian raids and had therefore felt more inclined to sell their land than build permanent houses. In these raids they had

[12] *ibid.*, p. 134.

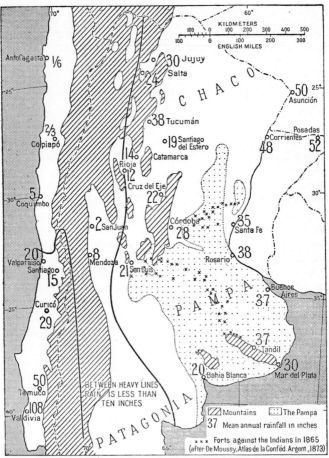

FIG. 37—General map of the Argentine Republic and Chile showing the mountains, the Pampa, and the distribution of rainfall. Scale, 1: 19,000,000.

always got back the cattle the Indians had tried to drive off and had been able to punish the raiders, thanks to their skill with the rifle. But when Alejandra colony was founded north of them in 1870, they felt more secure and at the time of Wilcken's visit had built brick kilns and made enough bricks to build themselves permanent houses. I have not been able to learn anything of the later history of this group of Americans.

THE INDIANS OF THE PAMPA AND THEIR SUBJUGATION

Always in those days the lands that the national or provincial government had to dispose of were those that were left, the less desirable lands, lands the influential Creoles had not taken possession of, whether the defect were scrub, swampiness, or Indian raids. The lines of black crosses in Figure 37 show where De Moussy delineated the barrier forts in 1865, the only defense the settlers on the Pampa had till Roca's day. In the north the Indians came near to the city of Santa Fe itself. In the south they withheld the southwest half of the Province of Buenos Aires from settlement and held the whole of the Territory of the Pampa, all excellent wheat land.

Corrientes and Entre Ríos Provinces, which lie between the broad streams of the Paraná on the west and the Uruguay on the east, making up the Argentine Mesopotamia, had always been safe from raids by Pampa Indians behind the wide marsh barrier of the Paraná (Fig. 21). The Guaraní Indian of this Mesopotamia was less warlike and entered into the "civilized" population of both provinces. This immunity from Indian attack accounts for the early wealth and growth of towns in those two provinces at a time when Córdoba and Buenos Aires had so few.[13]

[13] NUMBER OF TOWNS OF 1000 OR MORE PEOPLE*

Province	in 1869†	in 1895‡	in 1914§
Corrientes	15	17	18
Entre Ríos	11	15	19
Córdoba	7	14	43
Buenos Aires	12	73	89

* See also Pl. I, on which the numbers of towns does not necessarily tally with these figures, as towns of over 900 have been included in those shown by the 1000-inhabitant symbol. On the other hand not all the towns of 1000 or more people indicated in the three censuses as existing in Buenos Aires Province are enumerated in this list or shown on the map because many of them were not really urban agglomerations.   (*For continuation of footnote, see next page.*)

In 1869 Mesopotamia had an importance that it has quite lost (Fig. 38) since the railways have made the whole Pampa tributary to the port of Buenos Aires. Most of the towns of Corrientes and Entre Ríos were on a navigable river, so that before the railway came they had a great advantage over all Córdoba towns and most of those of Buenos Aires.

It was toward the close of the period of the earlier Santa Fe colonies that Roca pushed the Indians out of the southern area by the campaigns of 1879 to 1884. They were resounding words that the general wrote into his order of the day of

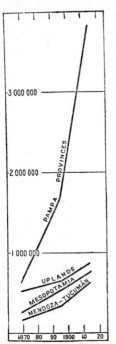

FIG. 38. (Explanation at the right.)

Diagram showing the population growth of Argentine regions at the censuses of 1869, 1895, and 1914.

POPULATION IN THOUSANDS				PER CENT INCREASE 1869–1914
	1869	1895	1914	
Uplands	504	655	885	175
Mendoza-Tucumán	174	332	610	357
Mesopotamia	263	532	772	294
Pampa Provinces	607	1695	3802	626

Uplands: Jujuy, Salta, Santiago, Catamarca, La Rioja, San Juan, and San Luis.

Mendoza-Tucumán: Mendoza and Tucumán.

Mesopotamia: Corrientes and Entre Ríos.

Pampa Provinces: Córdoba, Santa Fe, Buenos Aires, La Pampa.

Really in 1869 Córdoba, Tucumán, Mendoza belonged to the Uplands, which so considered had a population of 889 thousand—far more people than the Pampa.

Immigration has developed mainly the Pampa

April 26, 1879: "When the wave of humanity invades these desolate fields that were yesterday the stage of sanguinary and dev-

Continuation of footnote 13.

† Primer censo de la República Argentina, 1869, Buenos Aires, 1872, pp. 216, 172, 256, and 90–92 (also pp. 674–683).

‡ Segundo censo de la República Argentina, 1895, Vol. 2: Población, Buenos Aires, 1898, pp. 231, 195, 271, and 60–62.

§ Tercer censo nacional, 1914, Vol. 4: Población, Buenos Aires, 1916, pp. 469–475 (only cities of 2000 or more inhabitants are listed in this census).

astating raids to turn them into markets of wealth and flourishing towns, in which millions of men may live rich and happy—then and not till then the true worth of your efforts will be perceived. Destroying these nests of land pirates and taking effective possession of the vast region that shelters them, you have opened and widened the horizons of your country toward the southland, tracing as it were with your bayonets an immense field for the development of future greatness."[14]

That was the end of the Indian peril on the Pampa, which had been intensified by the receptiveness of the Chilean market for animals that the Indians could steal from Argentine *estancias*. Puelma of San Carlos said from his seat in the Chilean Chamber of Deputies in 1870: "As for the trade [with the Araucanian Indians] we see that it is of animals that they have stolen from the Argentine Republic. It is known that forty thousand animals, more or less, have been stolen there lately. And we, knowing that they have been stolen, buy them without any scruple."[15]

Roca's campaign was a great sweep of Argentine troops along the whole line of the southwest frontier, destroying every Indian settlement north of the Río Negro, capturing men, women, and children, and bringing great numbers of them prisoners to be used in the navy and in the agricultural colonies of Santa Fe and Entre Ríos. Not a single seat of Indian life was left on the southern Pampa to serve as a starting point for further Indian raids. The passes of the Andes were taken possession of and made secure for the cattle men of Mendoza, San Luis, and Córdoba to drive their own cattle for sale where only a year before Indian thieves had been wont to take them as stolen animals.

Railway Land Colonizing

The direct result of this campaign was the widening of the Province of Buenos Aires and the creation of the National

[14] W. J. Molins: La Pampa, Buenos Aires, 1918, pp. 5–6.
[15] *ibid.*, p. 10.

Territory of La Pampa, giving the nation a wealth of new and fertile lands to squander on its favorites. But the indirect result, the elimination of raids from the south into the Pampa between Buenos Aires and Córdoba, was no less helpful to the progress of the country, for it greatly facilitated the agricultural colonization that was going on, made possible the construction of railways, and opened up for settlement lands farther and farther back from the *barranca* of the Paraná. The first really important line built in the Argentine Republic, the Ferrocarril Central Argentino, was built between 1863 and 1870 (see Pl. IA) by the American Wheelwright with English capital, connecting Rosario on the Paraná with Córdoba in the interior.[16] The concession guaranteed the company 7 per cent interest on their $8,000,000 capital and a strip of land three miles wide on each side of the line.[17] Santa Fe Province contributed 89 square leagues (925 square miles) of land for this purpose. The country needed railroads and paid for them with its only wealth. Though the land bounty was really of huge value, it was the moderate cash guarantee that the government had much trouble at first to pay. Ready money was very scarce.

The colonizing of this strip of land helped the railroad greatly in the early days before traffic had developed importance. The railway company had an organization that was able to handle its colonizing much more efficiently than the state had been able to. Concessions of 83 acres were sold at $400 in annual payments spread over four years, or rented on a basis of 5 per cent of that sum, rental payments to count toward subsequent purchase if desired.[18] This made the square league of land worth $640,000 and the Santa Fe contribution to the railway $57,000,000! Through its supply and construction departments the railway was able to deliver necessary tools and materials to the colonists with a punctuality hitherto unknown. Perkins, the general manager of colonies,

[16] F. M. Halsey: Railway Expansion in Latin America, New York, 1916, p. 11.
[17] *Argentine Year Book*, 10th edit., 1915–16, Buenos Aires, 1916, p. 254 ff.
[18] Wilcken, *op. cit.*, p. 149.

reached Roldán, 15 miles west of Rosario (Fig. 28), only two weeks before the first twenty-five families arrived in March, 1870, but he had everything ready to receive them, wooden houses, wire for fences, tools, and provisions, "so that the colonists could get to work an hour after arriving at the colony."[19] The company planned to put a station—as center of a colony—every 2½ leagues (8 miles), beginning with Roldán (originally "Bernstadt"). So cut-and-dried a scheme of locating towns corresponds very well with the featureless monotony of the Pampa, all good farm land where there is rain enough. Today, half a century later, the 19 stations between Córdoba city and the boundary of Santa Fe Province average 9 miles apart.[20]

COLONIZING FOR PROFIT: LEHMANN'S COLONIES

In telling the story of these colonies I have tried to give actual events where ascertainable. Decrees and laws governing immigration and colonizing abound and have a certain interest, but they were rarely put into effect as they read. A friend of the governor receives, according to the law of 1864, his donation of 20 leagues of land for founding a colony with 200 colonists—and fails to found any! Another buys 108 square leagues (1123 square miles!) at the price of 300 *bolivianos* and also never puts a single colonist on it and keeps the land![21] What matter the law?

Associated with the settlement at Esperanza is the name of Guillermo Lehmann, an amiable German Swiss long employed in the offices of the administration there (see, above, p. 70). In the ten years between 1875 and 1885 he founded no less than ten colonies,[22] covering nearly 59 square leagues of land

[19] Wilcken, *op. cit.*, p. 148.

[20] See Ulrico Greiner: Mapa de la Provincia de Córdoba, 1: 750,000, 3rd edit., Buenos Aires, 1912. This map shows the colonies.

[21] Nicasio Oroño: Defensa y reclamación de derechos de las tierras de la Colonia General Oroño, Buenos Aires, 1900, p. 225.

[22] Pilar, 1875; Nuevo Torino, 1876; Aurelia, 1881; Susana, 1881; Saguier, 1882; Presidente Roca, 1882; Lehmann, 1882; Rafaela, 1883; Umberto I°, 1884; Virginia, 1885 (see Fig. 39, on which the size of each colony is also given in a table; on Fig. 28 their general location west of Esperanza can be identified by means of these dates).

about 20 miles west of Esperanza, at first—Pilar, 1875, and Nuevo Torino, 1876—in association with Carlos Christiani, and then alone. He did this for profit and made money out of it, but he seems to have taken excellent care of his colonists as well. If the law of 1864 had operated in his favor he would have been entitled to 200 square leagues for his ten colonies. With much less he would have been wealthy.

Five of these colonies were founded in the governorship of Dr. Simón de Iriondo, whose protection Lehmann very probably enjoyed. The Lehmann colonies (Fig. 39) constituted a single block of land of irregular shape, with one section, the Estancia Lehmann of two or three square leagues area adjoining the Colonia Lehmann on the east, that seems to be still in the hands of the family. A very large number of commercial colonies like these were now founded. The authorities of Esperanza have honored Lehmann by placing his name on the colonization monument in their central plaza. It is this man's son, also married into a good Creole family, who was governor of Santa Fe Province in 1918 (see p. 70). Eight of these colonies—all except Aurelia and Virginia—are reported in the census of 1914[23] with a population of 22,754, which gives them a population density of 40 persons to the square mile, about like that of our purely agricultural regions in the West and South—Iowa, Alabama, and Georgia.

PROPORTION OF LANDOWNERS AND SIZE OF HOLDINGS

It is not reported how many of these settlers nowadays own their land. In the Department Castellanos, where most of the Lehmann colonies are situated, the census of 1914 reported[24] 8724 owners of land in a total population of 47,587 men, women, and children. Six persons to a family would not be an unreasonable assumption, as the San Carlos colony averaged that in 1872, and we might proceed to argue that almost every family owned land. The Department Las Colonias shows

[23] Tercer censo nacional, Vol. 2, pp. 38, 39, and 40.
[24] ibid., Vol. 4, p. 25 (population in Vol. 2, p. 39).

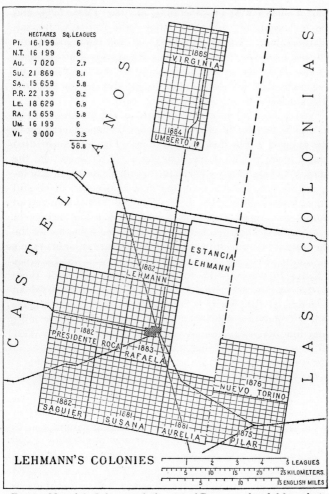

	HECTARES	SQ. LEAGUES
PI.	16 199	6
N.T.	16 199	6
AU.	7 020	2.7
SU.	21 869	8.1
SA.	15 659	5.8
P.R.	22 139	8.2
LE.	18 629	6.9
RA.	15 659	5.8
UM.	16 199	6
VI.	9 000	3.3
		58.8

LEHMANN'S COLONIES

FIG. 39—Map of the Lehmann colonies west of Esperanza: founded for private profit by Guillermo Lehmann but to the advantage of the colonists, too. Scale, 1: 750,000. (Based on the map cited above on p. 66 in footnote 22; the areas from the publication by Carrasco cited below on p. 100.)

about the same figures:[25] 7319 owners and 44,712 population.
Of the Argentines in this department one in eight is a landowner, of the foreigners one in three. For the whole Province
of Santa Fe one in eleven of the Argentines are landowners,
of the foreigners one in six. For the Province of Buenos Aires
one in ten of the natives owns land, and one in five of the
foreigners.[26]

Unfortunately we can learn nothing definite about the size
of the properties in relation to ownership by Argentines and
foreigners.[27] The European is eager to acquire land always,
but probably most of the holdings are very small. We have
seen the early Santa Fe farms running certainly not over
100 acres in size, and there are many smaller properties that
have arisen since. Many of the colony concessions are subdivided, as for instance at Esperanza, where three-fifths of the
original lots were subdivided by 1872, according to the plan
in Wilcken's report.[28] Nevertheless the average size of landed
property in the Argentine Republic is 1297 acres,[29] over nine

[25] Tercer censo nacional, Vol. 4, p. 25 (population, Vol. 2, p. 41).

[26] On the nationality of the land owners see Tercer censo nacional, Vol. 4, pp.
25, 27, 24, Vol. 2, pp. 41, 45, 37, and Vol. 5, pp. 357, 310, 309.

[27] The only figures that seem to be available give the number of agricultural
properties by size groups and the number of Argentines and foreigners who are
"*directores*" (operators) of properties (1914 Census, Vol. 5). For the three terri-
torial divisions here discussed these figures are as follows:

Size	Dept. Las Colonias (p. 144)	Santa Fe Prov. (p. 74)	Buenos Aires Prov. (p. 73)
Under 62 acres . . .	417	6,777	20,133
62–125 acres	276	5,356	8,799
125–250 acres	833	10,533	12,930
250–1250 acres . . .	1,847	15,059	27,425
Over 1250 acres . . .	121	1,712	9,381

The number of "*directores*" is as follows: Las Colonias, 1383 Argentines, 1734
foreigners (*ibid.*, p. 357); Santa Fe, 9428 Argentines, 27,290 foreigners (p. 310);
Buenos Aires, 26,395 Argentines, 43,483 foreigners (p. 309).

On the general problem indicated by its title see Egidia Ferrari: The Problem of
Small Occupying Ownership in Argentina, *Internatl. Rev. of Agric. Economics*,
N.S., Vol. 2, 1924, pp. 377–395.—EDIT. NOTE.

[28] *op. cit.*, facing p. 28, scale about 1 : 18,000.

[29] E. W. Schmidt: Die agrarische Exportwirtschaft Argentiniens (Probleme der
Weltwirtschaft: Schriften des Instituts für Seeverkehr und Weltwirtschaft an der
Universität Kiel, Vol. 33), Jena, 1920, p. 120.

times as large as in the United States at the same time (138 acres, 1910; 148 acres, 1920).[30] Schmidt has pointed out[31] the misleading character of the Argentine statistics, which officially minimize the numerous and undeniable *latifundia*. Certainly the area owned by Argentines is much larger than that owned by foreigners.

NATIONALITY OF THE COLONISTS

At the time of Wilcken's inspection, 1872, the results of which are embodied in the report to which we have made frequent reference—one of the most reliable pieces of statistical work ever published by the Argentine government—there had been colonized in Córdoba Province 8 square leagues,[32] in Entre Ríos 10 square leagues, in Santa Fe 135½ square leagues of land, by nearly 17,000 colonists made up as follows:[33]

Northern Stocks		per cent	Southern Stocks		per cent
Swiss	5,857	35.1	Italians	4,157	24.9
Germans	1,483	8.9	Argentines	2,364	14.1
English	486	2.9	French	1,889	11.3
North Americans	82	.5	Spaniards	215	1.6
Belgians	54	.3	Other South		
Danes	42	.2	Americans	33	.2
Swedes	10		Others	6	
	8,014	47.9		8,664	52.1

During the period (1857–1872) in which these 17,000 settled as farmers the total number of immigrants to the country was in round numbers 221,000, of whom about 103,000 stayed in

[30] Fourteenth Census of the United States, 1920, Vol. 5: Agriculture, General Report, Washington, 1922, p. 66.

[31] *op. cit.*, pp. 120–121.

[32] Córdoba Province is included in Wilcken's enumeration only because of Colonia Tortugas, at that time the westernmost of the colonies on the Central Argentine Railway. It was then considered to lie in Córdoba (Wilcken, p. 154 and map of Santa Fe colonies opp. p. 204; see also below, p. 107). The name is now applied to a colony lying almost wholly within Santa Fe (map referred to above in Ch. III, footnote 22), the original tract seemingly having been situated farther west, in what is now parts of General Roca and Marcos Juárez colonies in Córdoba Province (see the map referred to above in footnote 20).

[33] Wilcken, *op. cit.*, p. 296.

the country.[34] Inasmuch as Sante Fe and Entre Ríos Provinces include practically all of the land that was open to agricultural occupation at that time, it may be said that *only one-sixth of the immigrants of that, the golden era of Argentine colonization, settled on the land*, the rest going to swell the population of the towns.

It is striking to see the large proportion of Northern settlers, nearly half of the whole. As for the nationalities of the immigrants to the Republic during the same period the figures for those who stayed are given as follows.[35] They show interesting contrasts with those above as to the ratio between Northern and Southern stocks and otherwise.

Northern Stocks		per cent	Southern Stocks		per cent
Swiss	1,732	1.7	Italians	63,825	61.0
Germans	990	0.9	Spaniards	21,416	20.5
Austrians	666	0.6	Portuguese	510	0.5
English	2,604	2.5	French	7,055	6.7
Belgians	392	0.4			
Dutch	67	0.1			
	6,451	6.2		92,806	88.7

Others about 5400

The unsatisfactory character of the statistics is evident enough, even when allowance is made for natural increase, a total of 1732 Swiss staying in the country (out of 3339 arriving) during a period that saw 5857 Swiss established in colonies on its soil! The latter figure is certainly to be preferred. I have much more confidence in Wilcken than in the Argentine official statisticians. The relatively large number of English might include engineers and construction men on the Central Argentine Railway. The Italians, however, were largely

[34] Resumen estadístico del movimiento migratorio en la República Argentina, años 1857–1924, Direcc. Gen. de Inmigración, Buenos Aires, 1925, pp. 3 (decadal figures) and 32–33 (annual figures). "Immigrants" and "emigrants" are defined as second- and third-class passengers. The emigrant figures on p. 33 include first-class passengers. We have therefore taken the figures for 1871 and 1872 from those kindly supplied for this inquiry by Señor Jorge Meneclier, chief of immigration statistics of the Dirección General de Inmigración, Buenos Aires.

[35] *ibid.*, pp. 4–5 (decadal figures), pp. 6–18 (annual figures).

staying in the city. The census of 1869[36] reports 80,000 foreigners (excepting other Latin Americans) in the city of Buenos Aires in that year. That the bulk of the immigration stayed in the cities may not be so unmitigated an evil as is often supposed. There were industries and trades to be carried on that had been unattended to. Railway work also needed immigrants and doubtless got them. The Creole was of little use for such tasks. The sons and daughters born in the colonies count as Argentines. The Italians of the colonies were all from Piedmont in the north of Italy. The other Italians were mostly, I infer, from the south.

PROTESTANT COLONISTS FROM NORTHERN EUROPE AND OROÑO'S SUPPORT OF THEM

The number of colonies[37] at that time was 34, containing 3185 families averaging 5.3 persons each, a great many of them owners of their lots. Their capital was 3500 *bolivianos* a family, 11,000,000 in all, and the last harvest, 1871–1872, yielded 795,000 bushels of wheat and 392,000 bushels of maize. About a fifth of them, 3595 individuals, were Protestants. There were only thirteen churches in the 34 colonies, of which five were Protestant, and three of these were closed for lack of funds to pay the minister. The Catholics were greatly shocked at the unwillingness of the Protestants to spend anything on religion; but the Catholics, too, appear to have lacked religious zeal. Of course the Catholic churches were supported from the taxes that all paid alike, and the Protestants were quite unwilling to contribute anything to support their own churches and were of so many sects and so hostile that they could not act together. In spite of the prosperity of the colonists, Protestant ministers had to leave them or starve. Oroño and Creoles of his type desired to have the government aid the Protestants in this respect. They felt that the Northern colonists were worth attracting.

[36] pp. 26–27.
[37] The statements in this paragraph are based on Wilcken, *op. cit.*, pp. 296–303.

Education was as badly off. The constitution of Santa Fe made primary education compulsory and imposed penalties, but there were only 16 schools in ten of the Santa Fe colonies (the remaining twenty having none), attended by 640 children, less than 5 per cent of the population[38] and 33 per cent of the children of school age.[39] The whole 34 colonies had 22 schools, attended by 1120 children,[40] 7 per cent of the population and 50 per cent of the children of school age. The governments succeeding Oroño, as they emanated from a revolution, "had to devote their whole attention and all the income of the state to keeping themselves in power, being always threatened by the party that fell with him."[41] Nicasio Oroño, governor[42] of Santa Fe from 1865 to 1868 and a great friend and protector of the settlers at Esperanza, who called him father of the colonists, was driven from office by a revolution. "My enemies made a pretext of my law of civil marriage and my plan for a school of agriculture in San Lorenzo."[43]

Reference has been made above (p. 57) to the hostility aroused in the Creole peasantry in 1856 by the donations of land and advancing of supplies to the colonists. In the following twelve years these jealousies became more intense and lost nothing in intensity as the Creoles became aware of the presence of Protestants among the newcomers. It was a feeble

[38] Wilcken, *op. cit.*, p. 303.
[39] If we assume that about one-seventh of a population is between 7 and 14 years old as in the United States (Fourteenth Census of the United States, 1920, Vol. 2: Population, General·Report, Washington, 1922, diagram on p. 151).
[40] Wilcken, *op. cit.*, Table 3 at end.
[41] *ibid.*, p. 304.

[42] GOVERNORS OF SANTA FE AND NUMBER OF COLONIES
FOUNDED IN THEIR TERMS*

1851–54	Domingo Crespo	0	1869–71	Mariano Cabal	23
1855–56	José M. Cullen	1	1872–74	Simón de Iriondo	15
1857–58	J. Pablo Lopez	1	1875–78	Servando Bayo	16
1859–60	Rosendo M. Fraga	1	1879–82	Simón de Iriondo	25
1860–61	Pascual Rosas	1	1883–86	Manuel M. Zavalla	63
1862–65	Patricio Cullen	2	1887–90	José Galvez	99
1866–68	Nicasio Oroño	8	1891–93	Juan M. Cafferata	84

*Gabriel Carrasco: La colonización agrícola en la Provincia de Santa-Fé: Cuadro general conteniendo el nombre, situación, extensión, fecha y fundador de las colonias existentes hasta el 1º de junio de 1893, Minist. de Agric., Justicia é Instrucc. Pública, Santa Fe, 1893, p. 34.

[43] Oroño, *op. cit.*, p. 6.

sort of Protestantism, not vigorous enough to exert itself for its own support. It could not have annoyed the Catholic country folk in any active way. The gaucho was a poor observer of religion himself and entirely tolerant of others. I remember well the story told me by an old Córdoba gentleman in the presence of his devout and annoyed daughter-in-law, who did her best to make him stop, of the prayer offered by a rich but ignorant landholder in some access of religious enthusiasm. Holding his rosary in one hand he pushed the beads by with one finger of the other, saying *Pase Vos* to the little ones and *Pase Vuesa Merced* to the big one—"You go by" and "Your Grace go by!"

Oroño was a firm believer in the need of colonists from the north of Europe. He knew the benefits that had accrued to the United States from northern immigrants and believed that the southern races would never give the Republic what it needed, for the northern people alone "are distinguished by the qualities which are necessary to counterbalance the social and political defects which unfortunately mark the agitated history of our South American continent since the epoch of independence."[44] These qualities were perseverance and strength of will enough to conquer the desert and keep the country free, and they were to be found only in the people of the north, which demanded consideration for their institutions. No doubt the power of the Catholic Church was used against Oroño, for the attack centered on his law of *matrimonio civil*, which was passed in 1868. We read in the story of Esperanza[45] of Louis Tabornig, the Austrian blacksmith who invented and manufactured a plow that rivaled the famous North American plows and was widely used in the province. He was the only person in Esperanza married by the civil authorities. Writing in 1900, when his persecutions were things of the past, Oroño argues:[46] "The people of northern Europe generally profess a faith different from ours. They belong to the reformed,

[44] *ibid.*, p. 7.
[45] Wilcken, *op. cit.*, p. 26.
[46] Oroño, *op. cit.*, pp. 8–9.

evangelical religion, the religion that is emancipated from Rome, though really as Christian as we are. And these individuals would not come to our country for all the advantages we could offer them unless they could count on professing their faith freely. True, the constitution assures liberty of conscience and faith, but it only states the principle and leaves the legislators to make its application effective. Among those means was certainly the law of civil marriage, which emancipates the family from theocratic power and favors the fusion of the races, of nations, of individuals of different religion, because it puts the family above the ceremony and puts theological intolerance aside forever. Civil marriage, then, is highly social and highly moral. Moreover, it has the advantage of being free and makes the contract accessible to rich and poor alike, which is not true of the religious sacrament, with the result that many individuals live together unwedded because they cannot afford to legalize their union. Suppressed, therefore, should be the obstacle that poverty often cannot overcome, and suppressed, too, the still greater obstacle of difference of religion. How would the foreigners come here if they could not marry, if they could not create families? . . . Such are the considerations that militated in favor of the establishment of civil marriage among us and that made a great impression at that time on the governor of Santa Fe, a province whose future was dependent on colonization. It will be said that colonization went on in spite of all this. Undoubtedly, but it would have developed greater proportions if the admirable institution of civil marriage had been maintained, and the consequences would have been felt not only in Santa Fe but in the whole republic. All true friends of the country understand this, even the most learned jurists of Buenos Aires. The opposition of superstition was in a fair way to be overcome. Unfortunately there were political aspirations in the field which seized the occasion to overthrow a government that was progressive and animated by the best intentions, but which did not lend itself pliantly to the ambitious aims of its citizens."

Church Influence at San Lorenzo

Another point of attack in Oroño's administration was his project for a school of agriculture at San Lorenzo, about 15 miles north of Rosario. The Franciscans have a convent there, founded for the conversion of the Indians. But by 1867 the nearest Indians were north of the city of Santa Fe, entirely out of reach. It was Oroño's plan, apparently, to expropriate the lands of the Franciscans and remove their establishment to the Indian country in order to locate at San Lorenzo a school where the native Creoles could learn the practice of agriculture.

This probably stirred up the Church authorities more than the law of civil marriage. On visiting San Lorenzo in 1918 I had some conversation with a Syrian in a little store where I went to buy something to eat. He described himself as a Catholic Arab, from the port of Beirut. All the Arabs in the port were Catholics, he said. The Arabs of the interior of Syria were Mohammedan, and as they had the government on their side they persecuted the Catholic Arabs in every way, so that they could not endure life in Turkey after they embraced Christianity. He remarked that San Lorenzo was a horrid dead town! "What was the matter with it?" "Why, the friars." There were too many of them, and they wouldn't allow anything to be done. This feeling was held by others, too, for the next man we asked what was the matter with San Lorenzo also said it was the friars. It was not clear what the friars did to the people. The second man, being pressed, stated that they once owned all the land in town and still owned all the land along the bluff (barranca) of the Paraná and would not sell it nor do anything with it. This man professed that he was a good Catholic. There was certainly no air of anything going on in town.

Oroño's Troubles About the Ownership of His Lands

At any rate Oroño's government fell. For some years he was banished from the Province of Santa Fe. In 1872 he

founded the colony of Oroño,[47] west of Coronda and less than
ten miles south of the colony San Carlos. Instead of applying
under the law of 1864, referred to above (p. 93), for 20 square
leagues of land to found a colony of 200 individuals, he used
his own land that he had from his father and states that he
expended $20,000 of his own money in aiding the colonists.
That would be in the form of advances to be repaid with interest from their crops. He and his father had been occupying
this land for thirty-seven years. But his enemies did not let
him rest. Colonizing made men rich. To own a few leagues
of land in Creole days was nothing; many a man did that and
hardly knew where to lay hands on a dollar of ready money.
But a colony was a different matter. Within the year of founding his colony a Spaniard named Francisco María Torres
denounced Oroño's estate as fiscal land. If he could prove this
the law allowed him a sixth of the land for his trouble. Torres
claimed that the land had really belonged to the Jesuits by
purchase and that when the Jesuits were expelled, all their
property became the property of the province. Oroño's story[48]
is a very different one. Of course his interests lose nothing in
the telling, but he gives what seem to be copies of the original
documents, court decisions, letters, and reports of the land
surveyors.

The elder Oroño had been granted the land on his own
petition in 1836 as lieutenant of militia. As the Creole governments rarely had any money, that was the customary way of
paying the officers and men. The land was not at the time
definitely known to be provincial land, and there was no
surveyor available. The land was asked for and granted subject to that doubt. Here is the decree of governor Estanislao
Lopez—the briefest one, I think, ever issued by a Spaniard.

SANTA FE, April 8, 1836

Let there be granted to the petitioner the lands occupied by Don
Pedro Juan Vergara without prejudice to better rights and with the

[47] Wilcken, *op. cit.*, p. 96. Oroño colony is indicated on Fig. 28 by the figure 72.
[48] Told in the book cited above in footnote 21 of this chapter. Governor Lopez's
decree, referred to below, is reproduced on p. 60 of that book.

provision that when it is shown that said lands are public property and when they have been measured and marked out with the customary formalities the government will indicate the area of land which is donated to him, in which case the title that corresponds will be issued.

LOPEZ

[countersigned] Domingo Cúllen

In 1858, after occupying these lands twenty-two years, Santiago Oroño, now having the title of General for his part in the battle of Monte Caseros, which ended the long rule of the tyrant Rosas, became satisfied that his estate really belonged to the heirs of Melchor Martínez and bought their rights and received title from them. Had it been fiscal land there was a law that gave him title to half of it simply for his having been in occupation of it twenty years. Later he was shown to be right in his action by a report from the government surveyors that there had been two similar parcels of land each having a frontage of two leagues on the Santa Fe River and extending six leagues back. The one lay north of the village of Coronda and the other adjoined it on the south. The northern strip was the one the Jesuits came into possession of, and the southern was that of Melchor Martínez and had a remarkably clear chain of ownership down to the heirs from whom Oroño bought. Oroño's land was private property when he bought it and remained private still. What Oroño bought of the Melchor Martínez heirs was the back four leagues of their six leagues of depth. But the courts decided against him: that the decree of 1836 gave him no land but merely promised to give him some when some future condition was fulfilled, and that his titles of purchase were null and void because of certain erasures and conflicting dates. Oroño points out that this would not make it fiscal land but would throw it back into the hands of the Melchor Martínez heirs, and Torres' "denunciation" of it as fiscal land would have failed. Two of the five judges made a minority report to this effect, but three overruled them. The land was pronounced fiscal, taken from Oroño, and, later, Torres was awarded his sixth, which he asked for and obtained in the form of forty concessions in the Colonia Oroño. This, of course, caused the greatest upsetting in the colony. The Martínez heirs were not called into court, had not claimed the land, and presumably were in satisfied possession of the purchase price. The grant to Torres was in 1884, after Oroño had filed many petitions, written many letters, and published many articles in the newspapers in support of his claim. In 1875, for instance, he petitioned the province to give effect to the decree of 1836 on the ground that a great number of soldiers and officers had been granted land on much less service than his father had rendered and that Lopez had promised to grant him lands in the decree of 1836. The province refused. In 1881 Dr. Simón de Iriondo, who was the head and heart of the movement against Oroño, offered in a private letter to have the government recognize Oroño's right to half his land, less the sixth granted to Torres, if he would withdraw certain suits that he had before the courts. In 1887 it was proposed to grant Oroño, on the ground of the decree of 1836, his original land less the sixth awarded to Torres, regardless of the fact that this was not fiscal land and that the state could not give away what it did not own. Finally, on January 9, 1895, Governor Cafferata granted payment to Oroño for the parts of his property that the province sold. He continued pleading for the restoration of the rest. The narrative throws a distinct light on the nature of land-ownership in the Republic and on the relation of actual events to laws and decrees, likewise on the turns taken by politics in those times. Further, it serves to make us better acquainted with Oroño and introduces Iriondo.

INADEQUATE GOVERNMENT POLICY ABOUT LAND TITLES AND SURVEYS

Nothing is so essential to satisfactory immigration as ease of obtaining clear title to land. Government authorities in the Argentine Republic have always been dilatory and heedless in this matter and have thus detracted from the desirability of their land as a haven for immigrants. They expect colonists to be satisfied to occupy land for long years without any title at all in the hope of getting one in the end. This attitude is well exemplified in what is now going on in the way of colonizing national lands, if we may believe J. G. Velárdez, writing in a semi-official way and defending Argentine policies.[49] He states that he has seen a great deal of this in the Chaco. It "is colonization of a less regular kind, tolerated in the first instance and afterwards legalized by the government, taking the form of subdivision of land previously cultivated and its grant on liberal terms to the cultivator or occupier." Lands available "are taken up by squatters who settle in such a way as not to interfere with one another and so carry out the subdivision that each one holds a lot of one hundred hectares. ... The occupiers till the land and introduce capital in the form of fixtures and improvements such as houses and outbuildings, wire netting, wells, and so forth." Then the government legalizes matters by officially creating a colony and granting titles to the colonists. This, of course, throws the proper tasks of government on private individuals without giving them the security that government should afford.

The country also suffered inconvenience from the lack of some simple method of land survey, suitable for unsettled regions, like that applied to our territory northwest of the Ohio River. Santa Fe had easy initial points for a survey in the high *barranca* of the Paraná and the banks of its tributary rivers. The early Santa Fe colonists had quite definite titles granted them on precise enough surveys on the ground. The spreading of these colonies westward, shown on Figure 28, carried the network of these surveys across Santa Fe to the province of Córdoba, which it did not reach till the nineties. The only colony in Córdoba in 1872 was Tortugas on the line of the Central Argentine Railway, adjoining the Santa Fe colonies on that line. In general at that date the Topographic

[49] J. G. Velárdez: Land Settlement in the Argentine Republic, *Internatl. Rev. of Agric. Economics*, N. S., Vol. I, 1923, pp. 227-248.

Survey of Córdoba had no data about the province and did not know where government lands were even within eight or ten leagues of the capital city. It believed there were provincial lands in the Department Río Cuarto, but there had never been any land surveys there, and it was not known which lands were public and which were private.[50]

SUNCHALES COLONY AS AN EXAMPLE OF
FAILURE AT FIRST

Of course some colonies met disaster. Sometimes the persistence that was to win through to prosperity had to be supplied by later comers who started with the abandoned undertakings of their predecessors. Sunchales colony is a case in point.[51] On Figure 28 it is marked with its name and [18]86— the date of the last of its foundations—a little to the southeast of the boundary reëntrant in the northwest corner of the map. Originally a Jesuit post on the road from Santa Fe to Córdoba, it was abandoned about 1800, probably because the road was a roundabout one, and fell into ruin. The church seems to have been solidly enough built to make a really lasting ruin. In 1866 Governor Nicasio Oroño made up his mind to reopen the road and tried to found a colony on four square leagues of land at the old site. But he put it into the hands of incompetent commissioners, and they managed everything badly. For one thing, they never went near the place to acquaint themselves with actual conditions there. For another, they never managed to get anything there on time. Seed always arrived after planting was finished, and provisions were delayed until the colonists had eaten the seed. Much money was spent without getting what it was spent for. There were bitter complaints by the colonists, and the commissioners, instead of attending to the matters complained of, became indignant, made charges against the colonists without knowing how things really were at the colony,

[50] Wilcken, *op. cit.*, p. 242.
[51] *ibid.*, pp. 261–269.

and finally, having got things into an inextricable mess, sought to cure them by resigning.

In the days of Governor Cabal, the man who in 1869 acquired 800 square leagues of land in Santa Fe by his "industry," some seven hundred people were actually put down in the colony under one Carlos de Mot, with a grant of 20 square leagues of land. He was to have a bonus of 20 *bolivianos* for every colonist brought into the province. State management that was no better than that under Oroño gave title to De Mot and paid him 20,000 *bolivianos* for colonists supposed to be placed there without inquiring at Sunchales whether they had been received or not.

The director on the ground, Dr. Fablet, seems to have been as inefficient as his predecessors. In 1871 he made a wonderfully glowing report on the condition of the colony, reciting the numbers of colonists and enumerating harvests and crops in a variety never before heard of. Thus it happened that inspector Wilcken came to Santa Fe with high expectations for this colony. A concrete accomplishment of Fablet was the building in the colony of a beautiful palace which the books of the establishment credited to the wife of De Mot, the director. It was a two-story structure on the foundations of the Jesuit church with a sixteen-acre estate around it. Rare trees of the most exquisite fruit filled the orchards, and the gardens were stocked with strawberries, lettuce, asparagus, and a variety of other vegetables. In the midst of the estate was an artificial lagoon with an island in it, constructed at great cost to the administration of the colony, the whole place a very paradise in the midst of the desert. A foreman and twelve men had been kept at work on this for a long time. But the things the administrator should have attended to he had neglected. Anyone who offered himself had been accepted as a colonist without any investigation of the likelihood of his succeeding. De Mot had failed to supply the colonists with oxen, so that at first they had to till the ground with hoes and spades instead of plowing, a thing of inconceivable difficulty with the hard-baked soil of Santa Fe, but he had not stimulated them to work nor informed himself of their attention to work. Not knowing the facts or the truth, he had filled his reports with pleasing fictions. He classed as excellent colonists men who in two years had brought into cultivation only six of their twenty *cuadras* of land. He reported 715 persons present when his books had only 383 listed, and to these he had loaned money till their debt, apart from the 300 *bolivianos* for their land, amounted to almost 400 *bolivianos* apiece. When his funds were exhausted by such extravagances as these he could neither pay wages nor meet his ordinary obligations, to say nothing of helping his colonists through the emergencies that all young colonies encountered.

In March, 1872, when Wilcken drew near Sunchales on his tour of inspection, he met a caravan of frightened colonists full of rumors of attacking Indians, though none had been near in the last two years, in full flight from Sunchales, from their homes and standing crops, driving cattle that did not belong to them, carrying off from the colony anything they could lay hands on in spite of being heavily in debt, and filling the way with every sort of vehicle, including sleds on which the men drew the women and children, seeking the shelter of some settlement. In the colony were only the administrator and a dozen families, who were preparing to go and could not be persuaded to remain. These men gave in when others would have held out in the moments of trial that came to every agricultural settlement in the land. But if the Sunchales colony of 1872 perished, its components lived on, a new group of families occupying the site in 1886 under Carlos Christiani,[52] whom we have met in 1875 associated with Guillermo Lehmann in the founding of Nuevo Torino (p. 94). There is a station Sunchales today on the Tucumán branch of the Central Argentine Railway with a colony population in 1914 of 3520, of whom 1111 are listed as foreigners.[53] Such experiences as

[52] Carrasco, *op. cit.*, p. 15.
[53] Tercer censo nacional, Vol. 2, p. 39.

this flight from Sunchales sort out the families that undergo them into colonists for other sites and populace for the great cities, always a residuum of persons of lower moral fiber.

GRUETLI COLONY AND THE INDIAN MENACE

In the very days of this hegira it happened that the colony Gruetli (Fig. 28), northwest of Esperanza, was passing through great trials.[54] Gruetli was an unusually pleasant site where erosion had brought to the surface in flowing streams the waters that permeated the subsoil of the more level parts of the Pampa, where the colonists usually encountered it at depths of twenty to sixty feet. Its valleys were clad with excellent timber still offering good pasture land. Most of it had been taken up by colonists from San Carlos with their savings. They were trying to make it a colony exclusively of German Swiss, selling the concessions to them at a profit or renting to them. All had gone well till one day in 1870 two North American colonists were "treacherously murdered" by the Indians. It rather surprises the student of these narratives to hear so rarely of the killing of a colonist by Indians; attacks, alarms, raids on cattle abound, but killings are heard of rarely and more vaguely. The effect was immediate. A number of families that had settled at Gruetli moved away at once so that only thirteen families were left in 1872, and these so far apart as to be unable to help one another in case of need. Then on February 19, 1872, a Tyrolese farmer, drawing a load of wheat along the road in broad daylight, was likewise "assassinated." The common report ran that a band of twenty Indians "who could not be found" had committed the crime. The settlers were terribly upset and quite in the mood to break up their homes and abandon the colony when the collapse of Sunchales sent them ten families from there to swell their number and stimulate their courage, especially as more settlers were sent from San Carlos.

[54] Wilcken, *op. cit.*, pp. 111–113.

There is reason to believe that the killing at Gruetli two years earlier was what caused the rumor of Indian danger at Sunchales! An ironical fate led the fugitives from Sunchales right to the one point where the danger had really existed.

Note the detail of rented concessions at Gruetli. A colonist buys added lots, at first because he has not land enough; but presently he has more than he can cultivate, and so he puts a representative (*habilitado*) on it, who pays him with a share of the crop, the owner supplying the capital of tools, seed, and food. This was happening rather frequently. In some cases a colonist acquires twenty concessions. In one instance at Rafaela (Fig. 39) an immigrant had acquired by slow savings forty-two concessions with a total area of 1400 hectares (3460 acres).[55] The renting noted at Gruetli is of date of 1870 and is renting by a colonist.

[55] Antonio Franceschini: L'Emigrazione italiana nell' America del Sud: Studi sulla espansione coloniale transatlantica, Rome, 1908.

CHAPTER V

SOUTHERN SANTA FE COLONIES

Early one bright morning near the end of May, 1918, we took the train at Rosario for Villa Casilda, 28 miles to the westward. Argentine early morning trains have the great convenience of a dining car enabling the traveler to go from bed to the train without hurrying for an early breakfast. We had hardly taken our places at the wide window of the diner when the landscape was suddenly wrapped in dark mist blowing in from the Paraná, obviously because the river's tropical waters were so much warmer than the wintry southern land. It was ground mist. We could always see blue sky on looking up. A sudden east wind that had sprung up had brought air that had rested on the broad river until it contained much water vapor, and this was being condensed by contact with the cold ground. As the sun rose higher and began to warm the ground this mist "burned off," as we say. At Casilda we found the trees dripping water, though the sky was now clear. Easterly winds are common at Rosario—about 40 per cent of all the winds in autumn and winter (March to August, in the Argentine) and nearly half of them in spring and summer.[1] In Santa Fe they tell you that oranges may be grown as far west from the Paraná as these mists are blown. Beyond that mist frost destroys the blossoms. We saw oranges on the trees at San Lorenzo on the bluff and in patios at Villa Casilda, but they need protection so far south. The market supply comes from Corrientes (Fig. 40), 300 miles farther north, where frosts are not known.

[1] W. G. Davis: Climate of the Argentine Republic, Dept. of Agric., Buenos Aires, 1910, p. 42.

The Founding of Casilda Colony, Originally Candelaria, by Don Carlos Casado

Casilda colony,[2] originally Candelaria, was founded in 1870 by Carlos Casado del Alisal, a Spanish banker of Rosario (Fig. 42). He had come to the country poor and married a Señorita de Sastre, daughter of a Creole schoolmaster. Though succeeding at his business, he was not regarded as wealthy at the time of founding the colony. He acquired five square leagues of land from Octavio Grandoli for the colony, doubtless at a very modest price, for prices, as we shall see, everywhere ran low in those days. A novelty in the planning of this colony was that the section roads divided it into blocks of 100 hectares (247 acres), and each of these blocks was divided into four concessions of 25 hectares (62 acres) each instead of 33 as in the earlier colonies. For a town settlement two squares were left in the center of the colony (494 acres), each colonist being given a free town lot of 25 by 50 meters (82 by 164 feet).[3]

Renting a Practice Fostered by the Colonists Themselves

The concessions were sold at 500 Argentine gold pesos, about $485 of our money, i.e. at a little less than $8 an acre. These concessions proved to be too small, just as had been the case with the 83-acre ones farther north, and so we soon find colonists possessing two or three lots or even a whole block. Thus the 324 lots at Casilda were taken up by 95 families, on the average three or four lots to a family. The provision for rental, which we noticed in the colonies along the Central Argentine Railway (p. 92), was here of practical

[2] Guillermo Wilcken: Las colonias: Informe sobre el estado actual de las colonias agrícolas de la República Argentina presentado á la Comisión Central de Inmigración, Buenos Aires, 1873, pp. 191-201.

[3] It is of interest to compare this provision for a village site in the Argentine Republic with the provision being made at that same time in the Middle West of the United States for schools, viz. a reservation of 640 acres in each township, the townships being of about the same size as these Argentine colonies. The maximum provision for schools made in the Argentine colonies was the unusual construction of a very modest building and the allowance of $30 a month for a teacher—less than a laborer's wages at the time.

FIG. 40—Orange boats at Santa Fe city. They bring the fruit down the Paraná from Corrientes. The city is behind us; we are looking out along the new dredged channel that extends four miles from the port of Santa Fe to the Paraná ("Canal de Acceso" on Fig. 57).

FIG. 41 (left).—Carlos Brebbia, Italian immigrant, who from mason became railway contractor, respected citizen, father of significant Argentine sons.

FIG. 42 (right).—Don Carlos Casado del Alisal, founder of Colonia Candelaria (Villa Casilda). He was an unwearied protector of the interests of his colonists, who throve under his guidance and cherish his memory.

importance, for while, up to May, 1872, 47 lots had been sold for cash and 145 on time payments, 132 had been rented,[4] 148 still remaining in the hands of Casado. We must recognize that the colonists themselves initiated the practice of renting colonial lands which is now the greatest obstacle to the further progress of the country and commonly imputed to the selfishness of the great landowners. In those days renting was no evil. It was easy for anyone with a small capital to purchase land, and renting gave a chance to those who had not even that small amount of money. Moreover, it was stipulated that the amount paid for rent could be later applied for purchase if the renter desired. Today's difficulty is that the would-be colonist can find no small lots for sale. Nothing was commoner among the thriftier colonists than the purchase of extra lots as they saved money and the placing of *habilitados* upon them for a share of the harvest. I have heard them recount with honest pride the assistance they had given to less fortunate fellow countrymen. None of the earliest plans made provision for renting land. As just stated, it was a practice introduced by the colonists themselves. The Central Argentine Railway and afterwards Carlos Casado offered this arrangement to the colonists because they were demanding it; they wanted land to rent out to others because in Europe the ownership of land was as remote from them as the kingdom of heaven. In practice in America they found it an admirable thing to have others working for them, which is of course precisely the motive of the owner of large estates. Rather than take money for his land, which he must then invest at the risk of losing it, he prefers to keep it and have others work it for his advantage.

Casado's Help to the Colonists in the Early Years

Casado was the first colony founder to reserve to himself— for six years—the valuable privilege of all sales of supplies within the colony. No grocery, dry goods, or butcher shop

[4] Wilcken, *op. cit.*, p. 192.

could be set up without some arrangement with the administration. This might have been a means of exploiting the colonists, and the thing has actually happened since more than once. How it came out at Casilda may be seen from the fact that Casado forbade the sale of liquor in the colony—a rather extraordinary thing in a country where wine was and is still regarded as an essential part of daily food, yet I cannot learn that anyone complained,[5] probably because it was over fifty years ago! Furthermore, when it came to selling the settlers' products, Casado made no attempt to monopolize their handling, but all the colonists I talked to agreed that his business relations were so good and his interest in the welfare of the colony so keen that he never failed to get them better prices for their grain than was paid to others. His helpfulness was thoroughly believed in at Casilda. Casado became rich, but no one seemed to feel that he enriched himself through the colony. For that matter it is certain that land grants in connection with railroad building made him rich. On the contrary all expressed enthusiasm for the assistance he gave them. There is no question of his popularity in Casilda. It is intense today, twenty years after his death. I asked Don Carlos Brebbia, of whom more later (p. 121), if he knew him intimately, and he broke out at once: "If Carlos Casado had been a general—if you will pardon me—your soldiers would never have taken Cuba away from Spain! He was a man of wonderful force. Everything that he undertook had to succeed. He would admit no opposition. He would not see any difficulty. He had immense energy." They agreed that without him the colony could not have pulled through its hardest trials. They themselves had worked hard and earned the prosperity that had come to them, but they felt the importance of his constant help. "Above all he was always confident.

[5] On the contrary, Antonio Franceschini (L'Emigrazione italiana nell' America del Sud: Studi sulla espansione coloniale transatlantica, Rome, 1908, p. 363) quotes L. Petich, the Italian vice-consul in Rosario (Immigrazione nella Repubblica Argentina durante il 1873, *Boll. Consolare*, Vol. 10, pp. 589–633, Rome, Dec. 1874; reference on p. 615), to the effect that the prohibition made Casilda famous for "the undisturbed peace and tranquillity of public order."

Nothing discouraged him." Such men had difficulties to overcome. It is not enough for a government to give immigrants
access to the land. They have to be helped through the inevitable hard times which always come to them. Even in the
regions of the greatest prosperity, where everything is done
to make things go well with them, there are many who cannot
persevere through hardships and stay till wealth crowns their
efforts. Even with free passages and free land, as well as
diligent and effective intervention in case of need on the part
of a person deeply and constantly interested in the success of
the colony, many will fail, not merely in persistent hard labor
but in any persistence at all. Those who have just managed
to exist on their land through hard times have today a valuable
property. Those who worked hard and steadily in addition
have become affluent. Of course the colonists I talked with
were those who had stayed. Those who gave up and left the
colony may have had a different feeling for Casado. A few
colonists at Casilda paid for their land in two or three years.
Most took longer, and perhaps half of them never paid up at
all. These were persons who worked less, or encountered
misfortunes, or were drawn to the city or other colonies.

At first the colonists had cultivated wheat—it was in such
demand. For it must be remembered that at this time the
Argentine Republic was importing wheat from Chile, from the
United States, and from Europe. They kept on cultivating
it year after year as long as the crop came. When it began to
fall off from the impoverishment of the soil, some would not
hear of growing maize, as others had learned to do in rotation
with the familiar wheat, and went to seek other virgin soils to
continue to work the only crop they knew. Casado had supplied them everything, seed, house, materials, oxen, tools, and
credit for flour at the store. This debt Casado cancelled if
they wanted to go, a large amount of money at the time,
though the land they gave up came to be worth much more.
How Casado had driven, how he had helped them! He was
always a man who had great demands on him. He undertook

so many things and carried them through so successfully that
he was wanted at once for others. After the colonizing of
Candelaria he built the railroad from Rosario to Villa Casilda.
They needed that railroad badly! The government gave him
150 square leagues of land elsewhere in the province in payment, as well as concessions for stations along the line, which
proved very profitable to him. That was really where his
fortune was made. But it was hard for the government to
find anyone to build the road. He was needed badly. Then
he sold his banking business in Rosario to the Bank of London
and Río de La Plata, agreeing not to found another bank.
But the government of the province called him at once to be
manager of the Provincial Bank of Santa Fe. When bad
times came in 1889–1890 what would they have done without
Carlos Casado?

Always with these many things in hand he needed money.
So, in 1878, when the locusts ate up the wheat in September,
Casado did not know which way to turn for cash. Credit was
at that time being refused him in Rosario. The times were
bad, everybody was poor, and kind feelings were not governing
actions. He insisted on supplying seed to all who would plow
again. They must replant! He finally mortgaged his own
crop to get seed. Some did replant in October, almost time to
make the harvest (here in the southern hemisphere wheat is
harvested in December), and for the few *cuadras* that they
were able to seed got very good prices.

THE PLAGUE OF LOCUSTS

Among the injuries done by the locust Franceschini includes
the scarcity of fruit or shade trees in colonies on the Pampa of
Córdoba. He states that the *paraíso*, or paradise tree (*Melia
azedarach*), is the only shade tree that will withstand them,
which is the reason for its widespread use.[6] The locusts, he
says, make their appearance almost every year on those plains
—sometimes more than once—in numberless swarms, looking

[6] Franceschini, *op. cit.*, p. 409.

like a heavy snowfall in the air, a cloud that may stretch out ten or twelve miles in length and more than a mile in width, destroying everything green as they go, even the fruit trees. The only mitigating circumstance is that the area damaged by any one swarm is narrow, so that any particular field is not likely to be damaged more than occasionally. Mutual insurance appears to be an adequate remedy for losses by this voracious creature. The Argentine government has spent much money in fighting locusts and in devising methods of destroying them, with the result of putting some check to their ravages.

In three years' residence in the city of Córdoba the writer saw but one swarm of locusts. It was thick enough to obscure the sun as it passed across the sky, and the insects fell in the streets so thickly that we could not put our feet down without crushing one or two. On another occasion, coming down from Tucumán in the train, we were stopped in northern Córdoba Province by a small swarm crawling across the rails and making them so slippery with their crushed bodies that they had to be shoveled off to start the train again.

Iriondo's Support of Casado

It is usual, the bankers say, for the *colonizador* to look after his colonists closely; his own prosperity grows so much out of their success. But Casado did more than that: he impressed all these people with his constant interest in them. Later he had interest in quebracho lands in Paraguay and was much in Buenos Aires and Rosario. But he was apt to come to Casilda to see the colonists. Casilda was probably his first venture, and it is not believed he had any money to speak of when he started that. One thing that helped Casado greatly was the protection of Iriondo, whom we have met before (p. 106) as chief among the men who overthrew Governor Oroño in 1868. Iriondo's help was not with money but with political influence. Iriondo kept persons from bothering Casado through the courts, for the judges could not be persuaded to do anything against Iriondo. This was of the greatest use to Casado, of course, for he was always fighting someone. "The Administration always keeps this country back," one man exclaimed with real anger. "They never help anything, they always hinder." Well, in Casado's case Iriondo prevented that! They never could attack Casado through the courts.

RELATION OF THE CREOLE TO THE IMMIGRANT ELEMENT

There is a general feeling among the immigrants who have prospered by their work that the Creole lives a parasitic life, always trying to take toll of the efforts of the foreigner to develop the country without aiding or even facilitating those efforts himself, or even by hindering them if the toll be not in sight. It is certain it helps in business undertakings to have influential Creole allies.

Creoles, of course, make up almost the totality of political appointees, and some of these in public offices display a good deal of old-fashioned Creole incompetence, sending you to the next window or to some other official. The post office in the active and modern business city of Rosario is medieval in its appointments and service. Employees will exchange polite greetings with you. The Creoles have courtesy in their blood, but probably no one ever told a Creole employee that he existed to give the public quick and easy despatch of business, to his own inconvenience if necessary. A Creole statistician of Santa Fe notes in connection with the courts:[7] "Delays in procedure as well as in final decisions have been the inveterate defect of Argentine justice. The causes are many, but certainly one of the most important is the security of tenure in a badly managed office for those well related in prominent political circles who put private interests above the sacred interest of justice." An Italian whom we encountered near Díaz (northwest of Rosario; see below, p. 140) in charge of a small gang building brick culverts in the road asserted that all

[7] *Anuario de la Direcc. Gen. de Estadíst. de la Provincia de Santa Fé, 1913*, Rosario, 1914, p. 20.

posts like his were dual: a Creole head with a good salary, and a subordinate under him to do the work.

The Creole on the other hand, especially the class of Creoles which is not sharing freely in the increase of the national wealth, is wont to make much of the fact that so many immigrants who are now prosperous or wealthy came to America "with one hand before and another behind," as the Spanish phrase is, to cover their nakedness!

CARLOS BREBBIA OF CASILDA

Carlos Brebbia (Fig. 41) is an interesting man. A prosperous railway contractor of seventy-three, honored by the government with the charge of important works, respected by his fellow townsmen, modest, simple and affable, he has won his comfortable place in the land by a long life of useful labor. I found his house at Casilda easily from description by the pretty garden in front with its palm trees, quite like a villa in France or northern Italy. The garden enclosed the house on all sides, unlike the typical Creole house with its bare walls to the street, bars on the windows, and all the adornment and garden effect in the patios within (Fig. 43), which may succeed each other to the rear and end in a real fruit orchard shut off from the back street by another houselike wall.[8] There was painting going on at the front of the house and so we went around to the rear, where we found the owner at work getting the house ready for occupancy. He had just returned from a four months' stay in Italy, trying to get into service at the front. He had bought land at Casilda early but had never been an actual resident on the land himself, always putting a tenant on it, first on that lot and later on lots at other points as well as at Casilda. "I never crowded them. Some paid me when they could, and some never paid at all; but I never lost faith in agriculture as the future of this land." He was a mason by trade. Born in a little village near Como in northern

[8] See also Figs. 26, 29, 30, 33, and 34, above, and the writer's "Recent Colonization in Chile," *Amer. Geogr. Soc. Research Series No. 6*, 1921, Figs. 2 and 3.

Italy he worked on the Mont Cenis tunnel when sixteen years of age and came to the Argentine Republic about 1872. He was called to Casilda from Rosario to work on the administration building of the colony. It was money from this job that he invested in his first lot, and through this job he became acquainted with Don Carlos Casado, with whom he worked for the rest of Casado's life, for Casado's first need was always workers. When he built the railroad from Rosario to Casilda in 1883 it was Brebbia who did the mason work. Later Brebbia did railway building under him on the branches southward to Melincué, 1888, and westward to Juárez Celmán, 1889. In 1908 he was made sub-director of construction on the Patagonian road from San Antonio to Lake Nahuel Huapi.

Brebbia has great pride in having helped many a poor family of Italian workers to get land, buy seed, tools, and food—not a few of them now rich. If some of them did not pay him back it did not matter. Most of them did, although they had their hard times. The country had treated him well. He took pleasure, too, in his part in getting the national agricultural school located at Casilda during the three years that he was a member of the Comisión de Fomento. Someone had been entrusted by the government with the choice of the site of the school for Santa Fe. When this person came to Casilda they showed him a piece of land some kilometers away from the village, quite empty and unattractive, just open pampa, and he was not interested at all. He had just been looking at a place that the Governor wanted him to take near some land of his own. But Brebbia showed him a place on the outskirts of the village with a good building, trees, and growing crops, a really attractive place, and this pleased him at once. "If he could have that he would use all his influence with the minister to have it adopted." As a matter of fact Brebbia didn't own it or have an option to so much as an inch of it, but he went to work to get it and met obstacles immediately. People had no vision of what that school would mean to the town. Worst of all, Casado said no. Everybody said no.

But Brebbia persisted and finally got the block desired and the adjoining one as well, and there the school was put.

In 1892 he founded a company for mutual insurance against hail, which distributed more than half a million dollars for losses by hailstorms before the hostility of standard companies compelled it to go out of business.

Brebbia has six Argentine sons, the oldest a grain commission merchant in Rosario and secretary of the Stock Exchange. He married an Italian. The next is a commander in the Argentine navy, of whom I have heard elsewhere as the man trusted to take a valuable warship through the intricate passages beyond the Strait of Magellan. Another, whose wife is an Argentine of Spanish parentage, is managing a large flour mill at Melincué. Another, employed in the mill as accountant, married an Argentine of straight Creole family. These young men represent an addition to the blood of the Argentine nation that is worth while. This is immigration at its best—a skilled worker pays his own passage to the New World and goes to the work that awaits a man with a trade, today as in the past; he earns and saves and buys land. That opportunity was the happy condition of the Argentine Republic of forty years ago. Land at really low price was being offered to men who farm to get it farmed. Dr. Brougnes, the Frenchman, Castellanos of Salta, and Governors Cullen and Oroño in Santa Fe, who joined them in making land available, did the useful thing just there: enabling workers to get the land to work at the price it was then really worth. Not immigration agencies, not free passages, not money help to the newcomer unadjusted to any capacity he has shown to pay obligations, but a fair chance to buy land at actual present worth, unaugmented by speculative estimates of the value that his labor will some day give it, makes for successful settlement here as elsewhere. A nation that allows one group of its citizens, whether large or small, to withhold the land from those who will give it value, until they have paid to the withholders a great share of the value that is to be given it, is not in intelligent hands. The land must be purchasable at something near its taxable value; and it will be so purchasable when it is taxed at something near its selling price. Possible ownership of the land is the crucible wherein the foreigner who is worth while is transmuted into a citizen.

CASILDA IN 1918

Whether it be due to the fostering care of Don Carlos Casado or to the nearness of the port of Rosario, Casilda has come to be a place of some importance, with 10,000 people in the town and 2000 more in the colony around. Some hundreds of prosperous colonists have come into the town to live, leaving a son or a renter on the farm. They raise much wheat in the colony and a good deal of linseed but rather more maize than either.

Maize is now the dominant crop of Santa Fe, cultivated by renters who appear to live under conditions of much wretchedness. Maize is often said to be a renter's crop because it does not require so much expensive machinery as wheat. A factor that may have some influence is the seasonal distribution of the rainfall. At Carcarañá, a few miles north of Casilda, the average annual rainfall is 33.4 inches—11.5 in summer, December, January, and February; 10.1 in autumn, March, April, and May; 3.8 in winter, June, July, and August; and 8.0 in spring, September, October, and November.[9] As wheat is usually sown from the first to the fourth week in June and harvested toward the end of December, it has winter and spring for growing season, with a total rainfall of 11.8 inches. But maize is planted from September to December, according to the season, and harvested in March, and so its season of growth is spring and summer, with a total rainfall of 19.5 inches, almost twice as much as is available to grow wheat. Something of the same relation holds in all the cereal districts of the Re-

[9] Josef Chavanne: Die Temperatur- und Regenverhältnisse Argentiniens, *Veröffentl. der Deutschen Akad. Vereinigung zu Buenos Aires*, Vol. 1, No. 7 [about 1903], p. 33.

public.[10] When it is commonly said that Santa Fe has abandoned wheat for corn a change is referred to which should be put less strongly. Around Rosario, it is true, wheat is almost abandoned for corn, but in the province corn and alfalfa are produced on enormously greater areas than formerly, while wheat is falling off somewhat.[11] The larger changes in the twenty years from 1895 to 1915 are: a tenfold increase of alfalfa acreage, a sevenfold growth of the acreage in maize, a doubling of flaxseed, and a diminution of wheat by an eighth.

We found Casilda an active town with *paraíso* trees along the streets and in a public square. This is the old-time Santa Fe tree for town use, usually pollarded. But the square was also provided with a younger plantation of *ligustros* (privet). These are evergreen and have a dark green foliage which suits the climate very well, adding greatly to the winter aspect of the streets. The true old-Creole street is absolutely barren of vegetation (Fig. 30) except for the charming glimpses of patios through open street doors. The heavy wood folding doors at the house entrance are rarely closed except at night; those who want some walling off from the public on the street being content with an inner door of open iron work. The *ligustro* is pollarded to have a spherical head that will not interfere with the view from the second story. This is very ugly on deciduous trees like the *paraíso*, as the leaves are needed to cover the stumpy, misshapen twigs.

[10] The respective sums of rainfall in inches for the maize (Sept.-Feb.) and the wheat (June-Nov.) growing season at various points are: Santa Fe city, 20.8 and 13.4; San Nicolás on the Paraná, 18.8 and 14.2; Trenque Lauquén in southwest Buenos Aires Province, 16.2 and 9.9; Córdoba city, 20.5 and 8.6; Río Cuarto, 19.9 and 10.7; General Acha in Pampa Central, 10.4 and 6.0 (W. G. Davis: Argentine Meteorological Service: History and Organization, With a Condensed Summary of Results, Ministry of Agric., Buenos Aires, 1914, pp. 159, 160, 161, 166, 167, 168).

[11] Following are the areas in hectares in the principal crops of Santa Fe Province for 43 years (*Estadística Agrícola, 1915-16*, Direcc. Gen. de Econ. Rural y Estadist., Minist. de Agric., Buenos Aires, 1917, pp. 17, 18, 20):

	1872	1888	1895	1915
Wheat	35,861	401,652	1,030,898	903,000
Maize	1,695	60,901	185,898	1,275,650
Flaxseed	—	?	266,606	580,000
Alfalfa	—	29,551	133,730	1,320,000

Some of the Settlers of the Colony

Casilda has many prosperous colonists still living on their concessions, mostly Italians. We visited a number of them, accompanied by Director Spangenburg, the conscientious and enthusiastic head of the agricultural school. The first was that of an Italian living in a substantial house of brick (Figs. 44–45) with his name painted on the end. He and his wife (Fig. 46) were away the first day I called, but there were plenty of good workers on the job in his family of nine children, seven of them boys (Fig. 47). It is a 25-hectare (62-acre) lot that they have bought with the savings of twenty years of labor, estimated to be worth 25,000 Argentine dollars, *moneda nacional*,[12] i.e. paper pesos fixed at 44 per cent of the value of the gold peso (or, in United States currency, slightly less than $11,000). They are also farming a larger piece of land that they are now buying. Twenty-three *cuadras* of their land are in corn this year, six in alfalfa, and six in pasture—in all 59 acres under occupation.

The boys were at work when we came. The place was well fenced, had a good well, and a corral with a cement trough for the cattle. The smaller boys were barefoot, all very poorly dressed but not inappropriately for their work. They were not very quick to understand what was said, less so than other Italians we had talked to, for usually they are extremely vivacious. All but the oldest son were born in the Argentine. It was interesting to see that people like these in no case bought a Ford automobile unless it was clearly a money maker. They are slow to spend. In Italy they had to be so to keep alive, and here it has meant their rise in fortune. Hard, miserly parsimony has controlled their actions for years and still controls the actions of some of those who have reached real wealth. The astonishing thing is that so many moderately prosperous are hospitable and able to spend without regret. Of the free-handedness of the American middle class nothing is to be seen here unless the extravagance of the rich be brought into comparison.

[12] Abbreviated $ m/n.

Fig. 43—A Creole patio, in a hotel at Santiago del Estero. The church that looms behind is across the street. The attractive interior is in typical contrast to the blank street walls.

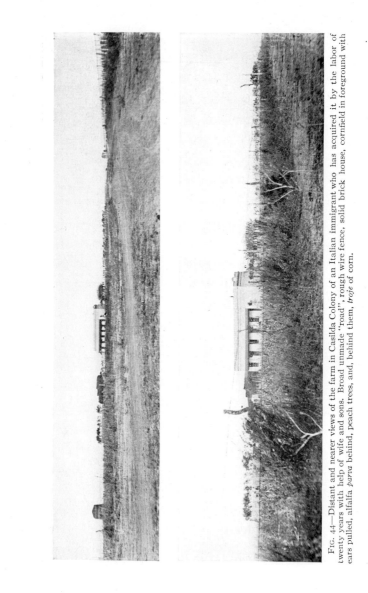

Fig. 44—Distant and nearer views of the farm in Casilda Colony of an Italian immigrant who has acquired it by the labor of twenty years with help of wife and sons. Broad unmade "road", rough wire fence, solid brick house, cornfield in foreground with ears pulled, alfalfa *parva* behind, peach trees, and, behind them, *troje* of corn.

FIG. 45.—The dwelling house on the Italian colonist's farm. Of good burned brick, all to be coated with stucco as under the porch. Roof of the type called *azotea*, i.e. slightly sloping and made of tiles set in cement, with 30-inch parapet around.

Fig. 46 (above)—The Italian colonist and his wife.

Fig. 47 (below)—Four of the Italian's seven sons. They came in from the field to be photographed. Only the oldest was born in Italy. The parents were away when this photograph was made, but the work was in the hands of the boys.

It is characteristic that all the children work. They brought that custom, too, from the Old World, and it is doubtful if it lasts to the next generation.

We also visited a colonist and his wife from Venice, thirty-eight years in the Argentine. They have eleven children, who now do the work while the parents take their ease (Fig. 48). The boys were out in the fields at the time. This man raised wheat and said he never had so good a harvest. Of course the fancy price helped. The wife, mother of eleven, was remarkably vigorous, rosy-faced, and full of fun. They invited us to have a glass of wine made from their own grapes by the head of the house. I did not meet an Italian colonist who spoke a good word for the wines of Mendoza, though the industry is largely in Italian hands. The house was very plain but well built, the floor of cement with a smooth, tilelike surface. On the wall hung a diploma awarded in some agricultural competition, the main decoration. This man's place had numerous black poplars in front besides the grape vines, and nearer the road a garden of flowers with fancy borders of leafy plants in the Italian fashion—quite an effervescence of prosperity for the country. There is no doubt of the contentment of these people and their doing what they wanted to. I asked the man if he did not want to go back to Italy. "Oh, yes, he would like to go back some time, but it was a long way off and now with the war!" Would he want to live there? "What, me? I am a better Argentine than many of them that were born here!" But he had no notion of being naturalized, saw no use in it.

Another colonist we visited was very prosperous, it was said—worth $50,000 m/n. He had just put electric lights in his house and had most attractive tiles in the floor of his portico. He also had an Aermotor windmill, but along with these signs of comfort went the report of the drunkenness that occasional immigrants fall victim to. All the men about here had prospered and had good houses of burnt bricks with solid roofs. All have been hard workers. They had worked the family hard, too. Distinctly, the family, the larger the better, has been the wealth of the colonist. All these houses are of quite different type from those of the renters and maize growers near Rosario. (It is agreed that wheat must be grown on cheaper land to counterbalance the high cost of the machinery needed to handle it.)

The Granja, or Complete Farm

We were entertained at a very good breakfast-noonday meal at the School of Agriculture and taken in the Ford of one of the professors, a most amiable man, to visit these farms. Director Spangenburg's ideal and that of most teachers and writers on agriculture in the Argentine Republic is the *granja*, or complete farm, with cattle, cereals, vegetables, orchard, hens, and pigs. Here there should be constant rotation of crops, and all the food of the family should be raised at home, so that they would be well fed whatever the caprice of the weather or the market for some one of their crops. There will rarely be a year when all the crops are poor. Another equally important advantage of the *granja* is that it keeps everybody busy all day throughout the year instead of permitting long periods of idleness between harvest and planting, the favorite opportunity for drunkenness and other vices.

The neglect of vegetable raising in wheat- and maize-growing families has been found to cause single families of colonists to spend $300 or $400 m/n a year at the store for vegetables that they might easily have raised themselves. It seems a general belief in the Argentine Republic that all farms in the United States are model *granjas*.

An Example of the Harmful Aspect of Child Labor

On our way back through town we had our shoes polished by a boy who reminded me of Lazarillo de Tormes, the hero of the sixteenth-century picaresque novel of that name. The boy was Argentine and bright; his master, an Italian, who didn't understand us very well or pretended not to. The

Fig. 48—Another Italian colonist of Casilda and his wife. They own their house and do not work (much!). There are eleven children to keep things going. They are very happy in their house with its grape vine. The bake oven behind.

FIG. 49—Students of the School of Agriculture of Santa Fe Province at Casilda. Creoles, Indians, foreign born, and sons of immigrants. All do daily tasks with their hands.

FIG. 50—Citizens of Casilda giving a farewell party to a municipal secretary, who sits in the middle of the front row of men. Three are Italians, the rest Argentines, but new Argentines. Their parents were foreigners. They would not be called Creoles by the old-time Creoles.

boy was ten years old and not attending school, though the man insisted that he was. The man said he could read, but Lazarillo said "only some words and phrases." The boy did most of the work and was a good worker. The man took the money and did nothing except argue unconvincingly that the boy had had plenty of schooling. That is an evil side of the institution of putting the family to work that is so helpful to the colonist acquiring land. It is to be seen all over Latin America.[13]

THE SCHOOL OF AGRICULTURE AT CASILDA

The agricultural school at Casilda is one of four special schools maintained by the Argentine national government: one for grape growing and wine making at Mendoza, one at Casilda for "agronomists," one at Córdoba for experts in agriculture and animal science, and one at Tucumán to train in sugar growing and manufacturing, the only one in territory that is still dominantly Creole.

The Casilda school stands in a handsome garden just at the edge of the town. The director was teaching a class, so the secretary and one of the professors entertained us until he appeared. Director Spangenburg takes a very earnest and devoted interest in the education of these young men. At the moment there were 75 students, all that there was room for. Applications had been filed by many more, and new dormitories were being built. The students are of many origins, as their picture shows, Figure 49. They pay an annual fee of $400 m/n ($176 United States money), but on statement from local authorities that their parents cannot afford it this is remitted, by granting them a *beca*, or scholarship, of that amount. I am told that application for this is not made by those who can really pay. The outfit that they must bring to school with them is of interest, its cost being estimated at $300 m/n: a new woolen mattress 6 feet by 2½; a new woolen

[13] Figure 2 in the writer's "Recent Colonization in Chile" (*Amer. Geogr. Soc. Research Series No. 6*, 1921) catches an illustration. The little boy is a servant at work, not a child at play.

pillow 12 by 30 inches, six sheets, three pillow cases, two new woolen blankets, one white cotton bedspread, one laundry bag, two bath towels, six towels, three woolen undershirts, six cotton or linen shirts, six pairs of drawers, a dozen pair of socks, three working shirts, either cotton or woolen, one woolen jersey, three dusters, two suits of *brin* (canvas) as seen in their picture, two pairs of heavy shoes, one of leather leggings, a Boy Scout hat, six napkins, and a napkin ring. To some of the students, apparently full-blooded Indians, the use of this outfit must be an education in itself. Others, however, are Creoles of more than a few generations. At Córdoba I found a recent graduate agronomist from the Córdoba school of agriculture who was a son of an old-time lawyer friend of mine, Creoles of old family like his wife. The young man was enthusiastic about his work in horticulture, though the family felt well provided for by the inherited farm of 365 hectares (902 acres). Nothing could be more hopeful for the Republic than that young Creoles of the upper class should turn with zeal to agriculture and industry, especially in conservative Córdoba. I saw other illustrations of this; still, I regard them as exceptional.

At Casilda the students have to attend classes part of the day and work in the fields or farm buildings the rest. They rise at 4:30 in summer, 5:45 in winter, going to bed at 8:30 and 8:45, with an hour out at noon for recreation and play. All the work of the school they do with their own hands. There is a foreman to direct their outside work in detail, under the general management of the director and faculty, and they make no trouble at all about this manual work, although it is utterly opposed to old-Creole conceptions of dignity. The students are fine young fellows and carry themselves very well.

The school course is of three years, supplemented by a year of practical farm work under some employer, with monthly reports, after which they may get their title of *administrador rural*. All the alumni are placed in these trial positions and get from $50 to $250 m/n a month for it. This trial year they call their "stage," under the impression, I think, that they are using an English word. The demand for these young men is greater than the supply, to manage estates in whole or in part.

All the work of the school is modeled on similar work in the United States, at least in intention, but obviously not in the extent to which the faculty disposes of the time of the students. The students make their own beds; they sleep in great open halls something like barracks and, while these are being enlarged, in the museum. They are constantly controlled and seem to have none of the liberties of our students. They are called by bells that resound noisily, and they are moved about in military formation. They have football and other games and shower baths but with no hot water! For study they must use the recitation rooms. There is no luxury of appointments as in so many of our newer schools. On the other hand they seem to have plenty of farm fields, plantations, buildings, and machinery. Two American silos figure in the equipment, and they advocate earnestly the use of a cheaper one that they call a *parva silo*. *Parva* is a stack (of alfalfa). For the *parva silo* they dig a trench in the ground six feet deep, fill it with cut maize for four and a half feet above ground, capping this with about three feet of earth contained within a wooden frame. This without walls of any sort serves in that mild climate to keep the maize and is regarded as essential to the cheap production of milk. For milk, which was scarce in this cattle country thirty years ago, is now produced abundantly, well cared for, and obtainable everywhere. Many cows the director says give their average of two liters—a shade over two quarts—of milk a day the year through.

Argentine Maize

Many experiments are made in selecting and planting maize. They use many American varieties, but they never seem to get a very fine large ear. Most of what we saw in the fields was small and scrubby. It is to be remembered that Argentine maize can get to Europe only by a journey of twenty or thirty days across the equator and must be able to stand the heat, an experience that North American corn escapes. The fields are usually full of weeds, which often fairly smother the crop. As we drew near Casilda on the train it had seemed to me that the fields were distinctly cleaner, as if the school had influence on the country round about. In some fields the maize stood six or seven feet high. Usually it had been very short. There was general disgust with the results of the 1917–1918 crop. No one seemed to think it worth anything. Certainly, during those war times, there was no price that tempted sale. We were told by a British commissioner that practically all the maize exported before the war went to Germany for distillation. Naturally the British Royal Commission had no interest in bagging maize for the Germans. The commission sold new bags for wheat at 75 centavos m/n each. A commercial commission in the Argentine got hold of all the old bags and mended them. Maize is almost exclusively bagged in old wheat bags. The Comisión de Aforo, the Argentine one referred to, estimated the value of used bags at 85 to 95 centavos, though they had brought but 10 or 12 centavos a few years back. If these prices do not accord very well they make it clear that at that time bags were so high that the maize buyers, who had to shell and bag the maize that they bought in the *trojes* where it is stored, put a high estimate of this cost into the price they were willing to pay for the maize when they offered the grower but two and a half to three pesos a quintal. At that time maize was being burned for fuel in small factories and to generate electric power for the street railway lines in Buenos Aires, for while maize was "down" all sorts of fuel were "up." Anthracite coal was unobtainable but quoted at 300 pesos a ton. Everyone who could get it was using *quebracho colorado*, and trains were loaded with it everywhere.

The ear of their maize is small although they call it a good quality. It seems much inferior in appearance to ours. But they think much of American varieties and use some sixty of them in the agricultural school. In France and Belgium

Argentine corn, however, is preferred to ours because "(1) the kernels are smaller, making it better adapted to poultry feeding; (2) it is sweeter and so is preferred as horse feed; and (3) it contains 3 to 4 per cent less moisture, so will ship and keep in good condition longer. Price seems to have nothing to do with the preference for the South American product, for at present Argentine corn sells for 8 to 10 cents a bushel more than American corn."[14]

Customary Usage in Wheat Cultivation

The customary usage in growing wheat and maize in Santa Fe is about as follows, according to a highly esteemed agronomist, Hugo Miatello, who wrote a book on the Santa Fe farm of 1905[15]: With wheat, rotation is common in four fields: of linseed one year and wheat three, shifting the linseed each year to a field that has been three years in wheat. New land is plowed first in February, a second time at sowing. At this time the ground is so hard that often three or four yoke of oxen must be used. Ordinarily one plowing only is given, followed by one or two harrowings across the furrows. Wheat is sowed in panels 60 to 80 meters wide and 800 to 1000 long. It is usually sown by hand and badly done. The seed is covered by a common toothed harrow driven at right angles to the furrows. Planting in lines is not usual because of the cost of machines.

Seed is not selected. The best grain is sold and the worst kept for seed. Instead of a reasonable 95 per cent of germinations they often get as low as 42. The seed is almost always full of weeds, with resultant weedy fields. The wheat is usually sown from the first to the fourth week of June, at latest mid-June to the end of July. It is harvested in blocks of 12 to 15 hectares (30 to 37 acres) through which roads are cut to meet at the middle, which is called the *corral*. Here they stack the *parvas* of wheat after leaving the shocks stacked on

[14] *U. S. Dept. of Agric. Year Book, 1921*, Washington, 1922, p. 207.
[15] La chacra santafecina en 1905, Buenos Aires, 1905, pp. 203–231.

end on the ground for eight or ten days, and here the threshing
is done. The grain is harvested in December; threshing toward the end of December lasts from forty to sixty days, to
the end of February. As recently as 1905 nine-tenths of the
threshing machines in Santa Fe Province were English, but
I believe the Americans have since made great gains.

MAIZE CULTIVATION PRACTICE

Maize is cultivated to some extent all over Santa Fe, but
especially in the south. In the Department Caseros 43 per
cent of the cultivated land is in maize, in San Lorenzo 66,
and in Rosario 82,[16] these three departments stretching across
the province in the latitude of Rosario. About half the maize
is cultivated by owners and half by renters.[17]

From June to August the ground is prepared by one plowing to a depth of four to six inches. Panels of corn in the
field are usually 40 to 80 meters wide and 500 to 800 meters
long. A great variety of plows is used. Then the ground is
gone over once or twice with the tooth harrow in three pieces,
rarely with a disk harrow. In the north the seeding is done by
hand, "tossing" they call it, and the yield is of no account.
In the south more use is made of the one-furrow seeding machine that plows a furrow, puts in seed, and covers by plowing
alongside. The Champion three-furrow seeder is also used.
It furrows across the earlier plowing. Local seed is poorly
selected if at all, but the agricultural schools are laying much
emphasis on selection. The customary width between furrows is 40 to 50 centimeters, but it ought in good land to be
70 or 80 to give the shallow roots more ground from which to
draw moisture in droughts. They use 20 to 25 kilograms of
seed to the acre, though 15 to 20 would be enough with better
chosen seed. The seeding is done from September to December, the earlier date being better even in spite of the danger
of drought. After being seeded the ground is harrowed across

16 These figures, from Miatello, *op. cit.*, p. 203, refer to 1904–1905.
17 From the writer's conversations with the colonists.

FIG. 51—Maize farm rented by an Italian at Roldán, 13 miles west of Rosario. A typical maize house-place. The most conspicuous thing is the little clump of trees, usually *paraísos*, with a windmill, a *troje*, or corn crib (to the left of the trees), and a *parva* of alfalfa (at the left margin).

Fig. 52—Closer view of the *trojes*. The one on the left is full of ears of corn. The other is just beginning to be filled. When the top of the first tier of cornstalks has been reached, another tier of stalks will be woven into wires that run around the posts. This is the customary type of corn crib of the maize renter in the Argentine.

at right angles to the furrows to level off the surface. When
the young plants are 8 to 10 centimeters high the ground is
harrowed as lightly as possible across the furrows to break
the crust and destroy weeds. This is common only in the
south. In the north no cultivation of any sort is given after
sowing. In October, with the plants 15 to 20 centimeters high,
they cultivate with a cultivator drawn by two horses, after
the ground has dried out, but not deeply if it has rained.

This account of actual field practice by one of the best-
esteemed local observers leaves no doubt that the agriculture
brought by the immigrant is not particularly intelligent. What
he has brought to the country is not so much knowledge of
farming as willingness to work on a farm.

Method of Storing Maize

All the way up from Rufino, in the southwestern corner of
the Province of Santa Fe, to Rosario, we saw maize being
harvested, but almost no wheat. We saw the maize everywhere being pulled by hand from the stalks where they stood,
put into sacks stuck up in the fields, and carted to the neighborhood of the houses, there to be placed in the *trojes*, or open-
air granaries, in which it is stored. They are bins about 20
feet across and as many high, made of cornstalks wattled into
wires stretched between five or six upright poles. Figure 52
shows two of them; the tall one full of ears of corn and the
other a tier of cornstalks high. It will be filled up to that height,
and then another tier of stalks will be woven on. When the
trojes get very high they are loaded with an "automatic" (Fig.
54) until full and heaped up in the middle with the reddish-
yellow ears. There is a great difference in the workmanship of
these *trojes*, reflecting the willingness of the renter to take
pains. Some are so flimsy it seems as if they would not hold
together, others are beautifully sound and solid. Occasionally
one sees a square one roofed with good corrugated iron. The
corn will keep four or five months in them. When the hot
weather comes it begins to get wormy if left in *trojes*. Out of

many hundred *trojes* we saw but one that was roofed over with thatch. They are usually left to the weather and damaged, just as the wheat is where it stands out at the railroad stations in piles of bags. Corrugated iron is the material that in old days would have been used to cover them, but the war made iron excessively dear. The corn was sold in the *troje*, the buyer offering what he chose, which at that time was very little. It was said there had been no crop of corn. There may have been no profit in it, but we saw immense quantities of it throughout the southern part of Santa Fe Province. The province's wheat is produced mainly farther north and west.

Failure of San Lorenzo to Develop As Entrepôt of Its Region

We went on May 14 to San Lorenzo, about 15 miles north of Rosario. As we moved out of the station of the Central Argentine Railway in Rosario we saw great stacks of wheat sacks, more wheat I suppose than I ever saw in my life, piled up not only under sheds with galvanized iron roofs but also out in the open air with only tarpaulins over them. There was much talk at that war time of lack of ships to take it abroad. All the wheat, we understood, was controlled by the British government. Certainly there was much dock front visible under our windows at the Savoy Hotel with almost no ships in sight.

The town of San Lorenzo gets no profit from the farmers because they take their wheat either to Rosario or to Puerto San Martín a mile or so farther up the river bank. There storehouses and elevators have been built. Perhaps this was what the friars would not do at San Lorenzo (see, above, p. 103), where they owned all the Paraná bank. At any rate they had not done it, and the new town was getting the business. An Englishman named John Kirk built the first elevator forty years ago when the colony was founded. Characteristically, before the war the Germans had come to be the largest owners in the elevators and landing places. There was only a single German in the locality now, a butcher. Italians were the most numerous. An Italian station master near by said they were "as common as pigweed." Didn't he think it unpatriotic to talk of his country like that? His country, he couldn't think much of his country. Did it feed him? "Well, do you till its soil?" "No, but my lot is cast over here."

English Ownership of Argentine Railways

In this corner of Santa Fe one travels by the "French Line," a railway from Rosario to Santa Fe and thence north. Most of the railways are English, like the Central Argentine, an extremely English line. English money was invested in railways in the United States, too, but imagine a company calling itself English there! Of course, these companies are different in that they are wholly English, organized in England by Englishmen with English money and using English locomotives and rolling stock till the superior adaptability of American locomotives to poorly laid tracks proved itself. No one who rides on the railway can fail to detect its English ownership for a moment. The English do not withhold any of their national ways for fear foreigners will not like them. Not at all. They have not come in as poor immigrants asking favors, but as capitalists, benefactors, and bearers of English civilization. English clerks and employees working for English companies have put on white flannels on their holidays and played cricket and football as if they were "at home." The Argentines used to scoff at the English in 1886, but in 1918 they are dressing up in flannels themselves and play cricket and football, too. Incidentally the English do a comfortable business selling them the equipment, and the Spanish-American vocabulary is enriched with such words as "footballer," "foul," "box," "referee," "match," and "atlhetic" (*sic*).

Maize Farms near Rosario

What is being produced in any Argentine region was plain enough from afar in this month of May, 1918. In southern

Córdoba one saw the wheat sacks piled up high beside the railroad, in southern Santa Fe the *trojes* of maize, and now along the Central Argentine Railway from Rosario for some fifteen miles west the rectangular stacks, or *parvas*, of brown alfalfa. If the alfalfa is well packed the brown color is limited to the outer four or five inches. Within, it remains fresh and green. Some of these *parvas* are over 100 feet long, and there are two or more to each *chacra* (farm) about here. The alfalfa is said to keep fifteen years in a good *parva*. In these districts any one of the three is bigger than a house, barns not being needed (as they believe) or used. Since the planting of trees is as yet very limited, the heaped-up harvest looms afar. For illustrations see the farm shown on Figure 51, in which a *parva* of alfalfa appears on the left, the house standing in a clump of *paraíso* trees. The windmill is an important item. Water at 60 feet is abundant enough, but it takes power to lift it. The foreground is a field of corn that has been crushed down by running a drag over it to get it ready for burning. This is rather customarily done with cornstalks after the ears have been pulled and horses and cattle turned in to eat what they will. With wheat and flax it is obligatory to burn the straw, which is said to breed an unendurable nuisance of flies if it is left to rot on the ground.

AN ITALIAN RENTER'S MAIZE FARM NEAR ROSARIO

This farm, which is at Roldán, 13 miles west of Rosario, is rented by an Italian from Ancona. The owner is a colonist in moderate circumstances who lives near by on 80 acres farmed by himself. The tenants have lived in this country thirteen years, brought a boy of five with them, and have several Argentine-born children. They rent 143 acres—the owner will not sell the land. Two-thirds of it is in maize, the rest in flax. The flaxseed sold for $2250 m/n (slightly less than $990 United States currency), paying the whole rent of $2220 m/n. The father, eighteen-year-old son, and the next girl all work in the field. The mother cooks and takes care of the horses. The

younger children go to school. Some drought in summer made
the corn crop short. They have already 400 quintals[18] in one
troje; and the other, which they have just started, will receive
700 to 800 quintals more, which will have to pay their living
expenses and profits. These statements were checked up by
those of a neighbor. The hut was pretty poor, and the ground
all around was dirty and littered. Perhaps they were acquiring property—I suspected they were saving money towards
it. Meanwhile they were living on a pretty low scale. The
real question is, of course, Was it higher than what they had
known in Italy? The chances are that it was. Certainly they
did have in this case the actual control—humanly speaking—
of 143 acres of land where they could do as they pleased, for
they paid a cash rental; and they had a very fair chance in
good seasons to make a large sum of money, which would be
all theirs to spend as they chose. They could never have
matched that in Italy. Often the Italians are accused of living
on *polenta*, just as at home. At any rate they do it with their
eyes fixed on a goal that is being attained by others and that
they too may very possibly attain—ownership of enough land
to give them food as long as they live and a surplus of no
mean proportions. This was something no amount of sacrifice
in Italy would have made possible.

The wife used to want to go back. The women suffer a good
deal from homesickness. They are alone more than the men,
but she is content here *now* because the war has seemed to
move Italy a long distance off. Her brother had been in the
Argentine for eleven years. He went back for his service, and
now he has been wounded. She is vexed at the war, which she
admits she does not understand. Who does? She has heard
nothing definite about it. They are very ignorant, all these
people. The difference between Italians and Argentines has
become clear to them, but they have also discovered more
different kinds of Italians than they ever met in Italy. The
difference between English and Americans and Germans is

18 Of 100 kilograms, or 220 pounds, each.

quite beyond them, and of different countries vaguest of vague concepts exist.

The wife said that neighboring land had been sold at $400 and $500 m/n a *cuadra* (4.17 acres). At that rate their 143 acres are worth $14,800 to $18,500 m/n. Their rent is 12 to 15 per cent of this, and we hear of 25 to 35 being asked; but that may have been before the war. If the corn brings $3.50 m/n a quintal the total return will be $5220 m/n, and they will get a total of 28 per cent on the assumed value. Unfortunately they cannot buy the land. Even if they can save the money they must keep looking about a long time before they find a chance to buy. All the houses in the maize country are poor. Practically all of them are houses of renters, either Spanish or Italian. Of course the renter spends no money and little labor on the house. His business is a gamble on the weather. If the weather is good, the all-important thing being rain enough at the right time and no deluges, and if the hail or locust does not destroy his crop, he will make a fortune in a year. When that good year comes he is "on easy street." Happy he, then, if he has sown much land. The amount of cultivation he has given it is less important. So renters spread themselves excessively, cultivate too much land, and do it badly.

A SPANISH RENTER'S FARM IN DÍAZ COLONY

One of these farms at Díaz colony, about fifty miles northwest of Rosario (founded in 1886, Fig. 28), is that of a Spanish renter. Figures 53–56 are views of the farm. Figure 53 shows two men pulling corn in the field. This renter came twelve years ago from Catalonia, the district about Barcelona, with his women folk, who are lonesome. You will see from the place that housework is not extensive, and there are neither hens, pigs, nor cows. Unless the wife works in the fields she is bound to find the time very heavy. The farm, rented on the percentage plan from a widow who lives near, is of 50 *cuadras* (209 acres), mostly in maize. He had planted

Fig. 53 (above).—A Spanish maize renter's farm at Colonia Díaz, 50 miles northwest of Rosario, from a distance. Note the two men pulling corn in the field.

Fig. 54 (below).—Nearer view, showing the house, the *trojes*, and the "automatic" loading machine for the *troje*. The two views give a very typical impression of the Pampa here in 1918.

FIG. 55 (above)—Somewhat closer view of the house and maize-filled *troje*.

FIG. 56 (below)—The house of the Spanish maize renter at Colonia Díaz, with wife and child. The house is built of sundried brick. Within there are a dirt floor and the scantiest of furniture. Typical of the poverty of the maize renters.

what flax he had seed for. His little flax had paid so well that he wished he had planted more. The government offered to supply seed but on terms that he was afraid of. The price of flaxseed varies greatly, and it is hard to tell when the crop will pay. In Figure 55 the two *trojes* show somewhat in detail, with the loading apparatus, called *automática* apparently because the box on wires can be pulled up from below and unloaded into the *troje*.

Of the dwelling on the left a nearer view is given in Figure 56. The material is sundried brick, the roof very like corrugated iron. The shoes and stockings of the woman and child indicate winter cold. Within, the house has a floor of bare earth and most meager equipment of chair, table, and bed. The bit of vine is unusual. So is the lack of trees. The usual thing is enough trees to make a distinct clump, which as often as not conceals the house. In summer the heat at this place must be terrific. The men were just pulling the ears of corn from the stalks in the fields to bring it in carts to the *trojes*. These people may have money in the bank. Their scale of life is pretty low.

THE EVILS OF THE RENTING SYSTEM PERPETUATED BY THE COLONISTS THEMSELVES

The colonists rarely had any sort of motor car in 1918—a Ford, if any; the renters never. For one thing they are not spenders, for another the cost was about $1700, *moneda nacional* of course, but the national dollar of 44 gold centavos is bigger to the Argentine than our dollar is to us. The use of cars is limited to the well-to-do, and the total number in the Republic must be small. Gasoline was costing $1.80 m/n a gallon. On the other hand the fee for a license is but $1.

The renter is often an immigrant of many years standing. He is dependent on the owner of the land. Even in cases which we found where the same land had been occupied by the renter for forty years, the rent has of course not remained stable. In view of the enormous increase in the value of the land stability is inconceivable. Change of ownership by sale or death may terminate an agreement at any moment and deprive a family of its accustomed base. Whether the renting is for cash or a proportion of crop, the terms are customarily made for only a year or two at the most, the alfalfa contract usually for five years.

It appears to be clear beyond doubt that renting as against purchase has been demanded by the immigrants. Paradoxical as it may sound, the immigrants' need and demand for small lots of land to buy is hindered by the immigrants' demand for land to rent. Of course there are immigrants and immigrants. But it is the competition of would-be renters for land on which to grow maize that has driven the rents in some cases up to 35 per cent of the sale value.

There can be no doubt of the present necessity of influencing the large landowner to part with some of his land to foster the increase of the too small present class of farmer owners, but he cannot be accused of having caused the present condition.

CHAPTER VI

COLONIES OF ENTRE RÍOS PROVINCE

The Argentine Mesopotamia and Its Cattle Industry

Eastward across the Paraná from Santa Fe lies the Argentine Mesopotamia—Corrientes and Entre Ríos Provinces (Fig. 21), with a quarter more territory between them than Santa Fe and a seventh fewer people;[1] not pampa this, for the soil is no longer the fine, wind-borne loess but deposits from the Paraná River. Lagoons and swamps are frequent, and the rain here is well over 40 inches a year;[2] but the same bright sky arches overhead as on the Pampa, and it is a pleasant land—greener far, of course; even in winter its greenness is pronounced. The northern province, Corrientes, has a strong admixture of the blood of the Guaraní Indians and is the most Indian of the Argentine provinces.

Both Corrientes and Entre Ríos are chiefly occupied in cattle raising, here still of the old-Creole type, for in this northern region the malaria-causing tick (see, below, p. 170) destroys the improved breeds of cattle which in the south and west are replacing the tough and scrubby Creole stock and making the exportation of chilled and frozen beef possible. In 1914 Corrientes had over 10 head of cattle for each inhabitant, and Entre Ríos had 5.5, Buenos Aires following with

[1]Comparison Between Santa Fe Province and
the Argentine Mesopotamia

Province	Area*	Population, 1914†
Corrientes	88,901 square kilometers	347,055
Entre Ríos	78,330 " "	425,373
Both together	167,231 square kilometers	772,428
Santa Fe	134,827 " "	899,640

*Tercer censo nacional, 1914, Vol. 1: Antecedentes y comentarios, Buenos Aires, 1916, p. 58.

†ibid., Vol. 2: Población, Buenos Aires, 1916, pp. 53, 48, and 45.

[2] W. G. Davis: Climate of the Argentine Republic, Dept. of Agric., Buenos Aires, 1910, Pl. 17 (map of mean annual rainfall).

4.4, and Santa Fe and Córdoba with 3.5 and 3.3[3] These are much larger figures than are known in other countries, and formerly they were larger still.   Men are few and cattle many; winter shelter is not needed, wild pasture abounds, and the cattle run nearly as uncontrolled as the buffaloes in their day on the plains of North America.   When the only use of Argentine cattle was to hunt them and slaughter them for their hides, reducing 48,000,000 (?) in 1780 to 6,000,000 in 1800,[4] any sort of curing of carcasses was a clear gain, and under Creole conditions the best that could be done was the extraction of grease, with an incidental preparation of *tasajo* (preserved meat) and extract of meat from selected animals.   The prejudice that forbids any self-respecting Argentine horseman to ride a mare sends 30,000 of these to the *graserías* every year. Tallow and fat were the chief products, though the establishments are called *saladeros* from the fact that *tasajo* is produced there by a process of salting and drying.   The relatively small number of animals whose flesh is up to even the low standard required for *carne tasajo* makes all the meat products minor parts of the output of these establishments.   This, I understand, is likewise true at the famous Liebig factory of Fray Bentos across the river in Uruguay.   For the Argentine *saladeros* the classification of products for the year 1909 deserves a glance.   More than half was grease; nearly a quarter extract of meat and meat flour for fertilizer.   The rest was margarine, preserved meat and tongues, condensed soup and gelatine.[5]

The *tasajo* is great slabs of beef, freed from the bones, piled fifteen feet high on a bed of horns, with salt strewn between

[3] RATIO OF CATTLE TO PEOPLE

Province	Number of Cattle, 1914*	Population, 1914†
Corrientes	3,543,395	347,005
Entre Ríos	2,334,372	425,373
Buenos Aires	9,090,536	2,066,165
Santa Fe	3,179,260	899,640
Córdoba	2,540,313	735,472

*Tercer censo nacional, 1914, Vol. 6: Censo ganadero, Buenos Aires, 1917, p. 3.
† *ibid.*, Vol. 2: Población, Buenos Aires, 1916, pp. 53, 48, 37, 45, and 59.

[4] F. T. Molinas: La colonización argentina y las industrias agropecuarias, Buenos Aires, [1910], pp. 21–22.

(*Footnote 5 on next page*)

the layers, and aired and repiled daily for over a month until it becomes thoroughly dry and also hard and black. Brazil and Cuba long used it to feed their slaves, and there is still a certain market in those countries, though it is likely to disappear with progress and prosperity. Its exportation from the Argentine Republic is rapidly falling off. For the six successive groups of five years beginning 1870 the quantities exported in thousands of tons were 169, 168, 116, 162, 212, and 179, with values in millions of Argentine gold pesos of 7, 12, 15, 20, 14, and 10.[6] In 1915 only 213 tons—not thousands of tons—were exported.[7] The season of the *saladeros* covers parts of two years. For the seven seasons concluding with 1914–1915 the thousands of animals slaughtered to make *tasajo* were 155, 157, 139, 130, 24, 3, and none.[8] Somewhat similarly in Uruguay for the same period and the same units the numbers were 545, 578, 449, 436, 254, 110, and 61, and in Brazil—on the border of the Uruguay River only—661, 703, 707, 902, 710, 518, and 454.[9] During the World War great quantities of frozen beef were supplied to the armies of the Allies, and it is possible that a good many animals were served as frozen beef that in other days would have been made into *tasajo*. That cannot be more than a contributory factor, however, because in the three regions together in 1911–1912 there were slaughtered for *tasajo* 1,467,400 animals and in 1912–1913,

[5] PRODUCTION OF THE ARGENTINE SALADEROS IN 1909*

Products	Amount in kilograms	Value in Argentine gold pesos
Gelatine	3,150	1,260
Concentrated soup	629,117	188,735
Preserved tongues	1,201,486	360,444
Preserved meat	6,390,124	639,013
Oleomargarine	4,882,949	732,442
Meat flour (fertilizer)	2,644,187	1,057,675
Extract of meat	1,351,494	2,702,988
Tallow and melted grease	54,325,123	7,573,230
	71,427,630	13,255,787

*Molinas, *op. cit.*, p. 196.

[6] *ibid.*, p. 192.

[7] *Estadística Agrícola, 1915–16*, Direcc. Gen. de Econ. Rural y Estadist., Minist. de Agric., Buenos Aires, 1917, p. 171.

[8] *ibid.*, p. 162. [9] *loc. cit.*

987,300[10]—a falling off of 480,100 animals before the war began. The *saladeros* continue a considerable elaboration of tallow and grease and meat extracts. The ten times more important business of packing chilled beef and mutton is limited to more southern regions in Santa Fe and Buenos Aires, where improved cattle can be raised without danger of the tick.

ENTRE RÍOS PROVINCE

Entre Ríos has made through its colonies important beginnings in agriculture, having had 385,000 hectares in wheat, maize, and flax in 1895, which had become 624,000 in 1916,[11] roughly 8 per cent of its area, while Santa Fe had 20 per cent. The largest towns in Entre Ríos are: Paraná, 36,089, and Concordia, 20,107. Santa Fe has Rosario, 222,592, and Santa Fe, 59,574.[12]

There are two main crossings on the Paraná, the principal commerce, now as always, running north and south: a thrice daily steamer from Santa Fe city to Paraná (Figs. 21 and 57), the smallness of the vessel indicating the insignificance of the traffic, and the great train ferry from Ibicuy in Entre Ríos to Zárate in Buenos Aires (Fig. 21), over which pass through trains between the Argentine capital and Asunción, Paraguay.

VISIT TO THE SO-CALLED RUSSIAN COLONIES

We made a little trip into Entre Ríos in June, 1918, to see something of the so-called Russian colonies. General information in Santa Fe, from the most reliable sources of information, was that the colonists were dirty, lazy people, living in wretchedness and neglecting their fields. We left Santa Fe at seven in the morning and as we traversed the straight canal of the new port to the Paraná, we heard from a passenger a new report on the Russian colonies, that they were very prosperous and that their land was kept in good order. He spoke especially of those near Diamante on the Paraná, 30 miles below Paraná

[10] *Estadística Agrícola, 1915-16*, p. 162.
[11] *Estadística Agrícola, 1916-17*, pp. 17 and 18.
[12] Tercer censo nacional, 1914, Vol. 4: Población, Buenos Aires, 1916, p. 469.

city, said he knew them personally, and we determined to
visit them. On the Santa Fe side the land is everywhere low
along this passage, but nearer Paraná it rises so abruptly that
the city stands 60 meters above the river. Idle lime kilns are
noticed halfway up this lofty bluff. It appears that there are

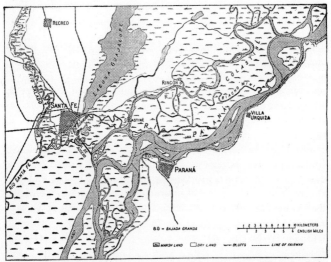

FIG. 57—Map of the channels between the cities of Santa Fe and Paraná. Scale,
1: 600,000. (Based mainly on Plano de Navegación del Río Paraná entre Esquina
y la desembocadura, 1: 100,000, Direcc. Gen. de Obras Hidraulicas, Minist. de
Obras Públicas, Buenos Aires, 1913.)
Very likely when Santa Fe was founded the Paraná River was flowing through
the westernmost of the channels here depicted. In this part of the river there is
no good site for a city on the western bank. Santa Fe is as near as it could be
placed and is liable to floods at that.

beds of fossil shells that were burned for lime with great advantage until the railway made available in 1872 the much
better lime from the mountains of Córdoba. The point marked
B. G. just west of the city on Figure 57 is Bajada Grande,
where a terrace above the river makes the loading so much
easier than at the high bluffs at Paraná and at Diamante that
the railway has now been extended over there. Over across

on the Santa Fe side Colastine has served as a point of embarkation for Santa Fe products up to the opening of the new port and channel at Santa Fe city.

At the hotel I found I could get out to the Russian colonies by motor car. It was a bad day for photographs, always cloudy and finally drizzling. The roads in the country were very fair for the Argentine, not smooth, but allowing a high rate of speed. As Paraná stands high above the river, dissection by rains has given the surrounding country an undulating surface. Quite contrary to our expectation we found it wonderfully tilled. There are substantial, at times attractive houses in sight in clumps of trees. Across valleys there are views of slopes beyond of beautiful green fields of alfalfa or no less beautiful fields—immense fields—of brownish-black plowed land. We noticed only one field of maize, and that weedy like those of Santa Fe. Except for the scarcity of trees, which were by no means absent, the scene might have been one in the United States. It is distinctly the pleasantest agricultural scene I have observed in the Argentine Republic. The rolling country is repellant to the people here—on the Pampa side—but agreeable to me, as it enables the eye to wander farther across the countryside. How singular the differences of tastes! When I first crossed the Andes in 1886 I had as companion a prosperous elderly gentleman of Buenos Aires, Don Pablo E. Díaz, who was a good traveler in all such matters as facing the discomforts of the mule trip but suffered greatly during the five days between Mendoza and Los Andes by being "shut up," as he expressed it, in the deep valleys that had to be followed. He was as homesick for the sight of the open plains as any Savoyard for his mountains. I had no sensation of the sort, only weariness of the dreary monotony of arid, plantless slopes.

The Russo-German Colony El Salto

The first of the Russian colonies, El Salto, lies almost halfway between Paraná and Diamante, fifteen miles from each.

It is a little village with almost no outlying houses. Near Rosario in Santa Fe Province we had become used to the house-clump of trees on each *chacra*, up to a score of trees around house, *troje*, *parva*, windmill, and well. You may count the clumps in sight at once and estimate from the number the characteristic size of holdings for the neighborhood. Here it is different. The village is central for residence, and the fields lie outside, as in many parts of Europe. El Salto is but one of six of these villages between Paraná and Diamante. I remember only the names El Salto, Los Prostestantes, and Pueblo Nuevo. The people are not really Russians at all, though they came from Russia. They were Germans in Russia in 1878, as they told me, and, objecting to military service, from which their ancestors had been promised exemption by Catherine II when she invited them to Russia, they had sent men to various parts of the New World to find a suitable home to which to move.[13] These men had liked the climate and prospects here in Entre Ríos. The province offered each colonist 104 acres of land for $120. They were also to have a yoke of oxen, plow, and other needed implements and food for two years, with ten years to repay it in. Their fare out they were to pay themselves. One hundred and fifty families of them came, and their families are large. They came from a German colony in the Russian government Saratov on the Volga. Among themselves all except the youngest speak their native German dialect still. Most of them acquired title to their land in the ten-year term and stayed on it. Some wandered off. Some made money and went to town to live. Many, many children have been born here, and these all speak Spanish. Almost everyone does except the women and a few old men. One young girl of eighteen, born here, professed not to understand Spanish at all, though the men said she was pretending, in

---

[13] Details on the Russo-German colonists of Entre Ríos Province and especially on their preference for living in central villages rather than on scattered farmhouses may be found in Karl Kaerger: Landwirtschaft und Kolonisation im Spanischen Amerika, Vol. 1: Die La Plata Staaten, Leipzig, 1901, pp. 422–423 and 495–500. Dr. Kaerger was at that time agricultural expert of the German Embassy in Buenos Aires.—EDIT. NOTE.

which case she was a good pretender. She didn't want to be photographed, as she had old clothes on; she had been washing! The women went barefoot, and the men treated them roughly. The men wore good enough clothes. The yards were well swept and the houses tidy, most of them of rough bricks not coated with stucco, as seen in the picture of the house in Figure 59. The ten or twelve houses that were coated over with stucco in the Creole fashion were gorgeously painted, the walls white and the window and door frames and shutters bright red, bright blue, or yellow and blue. You may imagine the trimmings of Figure 60 red! I never saw bright paints like these used in the Argentine, where the usual house colors are lime washes which quickly fade to the most delicate tints imaginable, however bright they may be when applied. These vivid colors are probably due to Russian influence. I am under the impression that they are oil colors, for they were all hard and bright.

There were many evidences of the low esteem in which the women were held. The nearest town being fifteen miles away and the nearest railway station eight, the colonists rarely meet anyone but Russian Germans like themselves. The men doubtless have errands that take them to town by horse or wagon, so that they have a certain amount of intercourse with the Creoles, a certain contact with Creole manners and institutions. The women do not find it possible to see much of the outside world, especially as they have large families.

All the German Russians at El Salto were Catholics. They were glad to see us, and all came crowding out in spite of the drizzle to hear what we had to say and talk to us. One man with the same name as his father and grandfather, and therefore called Tercero, came up and addressed me at once. His portrait is Figure 58. He was born here in 1880. He thought he looked very rough, called himself *muy bravo*, but had a most friendly eye. He looked older than his record to me. He said he had read about his fathers' country and they were very sad about what was happening there—I understood him

FIG. 58 (above)—A Russo-German colonist, born in Entre Ríos Province of German parents from a colony in Russia. Greatly changed from his peasant forbears.

FIG. 59 (below)—The Russo-German colonist's house, of well-burned brick, the roof of corrugated iron. When the photograph was being taken he put his wife and daughter where he wanted them and told them to stay there. They did.

FIG. 60 (above)—Brightly colored house showing Russian influence, at El Salto, a colony of Germans from Russia.   White, with blue or red shutters.

FIG. 61 (below)—Russo-German family at El Salto.   Their dress passes for Russian in the Argentine.

to mean Russia. I told him we were, too. He hoped for better things. "Our fathers were very ignorant, and we want our children to know more. We pay two school teachers and keep up two schools, one in the morning and one in the afternoon, as there are too many children for all to go at once." Probably the schooling was better than usual because they lived in a village. The Italians in the open country have no such chance. That is the great problem of Argentine education—how to get at the children of the widely scattered country population. This man corraled women and children for us and peremptorily ordered them to pose (Fig. 61). Finally he took me to his house (Fig. 59) at the end of the village. It was small but good, and wife and daughter were at work; the daughter, a girl of 17, shy before strangers but instantly obedient to her father's command to place herself so and so. I was ashamed for him and tried to interest her in the picture. She spoke Spanish and so did the wife. They seemed intelligent but extraordinarily submissive. Among the Italians we had always found the women practically in charge. Even the rather rough-looking Casilda colonist (Fig. 46) heeded what his spouse said instantly, and so did every Italian we talked with. None of their Italian women appeared shrewish, but they were certainly important members of their families.

My host had a large family—everybody did—but though the village was very German, or very foreign if you prefer, the children were all chattering in Spanish, and another generation will know little or nothing of German. It is not to be forgotten that these people in the colony are a residuum. Those who have gone, either because they have made money and gone to live in town or left because they thought they could make more elsewhere, are probably better assimilated to the country than these. The conservative, the old, the incompetent are sure to be preserved here in a backwater that will itself disappear with the improvement of means of transportation. The effectives, the people who can react to the country, are reacting. The foreigner is being absorbed, and a new nation is being born. The differences between what happens here and what has happened to immigrants to the United States are the environment—and that is immensely different—; the stock of the settlers, which differs fully as much; and the scarcity withal of foreigners who get land.

War time though it was, we Americans here among Germans speaking German were welcome and well received. As we were leaving the colonist's house he wanted to give me something. He had 132 acres in wheat, flax, and maize—a very little maize, consumed mostly on the place. He had a vegetable garden and pigs and hens. "Let me give you a chicken. You can eat it for your breakfast. I don't like a man like you to visit me and go away empty handed." I told him that his story and the pictures, if they came out well, would be recompense enough for coming.

El Salto had great numbers of dogs—huge, mastiff-like creatures—and they all seemed very savage and hungry. The Ford seemed to anger them. When we got out they paid little attention to us. A few weeks earlier my companion had been bitten by such a dog and had a much regretted rent torn in a needed pair of trousers. Our friend said the dogs only acted that way to strangers. "*He* was never troubled!"

We had been told of the towns of southern Chile, how German they were.[14] None of them are nearly as German as this village. In all of them most people speak Spanish and are Creoles, with no little touch of Indian blood. Here was nothing of the sort. It was all German stock, but with no Prussianism. Probably the agents of the modern empire had not thought these backwaters worth propagandizing. There had been no immigration since the original company. The information this man gave me he imparted in tolerable Spanish. We saw no Creoles at all. The chances are that the school-teachers were Creole and were feeling much isolated.

I noticed a good deal of plowing going on and many agricultural machines. The colonists are not averse to modern

[14] See the writer's "Recent Colonization in Chile," *Amer. Geogr. Soc. Research Series No. 6*, 1921, p. 8 ff.

methods. We had seen great piles of sacks of wheat awaiting shipment at Bajada Grande, as we came by. Now we saw many *parvas* of alfalfa.

I am inclined to think the village form of settlement, with the farms spread around, is full of suggestion for the Argentines. In the cattle days such settlements were uncalled for. In the agricultural stage they are entirely suitable. For the men they involve going considerable distances to and from work, but the men have horses and would go just as far to play *boliche*, or bowl, anyway. The women, on the other hand, have the society of other women; and, even if these are only of their own dialect-speakers, even if they remain isolated from the Creole culture of the country, they have society and find life much more tolerable; and that is as much as can well be expected for the immigrants. The Creole women who could influence them have no interest in them; rather, in the cities where they are numerous, these ladies resent their coming. "Are they *my* immigrants?" said a charming Creole indignantly. For the education of the children the village is much more promising, and this is of foremost importance.

It is not likely that the Russo-German we visited and his fellows call themselves Argentines. Certainly their women folk do not, yet the young people have no other language than Spanish. Hundreds from the colony have already scattered into other parts of the Republic where they have more contact with the Creoles, and another generation will see great changes. They have certainly here in El Salto come a long way from any Russian or German social condition. Their bearing, their knowledge of different nationalities, their conception of a country and of life itself have been utterly transformed, and along the same lines that the immigrant foreigner is transformed by life in the United States.

RETURN TO PARANÁ

The hotel in Paraná is not clean. Creole hotels never are. Their conception of sanitary arrangements, outside the great cities, is a nightmare, but good meals are served and the oranges are most delicious. When we asked for *bifes á caballo*, which are beefsteaks with fried eggs on them, there was some question of getting fresh eggs, and mention was made of eggs preserved in lime, the first time the point had come up. One gets fresh eggs everywhere in the Argentine and does not need to call them anything but eggs. It is no advantage to the consumer to have too many kinds of eggs. But it was getting pretty cold, and eggs were really scarce—in Paraná at this time 67 cents in American money a dozen. The very next day in a store in Santa Fe we saw fresh eggs (*huevos del día*) advertised, a phrase I never saw before. There are no plants for storing eggs as yet.

The boy who drove us out to El Salto was the son of a Spaniard, born in Buenos Aires and now five years up here and liking it very well. He drove rather fast, like all Argentine chauffeurs, but handled his car well. When he had trouble starting it he jacked up the rear axle and spun the rear wheel till the engine caught, all so expertly and quickly that it caused no delay.

The Jewish Colonies near Basavilbaso

The Russian colonies that had been named to us as especially degraded were at Basavilbaso over toward the Uruguay (Fig. 21). There we should find the farms ill-kept and the people indescribably dirty. A traveler on the train said the people preserved their national costume and were far more interesting than the Russian Germans of El Salto. We also heard that they had abandoned agriculture for cattle raising. But how, then, could they have ill-kept fields? It was beginning to be clear that somebody did not like them. Another version was that they had all gone to the cities to engage in trade!

Our visit made it clear that the objectionable persons are the Russian Jews of Baron Hirsch's charitable Jewish Colonization Association.[15]   They are not very numerous, less than ten thousand in all, and their essential offense is being Jews! Not Russians, but Jews from Russia—the men for whom Baron Hirsch provided $10,000,000 to rescue them from the wretched state of persecution in which they lived in that land, to put them on land of their own as agriculturists.   This is a different motive from those we have hitherto met in Argentine colonization, all directed to increasing the value of Argentine land to the nation, the province, or the landowner.   If an outsider, a non-Argentine, attempted colonizing, like the Swiss firm Beck and Herzog, who put so much forethought and care for their colonists into their effort, in the hope doubtless of making their own fortune, at least it was the already recognized motive of increasing the value of Argentine land to the Argentines that they tried to make use of; but here is a scheme to improve the lot of a nation of men without a country, a nation of men who have tilled the soil of trade and usury so exclusively that they have everywhere attained a hateful prominence in the art of exacting tribute from those who grow crops and make commodities.   Baron Hirsch wanted to make farmers of these men whom Russia hated and persecuted.

Direct observation in and near Basavilbaso[16] shows that the Jews are personally just as clean as the Creoles about them, while their houses are cleaner.   No doubt numbers of them have been true to Jewish instinct and left their farms for trade in cities and there have aroused intense hostility and gained much business by selling for much smaller profit than other tradesmen.   Creoles liked the prices and bought of them, but Creole merchants raged at them for upsetting the established scale of profits.

In its original contract with the settlers the Jewish Colonization Association required them to extend the period of payments for the land through twenty years and proposed not to

[15] In Kaerger, *op. cit.*, there is also some discussion, on pp. 423–429, of the Jewish colonies in Entre Ríos.   The present account, however, is based mainly on personal observation.

[16] Field work of Dr. Alfred Coester.

allow them to hasten the acquisition of title by more rapid or larger payments. The idea was to keep the Jew a farmer and discourage his selling out to take up other occupations. But Argentine law would not allow them to put off a colonist who offered cash for immediate title. There was in their deeds a stipulation that they could sell only to the Association itself. They have, however, often rented their land when they wanted to go away. Few of them gained possession in less than ten years, for the Jews did not make very good farmers. Their fields are weedy in the extreme, they plow too shallow, cultivate too little, limit themselves to wheat and flax, and pay no attention to selecting their seed. Because of the limitation of crops they have six idle months on their hands. This they spend not in drunkenness, like so many colonists of other nationalities, but in disputation and their "vice" of trade. A weedy field is called dirty, *sucio*; and so weedy crops have given the Jews a reputation of personal uncleanliness that the Creoles have no right to entertain of them. They keep their "national" costumes and do not assimilate, it is true. If you find a talented and charming young man of Jewish origin prominent in an Argentine ministry his name is not quite plainly Jewish, he has nothing to do with trade, and his religion is Catholic.

It is unfair to Baron Hirsch's great undertaking to stop with the declaration that Jews are not good farmers and that many Jews have left their farms to engage in petty trade in the city, for a great many Jews have actually been made into farmers of a sort who are doing well on farms of their own and mean to stay there. At the same time the 34 colonies of the Jewish Colonization Association together with the other 161 in Entre Ríos have given enormous value to the lands of that province, supplying it with money to spend and with opportunity for careers beyond any dream of the good old Creole days. Poor farming has been general in all the colonies, indeed is prevalent today in the best lands of Santa Fe. This is widely recognized by the Argentines, and much effort is being made by national and provincial governments to improve it through the work of the agricultural schools. Furthermore, in every race that has colonized there is a considerable percentage of failures, persons who will not persist long enough to succeed. Mr. Perkins, who handled the colonizing for the Central Argentine Railway, west of Rosario, estimated[17] the colonists he had encountered as 16 per cent admirable and 41 per cent good; and these were colonists he had selected as likely to make good farmers for the colonies of his railroad company, not as oppressed individuals needing assistance.

The land colonized by the Jewish Colonization Association was along the line of the railroad from Gualeguaychú to Concordia (Fig. 21), between the stations Gilbert and San Salvador and somewhat beyond, with a scattering of patches elsewhere. The earliest colonies were settled in groups of houses with land to be worked at varying distances. This was the case with colony Number One, about two miles north of Basavilbaso, where the photographs (Figs. 62–65) were taken. Each colonist was allotted 150 hectares for tillage and near his house seven hectares of *quinta* for garden and corral of animals. That was land enough to separate the houses considerably, as they were strung along a street 200 feet wide. There were twenty houses in Number One.

As this method of settlement in villages or groups gave some of the colonists land too far from their houses, an administrator named Feinberg soon altered that plan for one of lines or roads, each colonist still receiving 150 hectares of land, but the houses in fours at the crossroads. As the colonists were the poorest sort of people, they had been supplied with house, some animals, food, and seed, as well as transportation from Europe. The Association was able to win an agreement from the Russian government to exempt the colonists from all claims for military or other service. A few colonists, however, have come on their own account.

[17] W. Perkins: The Colonies of Santa Fe: Their Origin, Progress and Present Condition, With General Observations on Emigration to the Argentine Republic, Rosario de Santa Fe, 1864 (published in English and Spanish).

The Argentine government is taking much interest in the schools in these colonies. There had been some excesses of non-Argentine sentiment in some German Russian colonies in the province, debarring the "national language," as Spanish is officially called in the Republic, and making too much display of the Kaiser's portrait. This was stopped and the situation watched. All the teachers at Basavilbaso are Creoles, who are incidentally bitterly discontented with their social life. One judges they are maintaining no social settlement that sheds the light of Creole culture on the benighted foreigner. There is no doubt of the importance of these schools and the work they are doing. A Santa Fe newspaper man of Governor Oroño's day used to say that three sorts of education were needed in the Republic: one for the Argentines who lead a civilized life, another for the barbarians of the desert who need to be civilized, and still a third for the barbarians imported from Europe as immigrants.

The persons shown in Figure 63 are the wives of two brothers, Jewish farmers of Basavilbaso. One of them has spent all but six months of his twenty-five years in the colony and speaks only Spanish; he learned it in the schools. His father being dead, he is the head of the family. He is applying for more land. In the original allotment his land was right in the village, Colony Number One, just across the main street from the residence, so his father was given only 125 hectares, which Leon thought was too little for him and his brother with their families. They were content with the country and expected to stay on the property. He expected to get the 25 hectares from the allotment of someone who could not use what was assigned him. He told us about the seven hectares for a *quinta*, and we went out to look for his vegetables but found nothing but weeds. He had no outbuildings but spoke of his intention of building a *galpón de zinc* to house a fine new Deering reaper which was standing exposed to the weather. When asked if the reaper would not be injured by the weather, he thought not because he had taken all the wooden parts into the house!

Fig. 62 (above)—Farm house of two Jewish brothers at Basavilbaso, Entre Ríos Province.

Fig. 63 (below)—Interior of the house and the wives of the brothers. These people are supposed in the Argentine to live in filth and misery. The facts and the photographs do not bear out the belief.

FIG. 64 (above)—Springless Russian cart in the Russo-Jewish colony at Basavilbaso.

FIG. 65 (below)—Another Jewish farmer of Basavilbaso. His beard was highly objectionable to his Argentine neighbors, who condemned him on account of it.

Both he and the young women insisted on our coming into the house. It was the most civilized farmer's house seen in the Argentine. The dining room had relatively good chairs, table, and sideboard. On the walls were pictures, one a large crayon of the deceased father, and in addition there was a galaxy of small photographs, thirty or forty in the well-known wire arrangement for holding such photos. There was a sort of neat bagging, probably empty grain sacks, spread on the floor around the table where one would be likely to track in mud. A lace curtain portière separated this room from another. You may see in New England many more slovenly kept houses. Yet this colony had been characterized as *la mas sucia de todas*, the dirtiest of all.

Another Jewish farmer, whose portrait (Fig. 65) displays a beard that caused some adverse comment from Creoles, was a man of about fifty-five; he had been out of Russia twenty-three years and was actively farming. Some years he said he had had bad harvests, but this year he had been able to pay off $2500 from his wheat crop. In Russia he had been a farmer on one hectare. He was conscious of his improved circumstances here, but his wife thought some things in Russia were much nicer. That feeling is almost universal among the women of the colonies—until they have made a trip back there!

Two highly-thought-of business men in Paraná agreed that land in Entre Ríos was passing out of the hands of Creoles and into those of Russo-Germans and Russo-Jews. They plainly meant on a considerable scale, and it is the only province where such a thing is said.

CHAPTER VII

THE RAILROADS AND THE TRANSFORMATION OF AGRICULTURE

The Development of the Railroad Net

The spreading of farm colonies across the seventy-five-mile width of the Province of Santa Fe went hand in hand with the westward extension of the railways, which were essential to get the grain produced by the colonies to market. It is now called impracticable to haul wheat more than fifteen miles, though in colony days all sorts of impossible things were actually accomplished. We have seen that the first colonies were near the Paraná River, whose deep waters afforded a way out to Buenos Aires and to Europe. Successful agriculture farther back from the river demanded railways.

Agriculture had actually spread across the province by 1890. Córdoba, the next province to the west, had attempted as early as 1871 to encourage immigration and agriculture by the usual method of remitting taxes for a number of years. It was characteristic of the old times that treasuries were always empty, but it was no hardship to remit taxes on a community that did not yet exist and therefore had never paid any. However, very little came of it till the railway pushed into Cordobese territory from Santa Fe.[1]

[1] The number of colonies founded in Córdoba in the nineteenth century, according to Antonio Franceschini (L'Emigrazione italiana nell' America del Sud: Studi sulla espansione coloniale transatlantica, Rome, 1908, pp. 402–403), was:

1870–82	5	1888	11	1892	37	1896	7
1885	2	1889	6	1893	17	1897	6
1886	6	1890	10	1894	17	1898	3
1887	12	1891	7	1895	11	1900	4

This is somewhat less than indicated in another enumeration, also cited by Franceschini, p. 402 (O. Francisci: La colonizzazione nella provincia di Cordoba, Boll. Minist. degli Affari Esteri, July, 1900, Rome, pp. 4, 6, 7, 10), according to which the total number of colonies was: 5 in 1882; 31 in 1887; 69 in 1890; 146 in 1895; 157 in 1896; 164 in 1897; 176 in 1898.

From an extent of 319 miles in 1867 the Argentine railways grew to 7514 miles in 1892.[2]   Five distinct lines crossed Santa Fe to enter Córdoba and Santiago del Estero, which adjoin it on the west.   In the eastern two-thirds of central Santa Fe the network of rails was so close (see Pl. IB) that there was no point more than ten miles from the tracks.   From Rosario lines diverged in seven directions.   All this construction was due to the stimulus of the colonies, which supplied the roads with freight of grain.   In the ten years preceding the crisis year 1891 (Fig. 18) the railways added on an average 700 miles of track a year.   Their total freight in 1892 was about six million tons.[3]

The extension of these lines was an essential part of the process of opening up the Pampa to agriculture, and neither would have been possible without the other.[4]   The old-Creole régime had really no place for agriculture, colonies, or railways.   When you talked to the old-time Creole of colonists he thought of more peons, men who did his work readily and subserviently, men content with an utterly subordinate place in the community and with material surroundings that were little more than the bare necessities of existence.   They might have a few poor horses and cows and graze them on his land. They might even have the use of his land to farm.   He had always let his peons use what land they wanted.   Of course if the newcomers were to farm they must have land.   But he thought of it as *his* land that they were to use!   He did not imagine any considerable areas actually *owned* by these foreigners, taken out of his grazing land, and the owners left free to manage things as they pleased without consulting him.

However, the colonization of Santa Fe in the fifties and sixties of the last century did make a beginning of this very

---

[2] Tercer censo nacional, 1914, Vol. 10: Valores mobilarios y estadísticas diversas, Buenos Aires, 1917, p. 405.

[3] *ibid.*, p. 407.

[4] Franceschini (*op. cit.*, p. 290) thinks—1908—that the exorbitant rates of the English railways were a grave obstacle to the development of agriculture, but the way colonies were founded wherever the railway went shows the opposite to have been the case.

process of turning over considerable areas of land to immigrants. It was immigrant agriculture that caused the network of rails to spread to the farthest border of the tillable land. Today—1920—this network has covered its whole extent, to stop somewhat abruptly at the western border of the Pampa (Pl. Ic). Beyond are a few threads of space-traversing lines—the Transandine to Mendoza and Chile, three lines to Tucumán, and a single one to Catamarca, La Rioja, San Juan, beside the two Patagonian adventures that are creeping slowly westward to the well-watered Argentine Switzerland of the southwest, to Neuquén and Lake Nahuel Huapi on either side of the fortieth parallel. The overwhelming mass of the traffic is on the Pampa. It is not a continuous development of new western lands that will continue in the future as it has gone on in the past. Rather it is a chapter in Argentine development that is now closed. The net of rails has now covered the whole width of the belt of tillable lands. Everywhere it has reached the arid lands that bound it on the west. The lines that go farther traverse the desert. The Pampa is the rain land, and its border is definite enough. Irrigation adds something, it is true, even in the desert. It is old in the land. The Spaniard found it at Mendoza when he came. But when all the irrigable land is developed its area remains tiny. The Pampa contains the bulk of Argentine farming land.

The Pampa has about 200,000 square miles of most fertile soil, half of it already in agricultural use. The rest cannot be farmed unless it can be taken away from the cattle-raising Creoles who own it in vast estates of hundreds—sometimes thousands—of square miles and are well satisfied with things as they are. They control the country and have no idea of giving up their fundamental possession of the land to make room for land-tilling gringos.

The proposition that the Pampa is a limited area beyond which tillage and the rails attendant on tillage may not expand is simple enough, but it is not generally accepted in the country. There are a million and a third square miles of

Argentine territory, fully a million of them fairly level land. Tillage and railways have crept steadily across it for the last forty years, turning vast empty wastes into fertile fields. Eastern Córdoba looked sterile enough in 1885, yet superb fields of wheat and flax are growing there today. Surely the advance must go on just so across the whole national domain, argues the Argentine, for the rainfall boundary that limits the Pampa is an invisible thing. It is a gradation and not a line. This is, after all, only an average statement from observations of individual years. It does not impress the dweller on the spot. He knows of wet years. He is prone to believe more of them are coming. Yet there is in the landscape something to mark for the eye this border of sufficient average rains; the *monte*, the characteristic scrub of the dry lands, that begins beyond, as *chañar* in the west and northwest and *caldén* in the southwest. The network of rails has spread to the *monte* (Fig. 7). To expand farther westward the railway net must fray out into single threads that cross the arid lands, seeking something beyond. The net will fill in many of its opener meshes on the Pampa, especially if agriculture one day succeeds in weakening somewhat the hold that cattle raising now has on the powerful men of land, but it will expand no farther westward as a network. It is absolutely comparable to the western border of our own railway net in central Nebraska and South Dakota.

At this point the reader should examine the city and railway maps of 1867, 1892, and 1920 (Pl. IA, B, and C), with their indication of the permanent border of the Pampa.[5] In 1867,

[5] These maps are based on the following sources:

Size of cities. 1869: Primer censo de la República Argentina, 1869, Buenos Aires, 1872, pp. 674–683; 1895: Segundo censo de la República Argentina, 1895, Vol. 2: Población, Buenos Aires, 1898, pp. 60–62, 155–157, 195, 231, 271, 305, 339, 376, 413, 450, 487, 526, 566, 602, and 642; 1914: Tercer censo nacional, 1914 Vol. 4: Población, Buenos Aires, 1916, pp. 469–475 (see, however, remarks in footnote 13, p. 89, above). In Chile only the three largest cities are shown. For a complete 1907 cities map of central Chile see the writer's "Recent Colonization in Chile," *Amer. Geogr. Soc. Research Series No. 6*, 1921, facing p. 50.

Extension of railroad net. 1867: V. Martin de Moussy: Atlas de la Confédération Argentine, Paris, 1873, Pl. 5, 1:5,500,000. 1892: Mapa de los ferro carriles de
(For continuation of footnote, see next page.)

when the railways were in their beginning, the between-rivers country of Corrientes and Entre Ríos, the Argentine Mesopotamia, was the most accessible part of the republic, thanks to the broad, deep waterways of the Paraná and the Uruguay. The map shows the many river towns of 1869 resulting from this accessibility, important towns, though many of their inhabitants are of Guaraní Indian blood. The map shows also how great a proportion of the Pampa was still unoccupied and hence in the hands of the Indians prior to Roca's campaigns of the seventies (see also Fig. 37 and p. 90, above), lands that, once wrested from the Indians, were granted in vast estates to soldiers and citizens or sold under conditions of gifts, the origin of many of the *latifundia* of today. Most significant of all is the last map, showing the railways of 1920 and the population—in cities at any rate—of the last census, that of 1914, and bringing out the present filling up of the Pampa with the railway net as described, and the eight lines crossing the deserts farther west to reach little town clusters at the mountain borders, at Mendoza, San Juan, La Rioja, Catamarca, Tucumán, Salta, and Jujuy—larger at Mendoza and Tucumán, thanks to grapes and wine in the one case and to sugar in the other.

CREOLE MENTAL ATTITUDE TOWARD THE IMMIGRANT AS A CHECK TO COLONIZATION

It is agriculture, and agriculture in the hands of immigrants, that has spread this railway net across the land. From this agriculture have come the billion dollar grain and cattle exports, from this the significance of the Argentine Republic

Continuation of footnote 5.

la República Argentina construido por Dr. José Chavanne, 1:1,000,000, Direcc. de Ferro Carriles Nacionales, Buenos Aires, 1892 [a physical wall map primarily]. 1920: Mapa de communicaciones de la República Argentina compilado y construido por la División Cartográfica del Instituto Geográfico Militar, 1:1,000,000, Buenos Aires, 1920. In Chile all railroads at the approximate given dates are shown, according to the following sources. 1867: Same as for the Argentine. 1892: Mapa de la República de Chile por C. Opitz i Dr. H. Polakowsky, 1:2,500,000, Santiago, edición corréjida 1891. 1920: Mapa de los ferrocarriles, 1:4,600,000, in Guia de los ferrocarriles de Chile, Santiago, 1918.

as provisioner in meat and grain to a densely populated Old World, from this the wealth of the Creole landowner. We have referred to this man before. He is a most important factor in the situation that prevails. It cannot be too much emphasized that his mental attitude was and is quite different from that which theoretically at least prevails in the United States. Society is to him stratified into upper and lower classes. The upper class controls life for everybody. Not that it meddles tyrannically with the private affairs of the peon class, but in matters that affect all classes it expects to have its own way. Where we should think it natural and proper for the peon to insist upon his rights when any outcome of such upper-class arrangements bears too hard on him, the upper-class Creole mind conceives the relation quite differently, perhaps something like this: "Only the upper class is intelligent and responsible. Properly, therefore, they own the land and govern the community. A peon who finds he is having a hard time ought to apply to his patron and is entitled to get protection and help. The patron owes him this, and, if some individual patron should fail in this duty, in this feeling of *noblesse oblige*, probably it would be all right to have some court to which the peon should appeal. He must not, of course, ask to be taken out of his peon station in life." That is, the Creole recognizes that the patron has duties toward the peon, and actually has the habit of fulfilling this duty *in what he regards as sufficient measure*, but he has no very clear idea that the peon has *rights!* The glimpses of European society imparted by travel to some of the Creole upper class have not tended to change this mental attitude very much. In the peasants of Europe they see peons and like to regard themselves as Argentine representatives of Europe's landed aristocrats. I believe this attitude is at the back of the present check in settling the country and improving agriculture. If a considerable class of landowning peasants arose, with titles to their land under Argentine law, they would certainly have rights and come to know them. If these peasants were strangers to the traditions of serfdom, they would certainly show no hesitation in pressing their claims.

RATIO OF LANDOWNERSHIP TO TENANCY

At heart the Creole landowner has no sympathy with the immigrant's aspiration to a land title, and, as a matter of fact, he has not allowed the immigrant acquisition of land to go very far. It would be most interesting to know the actual area of tilled land in the Argentine Republic that belongs to those who till it, but this cannot be learned.[6] If Argentine statisticians had been definitely ordered to conceal this fact at all hazards, the figures could not withhold the information more completely. We know how many farms there are of a number of sizes, what is grown on them, and how many of the total number who work them are owners, renters, or share workers, but we do not know whether farms of a given size or crop are worked by the owners or not. We know the total area of tilled land in the chief agricultural provinces and their subdivisions, classified by crops and size of farms, but we have no information as to what part of this area is cultivated by its owners.[7]

[6] As to the area occupied by large holdings, a statement is illuminating that was made in the Chamber on September 21, 1903, by the Argentine deputy Joaquín Castellanos, who was campaigning against the keeping of land from use in *latifundia*. He said that in the National Territories 4000 square miles of farming land was being held idle by capitalists in lots of 154 to 309 square miles, and more than 12,000 square miles in blocks of over 309 square miles each—in all, more than 27,000 square miles, or 17,000,000 acres, in blocks larger than 39 square miles, or 24,710 acres, in extent (A. B. Martinez and Maurice Lewandowski: The Argentine in the Twentieth Century, transl. by Bernard Miall from the French of the 3rd edit., New York [1915], pp. 129–130).

[7] What statistics there are appear mainly in the official publication entitled *Estadística Agrícola*, issued by the Direcc. Gen. de Econ. Rural y Estadíst., Minist. de Agric., Buenos Aires, in the section entitled "Principales condiciones económicas de la producción de cereales: Modo de explotación." Tables there give, for most of the departments of the provinces of Buenos Aires, Santa Fe, Córdoba, Entre Ríos, and the Territory of La Pampa, the number of farms, the proportion worked by owners, renters, or share partners, the area harvested and the yield in tons of wheat, flax, oats, barley, millet, and rye, taken together as a unit.

Other published data that bear on this question indicate the size of the holdings in relation to the number of properties (1914 Census, Vol. 5, pp. 3–69 and 691–738), the number devoted to a given crop or to cattle raising (*ibid.*, pp. 73–306), and the acreage harvested in each of six principal crops, viz. wheat, maize, barley, oats,

(*For continuation of footnote, see next page.*)

In the case of numerous Argentine laws and decrees relating to landownership the reader will be careful to distinguish between their elevated aims and philanthropic language and the actuality of events.[8]

But, while the colonization in Santa Fe and Entre Ríos that has been here described did actually turn over a good deal of land to immigrants, the Pampa is still thinly settled. Agriculture is by no means in possession of all the good, tillable land. Not merely are large areas still untilled wastes, but the tillage of the land that is cropped is superficial, and the peopling of this land with a race of farmer owners that began so gallantly in the fifties at Esperanza has practically come to an end.

Growth of the Renting System

Agriculture itself has suffered a transformation in the land. When the first colonies were founded the domain was semi-desert, wandered over by scrubby cattle. The spaces were vast, measured not in acres but in leagues of nine square miles, browsed by great herds of cattle numbered in thousands of heads, but the leagues were well-nigh worthless and the cattle were little valued: the land at ten *bolivianos* a league and the cattle at a bare five dollars a head—merely what the hide would bring. Today the land is in hectares and valuable. In the seaboard province Buenos Aires six per cent of the cattle is English pedigreed stock of enormous value, and practically all the rest is improved with English crossings.[9]

Continuation of footnote 7

flax, and alfalfa (Agricultural and Pastoral Census of the Nation, Vol. 2: Stock-Breeding and Agriculture in 1908, Buenos Aires, 1909). There are also statistics on the nationality of those in control of the ranches and farms, the latter classified according to their crops (1914 Census, Vol. 5, pp. 309–450).—Edit. Note.

[8] This comes out well in J. G. Velárdez (Land Settlement in the Argentine Republic, *Internatl. Rev. of Agric. Economics*, N. S., Vol. 1, 1923, pp. 227–248). He signs himself "agricultural expert," which seems to give him a semi-official air. One supposes he is or was an employee of the Ministry of Agriculture. His paper contains abundant citations from laws as well as actual results in land-ownership.

[9] Agricultural and Pastoral Census of the Nation, 1908, Vol. 1: Stock Breeding, Buenos Aires, 1909, pp. xi and 134.

There is said to be no pure Creole stock left in the province. These huge values were introduced into the poverty-stricken land by Swiss and German farmers of a generation back. They were not remarkably good farmers, we recall. But their farming gave value to the cattle-poor land. And they paid for this land, made it theirs to own and to keep with a portion of the crops they raised on it. For instance, in the Department Marcos Juárez, Province of Córdoba, there were in 1906 a number of colonies, largely Italians.[10] The land had in 1890 belonged to five or six Argentines in the old-time cattle *latifundia* of moderate value but had come to be subdivided somewhat in colonizing. By 1906 a third of the different properties —but probably much less than a third of the area, since these would have been the small lots—belonged to Italian agricultural colonists. Another third belonged to Argentines, and the last third to Europeans not Italian—these two portions being in *latifundia* which attracted a good many Italian workers to Marcos Juárez. Undoubtedly it was stimulating to these men to see the Italian colonists on the little farms that they owned as well as tilled. They may well have hoped to have the same good fortune. But in this they were to be disappointed. They could have work there only as renters. There was no more land for sale. The *latifundia* were to be kept intact. The terms of rental were usually an eighth of the harvest, delivered at the railway station—very mild it seems compared with the portions demanded at Esperanza (p. 55) and other early colonies; but, unlike those portions, the payments gave no rights to the land, and the conditions of the contract were oppressive.

Long, long ago the Creole landowner found his leagues of worthless land had become a fortune and made up his mind to part with no more of them. They had, it appeared, an astonishing value—if gringos could be got to work them. He could get a lot of money for his land if he sold it, but what should he do with the money? He didn't know how to invest

[10] Franceschini, *op. cit.*, p. 417.

it. He might lose it; and wasn't the value of the land increasing every day? Better keep the land and let the gringo go on working it for him. Long before the colonies had crept from Santa Fe into Córdoba the colonies were *renters'* colonies, with little chance that the renter would acquire ownership. We have seen (pp. 114,141) how renting grew up spontaneously in earlier days, how the immigrants themselves acquired more land and rented it out, how the Central Argentine Railway allowed colonists to rent because they wanted to rent but also agreed to count the rentals toward payment if it was desired later to purchase (p. 92). How different the renting of the present day when purchase is out of the question!

Walle tells[11] of rentals of six and eight pesos a hectare paid in the Territory La Pampa in 1910 by colonists subrenting from an individual who had rented a large block from the landowner for two pesos a hectare. The owner avoided all bother with detail, and the large tenant paid himself four to six pesos a hectare for his troubles. If he had failed to collect half his rents—and he generally collected all of them—he would have fared very well, but over and above that he found excellent profit in supplying his colonists with provisions and advances of cash, in which he had the advantage of being the only grocer and banker on the ground, and drove very hard bargains with them in disposing of their crops.

The later immigrant found he had come to a land which his predecessors had made cattle-rich by their tillage, while a part, too large a part, of every crop he raised went to pay for mere permission for him to live and labor in this land of blooded cattle, where there was little hope of his ever owning an acre himself.

DEVELOPMENT OF STOCK BREEDING

About the year 1860 a beginning was made of exporting Argentine live cattle to England. But the Creole cattle, lineal descendants of animals escaped from the early Spaniards, were

[11] Paul Walle (Chargé de missions du Ministère de Commerce): L'Argentine telle qu'elle est, Paris, [1912], p. 495.

small, lean, and scrubby, half-wild animals self-raised on the Pampa. English taste rejected the meat. By 1870 the cattle-owning *estancieros*, realizing that they must improve their stock if they would sell it, began the importation of fine English stock. At the present time improved cattle are found everywhere in the south. North of a line that crosses south-central Córdoba and southern Santa Fe a cattle malaria, to which native cattle are immune, makes it impossible to keep the foreign breeds or native cattle that have been crossed with them.[12]

Since 1890 live animals have not been allowed to enter England on account of the foot-and-mouth disease, and so chilled and frozen meat is taking their place. The improved stock yields a beef that satisfied British taste. The business is a large one, and the product is about as important in exportation as the crop of cereals. Above all, the raising of fine stock as a business has a great appeal for the wealthy Creole landowners. The love of cattle and horses is a tradition in the land. In this single direction the British aristocracy has more appeal to the upper-class Argentines than does that of France. Possibly there is an Argentine gentleman of fortune or even of the respectable class (*gente decente*) who knows nothing of cattle and cannot ride a horse. I never heard of one, but if there is one I am sure he guards the shameful secret most zealously.

INFLUENCE OF STOCK BREEDING ON AGRICULTURE AND FORM OF LAND TENURE

But perhaps the most singular thing about this raising of fine cattle in the Argentine Republic, following on the agricultural valorization of the land, is the way it has transformed Argentine agriculture itself, so that we have today the cir-

[12] See the map, Pl. 3, and text, pp. 188–189, in Pierre Denis: La République Argentine: La mise en valeur du pays, Paris, 1920 (Engl. edition, map 3 facing p. 188 and text, pp. 188–189). On the general topic here discussed see also Herbert Gibson: The Evolution of Live-Stock Breeding in the Argentine, in: Agricultural and Pastoral Census of the Nation, Vol. 3: Monographs, Buenos Aires, 1909, pp. 55–106.

cumstance, unique in the world, that fully one-half the grain exported from the republic is an incident to cattle raising, being grown on grazing lands that are being prepared for seeding or reseeding with alfalfa to feed fine stock.

It was a merit of the old scrub Creole cattle that they fed well enough on the wild native grasses of the Pampa, well enough, that is, for stock of so little worth as they. Better stock immediately demanded better feed, and the necessity followed of replacing the wild Pampa grasses with alfalfa. The best method of doing this is to break up the soil and raise three or four crops of wheat on it. To this end a contract is made with a wheat grower, usually an Italian, to raise four crops of wheat and then seed the land to alfalfa with seed supplied by the landowner, all the work of the five years being done under the scrupulous inspection of the ranch foreman to see that it all tends to the best possible final result as a field of cattle feed. Agriculture has here become the handmaid of stock raising. Here are great numbers of farmers who are not progressing in the least toward owning their farms. A five-year term ends by dispossessing them. They must vacate to make room for fine cattle. The ranches of our Southwest gave place to farms. The *estancias* of the Argentine Republic absorbed the farmers for a spell, to cast them forth again presently till needed for further pastoral uses. Years later, when the alfalfa has run out, there will be another contract with a wandering renter to put in another four years of wheat to be followed by the cattle baron's alfalfa. Colonizing with farmer landowners has been replaced by farming by renters. On rented land grow the greater part of the great Argentine grain crops, and the rental is accompanied with restrictions that sadly handicap.

When I was a small boy in Massachusetts I once met a citi-fied-looking boy who was a stranger to me and wanted to run a race. It happened that I beat him; and he explained that it was not fair, I ought to have a handicap. I didn't know what he meant but assented and presently perceived that the hand-

icap meant that he was to have start enough to win. That is
the way the Argentine landowner gives the gringo land to
rent. Not that the method is especially Argentine. Foreigners
who own land do the same thing, but most of the land is owned
by Argentines. The gringo is usually the renter with the
handicap.

THE HARDSHIPS AND EVILS OF RENTING

Why should the renter be handicapped? Why shouldn't he
take his land and use it as he will, provided he pays the rental
agreed upon? Because the owner finds it possible to impose a
handicap and does so. The immigrant is ignorant. Half the
time he cannot read, even his own language. He persists
doggedly in any routine he happens to fall into. Often he
does not know the terms of his contract. He sees in the land
countrymen of his who have gained a competence perhaps in
the old days when land was to be had. It looks possible for
him, too. He knows nothing of agriculture but what he has
picked up in two or three harvests that he has worked through
at wages that seem to him fantastically high. They may
run as high as three American dollars a day and maintenance.
Living is also high. A Swede, who earned two riksdalers
(about 50 cents in our money) a day in his own land in 1870
but spent it all to live, was earning two to three gold pesos
(practically $2 to $3 in United States currency) in Córdoba
in 1885 but still found he had to spend it all to live, though
living now included a wife and children. But the Italian
field worker saved almost all his harvest wage. He had an
object in view. His needs were few, and doing without was
almost his second nature. The reader is not to get the idea
that all the Italians in the Argentine Republic go in rags and
are starving. The illustrations in this book will serve to
contradict any such idea. The Italians dress better than the
old-time gaucho. They wear good woolen garments in the
winter, when the gaucho wore only cotton, *brin*. They live
more economically than some other Europeans, just as other

Europeans live more cheaply than North Americans; but Hiller, who has looked into this matter, points[13] to $6,000,000 worth of Italian luxuries imported into the Republic in 1909, wines, olive oil, cheese, and cigars—luxuries, because cheaper substitutes are at hand. But the Italian who thrives as renter and becomes landowner must be able to carry economies to extremes.

Now he will rent a farm and work for himself. Half the harvest he must give up to pay for the use of the land. That much he knew. But his handicap begins to develop. He has to buy tools and equipment. Some of his money goes. Everything is dear. He finds himself bound by his contract to put so many hectares under the plow. He has rented under a contract that fixes everything. He can do nothing at will, he cannot accommodate himself to changing conditions. So much is to be accomplished that he hires labor. His money gone, he borrows at the store and long before his first harvest is deep in debt at an interest rate that is another handicap. Chances of the weather try the farmer's soul in every land. The Argentine has them in full measure, with the locust thrown in. In your prosperous year this scourge may eat half or all your crop. However, the chances are run and the crop is made, not a bad one perhaps. Now the custom of the land and the renter's lack of means compel the crop to be left exposed—if wheat, in sacks heaped up beside the railway at a station until cars can be found for it; if maize, on the ground in the rude *troje* of cornstalks, uncovered until it is taken away by the purchaser. Usually the winter is not rainy, but rains occur and rains spoil the grain. The contract says the owner is to receive his half of the grain "sound, clean, and dry." But most of the crop has none of these qualities. The renter has not skill enough at his craft to produce sound, clean grain; and he cannot keep it dry. Only good fortune would do that under his conditions. He may be obliged to buy grain to

[13] Georg Hiller: Einwanderung und Einwanderungspolitik in Argentinien, Berlin, 1912, p. 106.

pay the landlord his rent, for he will be held to his bargain. Of course, shouldn't the landowner have good marketable grain in return for the use of his land? The landowner knows more than the renter and imposes on him.

There are extraordinary fluctuations in Argentine harvests; and man has done very little to diminish the recurring hazards of the seasons, as witness the lack of storage for the grain product of the country. At Tres Arroyos, in the Province of Buenos Aires, a good many Italians had town subdivisions of 30 to 50 hectares, a size that in local practice did not suffice to support a family, and so they had to hire land elsewhere. Most of the country around was in *latifundia*, nine of them belonging to Italians. A succession of bad harvests following 1900 brought the farmers of Tres Arroyos almost to bankruptcy. A good harvest in 1904 produced $7,000,000 worth of grain in the neighborhood, but the colonists were so deep in debt that few crumbs of the harvest got to them. The merchants collected their accounts and then restricted their credits. The landowners increased their demands, and the farmers went on working, but more than ever for the merchants and landowners.[14]

Most of the gains of a good harvest go to landowner, middlemen, and railways under the present system. A renter farmer does not get up much enthusiasm for bumper crops. Until he can get land of his own that will bring the fruits of his labors into his own pockets he will have no great love of the country, and that will not be until the big *estancias* are broken up. The lucky ones who have managed to get land are prosperous enough. Every good harvest makes fortunes; every bad one, widespread disaster. In an unusual year a renter may overcome his handicap and even make something, sadly as the dice are loaded against him. In a bad year the roads are full of renters and their families carrying on their backs what possessions are left them. There have been renters' strikes in recent years that verged on civil war. Yet there are always

[14] Franceschini, *op. cit.*, p. 344.

some among these poor and ignorant men who succeed, by untiring industry and well-nigh incredible thrift.

DIFFICULTY OF SECURING TITLE TO LAND AS A FURTHER OBSTACLE TO COLONIZATION

Reference has already been made (p. 106) to the difficulty of obtaining title to land from the Argentine government. It is a very serious matter. The promise of the Argentine government to give land cannot be counted of much value. I do not see how any Argentine government or its representatives can escape the charge of essential dishonesty as long as no effort is made to fulfill definite promises. There have been numerous laws and projects for colonizing the national territory. The evidence comes from so many directions, from Argentines as well as foreigners, that one cannot doubt that probably thousands of individuals have fulfilled all the legal obligations, have cleared, cultivated, and are settled on land to which they have been promised title and cannot get it and of which they are in some cases even violently dispossessed. The most immediate need of the national government is to search out all such cases and act upon them at once. Huret tells the story for Neuquén.[16] "We have satisfied the conditions of the law," settlers at Lake Nahuel Huapi said to him, "cleared the land, built our dwelling, fenced and stocked our fields, brought a quarter and at times more of our land under tillage; all this ten, twelve, and fifteen years ago, but in spite of our demands we can get no titles." "What do they answer when you write to the ministry?" "They do not answer. In the last five years three different inspectors have been here, and we have complained to them and have never heard from them again." One of the complainants, although he had fulfilled all the requirements of Argentine law on colonization, was required to prove that he was an Argentine citizen. The Indians had burned his house with all his papers. He told them to look in

[15] Jules Huret: En Argentine (2 vols.: Vol. 1, De Buenos-Aires au Gran Chaco; Vol. 2, De La Plata à la Cordillère des Andes, Paris, 1912–13), Vol. 2, pp. 278–279.

the registers at the capital. "I was naturalized at Buenos Aires ten years ago. You must have the record there." It has never been Argentine policy to require settlers to be naturalized. Another colonist named Otto Goedeker is the oldest settler at Bariloche on the lake. He was induced to come by an offer of 250 hectares of land; this was reduced to 100 and then to 50. Meanwhile he has spent his money and cleared the land and worn himself out. At the same time men with influence come later and get larger properties at once.

We have recited the story of General Oroño's lands above (p. 103). According to W. Jaime Molins' "La Pampa," published in Buenos Aires in 1918,[16] the citizens of the town of Victorica, Territory of La Pampa, have been unable to get titles promised them about 1882, although they have complied with all the provisions of the law and paid for their land, many of them twice over. These people are Argentines by birth and descent. They came from Mercedes in San Luis Province as soon as the soldiers of Roca had driven the last Indians from the Pampa. Don Luis Gómez was one of those old settlers. He has a handsome house and place. He has two different titles to his lot and has paid for it twice over. Now he is summoned to clear his title within thirty days or vacate the lot! Doña Carmen Orozca, widow of the sergeant major of the troops who won the land from the Indians, has paid for her land four times over. As soon as the Indians were defeated the town was located, apparently as a half-military measure, an outpost of civilization against the savages. When the soldiers withdrew, provisional titles were given by the local authorities, as ordered by "superior authority." But investigation showed that Victorica had been located not on national land, as was supposed, but on land belonging to a cattle company. This situation the Argentine government has not been able to meet. There is no doubt that the settlers have fulfilled all their obligations toward the government, some of them several times over, yet they get no titles.

[16] pp. 309–313.

Very likely subordinates are at fault in this remissness in giving effect to law, but their superiors have the power to hold them to account. A Creole subordinate public officer is uncomfortable to deal with unless you come to him with evidence of standing well with his superiors. Otherwise he has an extraordinary capacity for not getting ahead with your affair. This is in part a Latin trait. One notices a good deal of it in France. Lord Bryce has suggested[17] that it comes from the fact that the employee has the favorable or unfavorable whim of his superior to take into account as well as the laws under which his office functions.

All observers agree that difficulty in obtaining land is a hindrance to settling desirable immigrants on Argentine lands today. Many projects are in the air for dividing the *latifundia* that certainly exist in too great numbers and are not to the public advantage. These projects may be difficult to pass and still more difficult to put into actual effect; indeed, putting any law in the matter into effect is so difficult at present that real progress must begin there. Nothing would be gained, for instance, by a law expropriating all large estates if public officials were allowed to turn the lands thus made available away from bona fide settlers into the hands of speculators and favorites, as they have always done in the past. If the men in power were only willing to take it, the real step needed would be easy enough. If it were only the will of the President and ministers of the Argentine Republic, supported by the Creole ruling class, that all officials should at once act on all applications pending for land titles claimed to be long due to colonists in occupation, with instructions to waive technicalities in cases of obvious and essential justice; and if this will were clearly and continuously made known to all the public officers concerned—men who are now accused of treating the immigrant with uniform contempt—it would do much to encourage the best possible class of immigrants, the only class worth receiving. It will be necessary to get land away

[17] James Bryce: Modern Democracies (2 vols., New York, 1921), Vol. 1, p. 275.

from speculators who hold any of it idle for speculation and not, as in the past, let it get into wrong hands again. Execution of present outstanding obligations of the government would be the best possible introduction to the national acquisition of lands now withheld from use. In general it is not to be expected, however, as I have said before, that a Creole should be willing to let an immigrant acquire land and participation in the government of the nation, and, while many *latifundia* and some of the most gigantic of them are in foreign hands, the government of this nation is completely Creole and the policies in force are those that Creoles find acceptable.

CHAPTER VIII

IMMIGRATION AS AN ASSET TO THE ARGENTINE

Having in the latter part of the preceding chapter discussed some of the factors that at present hinder a satisfactory fulfillment of Argentine colonization, let us in conclusion review the character and extent of the immigration that has made that colonization possible. In Chapter II we have already become acquainted with Argentine immigration in its broad outlines and in its relation to the political conditions of the day.

IMMIGRANTS' PASSAGE FARES

The cost oi passage from Europe has not affected immigration to the Argentine Republic so much as has often been supposed. In the earlier colonies the passages were usually paid by the colony manager, to be recovered later as the colonists made their first harvests. From those who were given land the amount was easily collected. It was as good a lien on their land as a tax or better, as it formed a prerequisite to the delivery of title. The considerable number who never completed the acquisition of title never repaid their passage money.

From those who had no title there was nothing on which to collect. The government's interest in this payment, like its interest in the country, prompted it to see that the immigrant was placed on land and began to get title, in order that the state might recover its advance as part of the new wealth wrested from the national soil. The man who came only because his passage was paid for him was probably never worth bringing. The man who has really proved worth while did not usually find the promise of payment of his transportation much of an attraction; at any rate it was not what decided him. In the earliest days he was induced to come by the representations of men like Aaron Castellanos that he could quickly acquire a large tract of good land, in a mild climate, where the products of the soil were in demand at a high price. Mechanics were attracted by the prospect of abundant work at good wages. Once a nucleus of prospering colonists was established, with actual title to land that brought them good returns, their letters home brought numbers out in their steps.

Fostering of Immigration by the Argentine Government

As soon as the advantage of colonization in the rapid valorization of the land was perceived by the Creoles, the government began to spend money in fostering immigration. A long history can be written of this official quest of immigrants in Europe.[1] Agents were employed abroad to collect them, agents appointed at Buenos Aires and Rosario to receive them, care for them, and move them into the interior. At one time agents in Europe were paid a bonus of $5 for every immigrant secured, provided he paid his own passage and actually arrived in the country. In the extravagant years just before 1890 the government gave free passages from Europe without scrutiny of the applicants. Millions of dollars were spent in that way; but the mass of the immigrants have come at their own expense—certainly the best elements have.

In Buenos Aires they are well treated and well cared for; occupation is found for them if desired, free maintenance for five days given them, and free passages into the interior if employment is found for them there. For a long time this was the work of a philanthropic society of citizens of Buenos Aires, aided by grants from the city, the province, and the nation—an admirable exhibition of the universal Creole kindness of heart that does not willingly see a stranger suffer at its door.

[1] The history of Argentine immigration policy is quite fully discussed in Georg Hiller: Einwanderung und Einwanderungspolitik in Argentinien, Berlin, 1912, Chs. I-V.

There are regulations excluding criminals and those afflicted with communicable disease or liable to become public charges. Possibly the regulations are not rigorously enforced.

The cities afford occupation and prosperity to large numbers of immigrant artisans but also shelter swarms of undesirables, as happens with us—a proletariat not of the New World. Altogether one encounters many more Italians and Spaniards in actual business affairs in Argentine cities than native Creoles.

ARGENTINE IMMIGRATION, 1857–1924

In the 68 years of record of Argentine immigration to 1924, inclusive, the average number of arrivals would be over 90,000 a year, though of course very unevenly distributed in time, mounting to over 300,000 in each of the two years immediately before the World War and passing 200,000 in each of the six years before that, as also in one other year, 1889. But very large numbers have also left the country, more than 100,000 in each of the years 1911, 1912, and 1913. In 1914 and 1915 the departures numbered respectively 178,684 and 111,459 when Europe was calling her soldiers to the colors. In no year since 1868 were those who left the country less than 8000.[2]

It would surprise many Americans to know that the same thing happens with us. Immigrants come, but emigrants also go. We cannot go back so far as the Argentines can. Our emigration record only dates from July 1, 1907. In the twelve months following that date (the fiscal year 1908 of the official calendar) 783,000 immigrants entered the United States, but 395,000 left it. Our greatest immigration in one year—1,218,000 in the wholly pre-war fiscal year 1914—was counterbalanced in some part by the departure of 303,000. These departures averaged 295,000 a year from 1908 to 1914 inclusive. Even in the first year (fiscal year 1922) after re-

[2] See, below, Appendix, Table I.

strictive immigration went into effect there were 199,000 departures, and in the three subsequent years for which these statistics are available the numbers were respectively 81,000, 77,000, and 93,000.[3] It is natural enough. Homesickness is terribly acute in the first year of the peasant's life in the New World. Success is always slow in coming. Everything seems to get worse with immigrants before even symptoms of betterment appear. And many never succeed at all. A few of those who succeed realize a long-cherished ambition to return and pass their last days in the native village. All these are motives for a strong returning current from New World shores. Bad times of course increase its volume. This is especially true of the Italians, who devote themselves mainly to agriculture; and it diminishes the number arriving in the year after a bad harvest and increases it after a good one.[4] Their departures vary in the opposite sense.

SEASONAL IMMIGRATION

The extensive wheat culture of the Argentine calls for large numbers of extra hands at harvest time for whom the country has no work at other seasons. There has long been some migration of labor within the country, as in the *ingenios* of Tucumán. Something of the same sort has happened in the wheat harvests. About 1906 bands of peons used to come every year from Santiago del Estero and Catamarca to the Department Marcos Juárez in Córdoba.[5] High fares on the railways hindered the movement, but those who had mules and horses came of their own accord, for the wages were fully three times those of the off season. It was estimated that

[3] All figures taken from *Annual Rept. of the Commissioner General of Immigration for the Fiscal Year Ended June 30, 1925*, Washington, 1925, Table 48 on p. 137. As to immigration restriction the two establishing acts are those of May 19, 1921 (annual quota of each nationality, 3 per cent of the number of residents of that nationality according to the Census of 1910) and May 26, 1924 (2 per cent according to Census of 1890). On these acts see the Commissioner's Report for 1921, pp. 16–17, and for 1924, pp. 24–30. A brief history of our immigration laws is given in the report for 1923, pp. 2–4.

[4] Hiller, *op. cit.*, pp. 101–102.

[5] Personal communication to the author in Córdoba.

there were then about 55,000 Italians in Córdoba Province,[6] almost all laborers, no doubt, but at harvest 17,000 to 20,000 more were needed. We hear, too, of some 4000 Italian laborers with headquarters around San Nicolás, in Buenos Aires Province, from April on, who spent the first three months of the year, the time of high wages, in the harvest fields. These men had organized themselves into compact squads of eight or ten for mutual aid and defense,[7] apparently to worry through the nine lean months without loss of their harvest earnings. One firm of grain merchants and importers in western Santa Fe used to send to Italy for temporary workers under a four months' contract for this harvest work. Besides high wages they gave their men a *puchero*, the Spanish thick stew of meat and vegetables, and a little Paraguay rum.[8] As their lodging was most casual almost every cent of their wages was saved to take back to Italy, which they reached in time to go to work on the northern harvest. Italians that come and go in this way are a much-talked-of feature of Argentine labor. From their seasonal migration they are known as *golondrinas*, or swallows. There are supposed to be 30,000 of them or more,[9] but this number appears to be exaggerated, and a good deal of the talk about them is fantastic and without foundation.

It is of course a very happy circumstance that the seasons of the northern hemisphere are six months later than those of the south, making possible two grain harvests and two winters in every year for those who care to cross the equator in search of them. Varied classes of European laborers do that very thing, noteworthy among them being opera stars and choruses, who thus get in two seasons of opera to the year. Madame Patti could and did sing in London and Paris in the winter and take steamer in March for Buenos Aires for another season of opera in June and July—the southern winter. Many

[6] Antonio Franceschini: L'Emigrazione italiana nell'America del Sud: Studi sulla espansione coloniale transatlantica, Rome, 1908, p. 399.
[7] *ibid.*, p. 340.
[8] *ibid.*, p. 416.
[9] According to statements made to the author in conversations with Argentines.

a famous musician has done the same. So did many a modest Italian company of small-city opera singers, chorus and all; for a South American city of 50,000 people would have felt disgraced if it had to go through the winter without a few weeks of opera. These people by their numbers were far more significant than the celebrities. Their paths of course would cross those of the rough-handed harvesters, who travel in pursuit of summers, flitting to Germany in June and to the Pampa in November. Some of them are said to have made the journey no less than seventeen times. When we asked the late Professor Ricchieri of Milan, the geographer, on the deck of the little steamer on Lake Maggiore how the people got their living in the tiny red-roofed villages nestling high on the slopes above, he answered *"emigrano,"* they emigrate! Those were the nests of these swallows.

Such men come to know the Argentine wheat harvests very well and how to organize for their own advantage. The Creole who undertakes to exploit them will find his work cut out for him. This, too, may have helped the growth of the legend that has sprung up around them. They are accused of injuring the country by carrying off huge sums of Argentine money and spending nothing in the land. This is mere detraction, of course, for labor such as they render is what the Argentine Republic must have for its very life. Everyone of them is an invaluable asset, even if he literally spends not a single cent in the country, which is most unlikely.

Hiller thinks[10] the migrating habit began with the crisis of 1890, which sent thousands of Italians away because they could get no work, to come again for the following harvest; but this is not possible, for ever since the record of Argentine immigration began there has been greater immigration in the November-to-March summer than in winter, though it has tended to settle more into November since 1890. We have records back to 1858 with a few gaps, giving the immigrant

[10] *op. cit.,* pp. 98–99.

arrivals at Buenos Aires every month.[11] In the decade 1861–1870 forty per cent of the year's immigrants came in the four months October, November, December, and January; in 1871–1880, forty-eight per cent; in 1881–1890, fifty per cent; in 1891–1900, fifty-four per cent; in 1901–1910, fifty-eight per cent, and in the three years leading up to the World War, fifty-three per cent—a general increase with the years. Even the dislocation of the war years (1914-1918) did not efface the preponderance of these months, with their forty per cent; and since the war the previous tendency has reasserted itself, the percentage being fifty-one in 1919–1924. This general increase is, I think, purely a reflection of Argentine economic conditions. It is getting harder and harder for an immigrant to get land of his own or to get really desirable employment at unskilled work, except at harvest time. Europeans intending immigration have accurate knowledge of these conditions by

[11] AVERAGE MONTHLY NUMBER OF IMMIGRANTS, 1858–1924

(Second- and third-class passengers in hundreds of individuals)

	Sept.	Oct.	Nov.	Dec.	Jan.	Feb.	Mar.	Apr.	May	June	July	Aug.	Year§
1858–1860*	4	3	4	5	7	5	6	3	3	3	4	4	50
1861–1870*	9	10	11	19	17	12	13	12	11	11	11	10	160
1871–1880†	15	28	36	37	25	20	20	20	19	15	14	13	261
1881–1890‡	49	92	111	119	95	68	59	53	56	50	41	48	841
1891–1900‡	47	87	115	98	53	42	39	33	35	32	34	34	648
1901–1910‡	119	244	355	292	126	100	104	94	93	84	69	83	1,764
1911–1913‡	219	367	437	450	258	213	197	150	149	146	122	129	2,837
1914–1918‡ (war)	26	36	44	39	62	50	44	38	33	28	25	22	451
1919–1924‡	93	143	187	178	91	76	86	67	70	65	63	63	1,184

*Computed from *Rejistro Estadist. de la República Argentina*, Buenos Aires, 1864–1873, as given in Hiller, *op. cit.*, p. 139. These values include the arrivals via Montevideo. The averages for 1861–1870 do not include 1869, as the figures for that year are not available.

†Computed from the monthly number of immigrants kindly communicated for this inquiry by Señor Meneclier (see, above, p. 98, footnote 34).

‡Computed from Resumen estadístico del movimiento migratorio en la República Argentina, años 1857-1924, Direcc. Gen. de Inmigración, Buenos Aires, 1925, pp. 28-29 and (for 1921-1924) p. 52.

Hiller, *op. cit.*, pp. 139-140, gives monthly arrivals covering the years 1858–1868, 1870-1873, 1882-1911, compiled from various official statistics. For the periods in which the two sources correspond, Hiller's figures and the Resumen's figures (including those communicated by Señor Meneclier) agree exactly in most cases and within a few units in a number of cases and not at all in a few isolated instances.

§ Determined from the annual and decadal totals in Resumen estadístico, p. 32.

word of mouth from returned relatives and acquaintances. If they are ready to start in July they know there is no hurry— the good pay doesn't begin till November; and they go on in Europe's best working season till the Argentine's best time draws on. If they seem likely to be ready in December, the drawing on of winter with its discomforts in the northern hemisphere and the knowledge that the good season begins in the Argentine with November hastens their start. It does not so much matter what the work is. City labor is best paid when farm labor is scarce. And when there is no work to be done on the farms there is a glut of labor in town.

That this analysis is accurate is shown by substantial facts. Spaniards in the Argentine take small part in farm labor, the French practically none, yet more of them come in November, like the Italians and like everybody else.[12] Spanish *golondrinas*, it is true, are known,[13] but no French ones. Periodicity in farm employment, however, must affect all employment in the country. It would in any country that is largely agricultural. It must affect immigration in the United States, for instance, and does, even more than in the Argentine Republic. From 1898 to 1913 our immigrants for March, April, May, and June exceeded the usual arrivals for four months on the average by 95,000 persons, 45 per cent of the annual immigration coming in those months. The Argentine excess of immigrants for October, November, and December during the same period was 42,000, 48 per cent of their year's total coming in the

[12]AVERAGE MONTHLY NUMBER OF IMMIGRANTS OF CERTAIN NATIONALITIES, 1901–1910*

(in hundreds of individuals)

	Sept.	Oct.	Nov.	Dec.	Jan.	Feb.	Mar.	Apr.	May	June	July	Aug.
All nationalities*	119	244	**355**	292	126	100	104	94	93	84	69	83
Italians†	51	119	**182**	133	56	42	49	39	39	31	24	32
Spaniards†	45	96	**132**	114	45	40	36	31	32	28	24	30
French†	3	4	**5**	5	3	2	2	2	2	2	2	2

*Computed from Resumen estadístico, p. 29.

†Computed from *Bol. Mens. de Estadís. Municipal de la Ciudad de Buenos Aires*, Buenos Aires, 1901–1910.

[13] See the note "Spanish Emigration," *Geogr. Rev.*, Vol. 12, 1922, pp. 309–310, and the report there mentioned: La emigración española transoceánica, 1911–1915, Consejo Superior de Emigración, Madrid, 1916.

three months. In Canada, too, the same thing happens, an excess of 60,000 immigrants over five months' average monthly immigration coming every year in March, April, May, June, and July.[14]

Proportion of the Sexes Among the Immigrants

Seasonal immigrants for agricultural labor would be men only. Had this sort of immigration, as Hiller thinks, begun in 1890, a preponderance of males should appear in the immigration with that date. All immigration shows an excess of males. Western European countries usually have fewer males than females in their population. About 1910 there were 94 males to a hundred females in England, 97 in France, Germany, and Switzerland, and 98 in Belgium and the Netherlands.[15] The United States had 106 in 1910, and the Argentine Republic 116 in 1914,[16] undoubtedly because of the operation of immigration; for, besides families of immigrants with the average proportion of the sexes that prevails in their home country, there come a good many unattached males. Fifty or sixty years ago our foreign born had 115 men to a hundred women.[17] In 1910 the number of males was 129,[17] and it had risen pretty gradually. We had been getting farther away

[14] AVERAGE MONTHLY NUMBER OF IMMIGRANTS TO THE
UNITED STATES AND CANADA
(in thousands of individuals)

	Mar.	Apr.	May	June	July	Aug.	Sept.	Oct.	Nov.	Dec.	Jan.	Feb.	Year	Month
To the United States (1898-1913)*	84	98	104	85	67	59	69	74	66	55	34	43	833	69
To Canada (1904-1913)†	27	41	43	31	23	20	19	17	12	8	6	8	255	21

*Annual Repts. of the Commissioner General of Immigration, Washington: for Fiscal Year Ended June 30, 1898, p. 28; 1899, p. 9; 1900, p. 9; 1901, p. 9; 1902, p. 12; 1903, p. 12; 1904, p. 11; 1905, p. 14; 1906, p. 16; 1907, p. 16; 1908, p. 13; 1909, p. 16; 1910, p. 14; 1911, p. 13; 1912, p. 67; 1913, p. 39; 1914, p. 36.

†Letter to the author from Mr. R. Fraser, Statistician, Canadian Department of Immigration and Colonization, Ottawa.

[15] Annuaire international de statistique, I: État de la population (Europe), Inst. Internat. de Statistique, The Hague, 1916, pp. 40-43.

[16] ibid., III: État de la population (Amérique), 1919, pp. 40-41.

[17] Fourteenth Census of the United States, 1920, Vol. 2: Population, General Report and Analytical Tables, Washington, 1922, p. 107.

from the habit of immigrant families. In 1912 our immigrants numbered 192 males to every hundred females; in 1923, 158.[18] From various references in Franceschini[19] I have gathered data on the sex of Italian immigrants to the Argentine from 1876 to 1900,[20] and there is no sign of the increase of males in 1890 which Hiller postulates. It is true that the disaster of 1890 sent crowds of them back,[21] and very likely some of these did come again in subsequent years, but instead of the excess of males increasing, as it would if temporary immigration of farm laborers began at that date, the males became less nu-

[18] *Annual Rept. of the Commissioner General of Immigration for the Fiscal Year Ended June 30, 1913*, Washington, 1913, p. 92; *for Fiscal Year Ended June 30, 1924*, Washington, 1924, p. 108. Both figures above are for the calendar years, not the fiscal years.

[19] *op. cit.*, pp. 251, 256, 258, 260. Franceschini's figures for 1880–1900 are seemingly taken from Marquis Malaspina: L'immigrazione nella Repubblica Argentina, *Boll. dell' Emigrazione*, Minist. degli Affari Esteri, Rome, 1902, No. 3 (pp. 3–24), p. 5. As a number of Franceschini's figures from internal evidence are incorrect and as the values for 1895 and 1896 are missing in his work the present table has been computed from Malaspina's figures. As to total annual Italian immigration to the Argentine, Malaspina tallies with the "Resumen estadístico," p. 8, except for 1887 and 1896, which there read respectively 65,139 and 75,202.

[20] PROPORTION OF THE SEXES AMONG ITALIAN IMMIGRANTS
TO THE ARGENTINE, 1876–1900*

Year	Total Ital. Immigr.	Males to 100 Females	Year	Total Ital. Immgr.	Males to 100 Females	Year	Total Ital. Imm.gr.	Males to 100 Females
1876	6,950	233	1884	31,983	233	1892	27,850	187
1877	7,556	253	1885	63,501	237	1893	37,977	196
1878	13,514	249	1886	43,328	156	1894	37,699	186
1879	22,774	235	1887	67,139	207	1895	41,203	205
1880	18,416	223	1888	75,029	230	1896	75,204	258
1881	20,506	222	1889	88,647	194	1897	44,678	226
1882	29,587	231	1890	39,122	186	1898	39,135	258
1883	37,043	192	1891	15,511	170	1899	53,295	304
						1900	52,143	304

*After Malaspina; see previous footnote.

[21] Italian emigrants: 1890, 47,408; 1891, 57,920 (Resumen estadístico, p. 8). From footnote 22, below, it will be noticed that the Resumen estadístico gives 48,794 as the number of all departing emigrants in 1890. This would leave only 1382 departures for all other nationalities. But the separate figures for each nationality in the Resumen (pp. 8–18) add up to 59,285 for 1890. There is hence here an inconsistency in the statistics, a point to which reference has already been made (p. 98). Hiller's (*op. cit.*, p. 137) figure of 62,355 for the total number of emigrants in 1890 is probably more reliable. As to total emigration in 1891 the Resumen's figure of 72,380 shows less discrepancy, as the separate nationality figures for that year add up to 74,856. Hiller (p. 137) also has 72,380 for total departures in 1891.

merous from 1886 to 1895. The effect of the crisis of 1890
was to halve the total Italian immigration twice running, but
the proportion of males also diminished in both years and
made no notable increase till 1898. The venturesome unattached males stayed away, it would seem. One may imagine
that in general the immigrants of unpromising years like that
were persons with obligations and contracts, wives and children
that had been sent for, for instance, and had their passages
paid. I suspect that if we could look into the sex proportion
of all emigrant *departures* from the Argentine in 1890 (63 per
cent as many as the arrivals of the year) or in 1891 (when they
were 256 per cent as many)[22] we should find the male pre-
dominance a very large one. For the unattached male moves
easily and is quick to take fright. The emigrants from the
United States in 1912 had 441 males to a hundred females and,
in 1923, 242,[23] much more than did the arrivals—192 and 158.

THE SEASON OF EMIGRATION

Departures of emigrant aliens from the Argentine Republic
are most numerous in March, April, May, and June,[24] almost
half of the out-go of the year occurring in those four months.
If all this excess consisted of returning seasonal laborers, it
would limit their number to about 7,500. I believe it was much
less, for the low wages of that season must recommend it to
many classes of people as a time for sailing. From what I can
learn of the matter, it looks to me as if there were rarely more
than a few thousand of these men that come and go, and that

[22] Second and third class arrivals, 1890: 77,815; 1891: 28,266.
"   "   "   "   departures, 1890: 48,794; 1891: 72,380.
(Resumen estadístico, pp. 28 and 30; see also our Fig. 18. Only of arrivals is
the sex indicated in the Resumen, namely on p. 19).
[23] Same references as in footnote 18 above: 1913, p. 93; 1924, p. 109. Both
figures are likewise for the calendar years.

[24] AVERAGE MONTHLY DEPARTURES OF EMIGRANT ALIENS
FROM THE ARGENTINE, 1891–1910*
(in hundreds of individuals)

Jan.	Feb.	Mar.	Apr.	May	June	July	Aug.	Sept.	Oct.	Nov.	Dec.	Year
26	38	55	59	63	60	52	36	28	24	23	22	486

*Computed from Resumen estadístico, p. 30 (year from p. 4).

it is a very fluctuating group, the individuals changing a good deal and very, very few coming with any regularity year after year. The experience of such men would quickly fit them to take advantage of the opportunities for permanent location that become available.

The steadiness of this (autumn) increase of departures is considerable. For nine of the twenty years (1891–1910) the month of largest figure was May; for five each, it was April and June (see Appendix, Table III). The phenomenon is probably normal. Winter is coming on in the south, and the fine weather in Europe. Just the same thing happens with the emigration from the United States. It increases very strikingly in November and December, so that on the average these months have an excess of 20,000 emigrants over the numbers usual for two months.[25] For most of the brief period before the World War since our immigration officers began to record the departures, the maximum occurred in those months. It will hardly be argued that we, too, have been getting seasonal workers without knowing it. It merely signifies that intending emigrants find November and December good months to leave the United States, and March to June to leave the Argentine. Figure 66 shows the facts of this fluctuation of Argentine receipts and losses of aliens from month to month in its actuality and will satisfy anyone of the regularity of the changes. The upsetting of the currents by the war is very plain, as well as the tendency to revert to the old form since the war ended.

The seasonal workers, whatever their number, have greatly assisted the Argentine people to make their harvests without burdening the labor market in the slack season.

[25] AVERAGE MONTHLY DEPARTURES OF EMIGRANT ALIENS FROM THE UNITED STATES, JULY 1, 1907–JUNE 30, 1914*
(in hundreds of individuals)

Jan.	Feb.	Mar.	Apr.	May	June	July	Aug.	Sept.	Oct.	Nov.	Dec.
229	158	179	220	222	257	261	245	235	251	349	342

*Computed from Annual Repts. of the Commissioner General of Immigration for the Fiscal Year Ended June 30, 1908, p. 13; 1909, p. 16; 1910, p. 14; 1911, p. 13; 1912, p. 67; 1913, p. 39; 1914, p. 36.

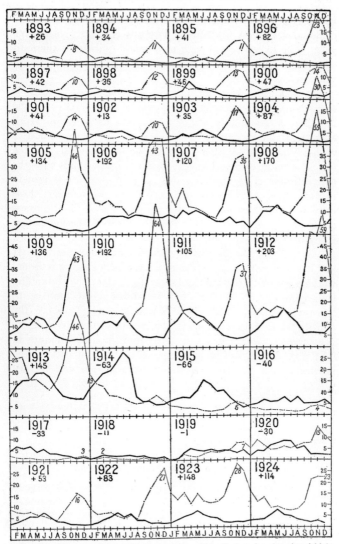

FIG. 66—Diagram of Argentine immigration (thin line) and emigration (thick line) in thousands by months, 1893-1924. (From the source cited below in the Appendix, Tables II and III, for the corresponding period.)

The number at the apex of each year's immigration curve indicates the maximum immigration during a month in that year; the number under each year, the gain (+) or loss (—) during that year.

NATIONALITY OF THE IMMIGRANTS

The Italians have been the most numerous of the immigrants in the long run, exceeding the Spaniards for the whole period of immigration in the proportion of the numbers 11 and 8. The French come next, but in much smaller numbers. For the three peoples, the numbers are as 11 to 8 to 1.[26] From 1908 to 1921 (except 1909) the Spaniards have each year somewhat outnumbered the Italians, having brought their greatest number—165,662—in 1912.[27] The greatest number of Italians coming in a single year was 127,348 in 1906, and of French 27,173 in 1889,[28] characteristic of the crest of the Celmán wave of spending, when the French were called in as "ministers of

[26] AVERAGE ANNUAL NUMBER OF IMMIGRANTS BY NATIONALITIES, 1857–1924*

(Second- and third-class passengers in hundreds of individuals)

	Italians	Spaniards	French	Austrians‡	Germans	Swiss	British	Russians	Average Total Immigration.†
1857–1860	31	8	3	0.7	0.6	0.7	1	0.3	50
1861–1865	67	13	3	0.7	0.8	1	2	0.4	94
1866–1870	160	32	13	0.9	2	3	6	0.5	225
1871–1875	166	57	45	1	4	7	12	0.5	297
1876–1880	139	32	21	8	4	5	8	0.4	224
1881–1885	365	46	41	11	12	11	10	0.2	510
1886–1890	622	271	146	22	16	14	22	8	1,172
1891–1895	321	73	22	5	9	5	3	30	473
1896–1900	529	191	29	13	9	4	5	13	824
1901–1905	579	293	28	27	12	4	7	40	1,052
1906–1910	1,013	1,012	40	48	27	6	18	130	2,476
1911–1913	844	1,356	49	52	42	9	23	164	2,837
1914–1918	110	242	12	5	6	2	6	14	451
1919–1924	504	398	17	9	6	6	13	10	1,184
Absolute totals in hundreds (not averages) 1857–1924§	26040	17803	2269	919	1007	370	644	1693	

*Computed from Resumen estadístico, pp. 8–14 and 16.
  †   "   "   "   "   p. 32.
‡All nationalities from Austria-Hungary. Hungarians were counted separately since 1905 according to Hiller, *op. cit.*, p. 143.
§Resumen estadístico, pp. 4–5.
[27] Resumen estadístico, p. 9. Totals for 1908–1921 (including 1909): Spaniards, 973,000; Italians, 676,000 (*ibid.*, pp. 8 and 9).
[28] *ibid.*, pp. 8 and 10 respectively.

luxury and extravagance" (German point of view). But the
French are entitled to claim to be the "aristocrats of immigration." They never came as unskilled laborers but as
skilled; and not merely as barbers and dressmakers and
pastry cooks but also as experts in the arts of civic adornment and engineering construction. They have contributed to
the Republic a service out of proportion to their numbers.

The war, of course, upset the regular currents of European
emigration, but they tend to reëstablish themselves along pre-
war lines except that the Germans are coming to the Argentine in
greater numbers than ever before.[29] It is strange that the French
and Russians maintained a considerable emigration throughout
the war, while the British, who had the ships, ceased sending a-
way their people almost as completely as their Austrian and German foes, who protested that the English were strangling them.

The Spaniards in the Argentine Republic have adopted city
labor as definitely as the Italians have made rural tasks their
own. They stand very much apart from the Creoles. The ties
of blood do not make the Spaniards especially attractive to
the Spanish Americans. I should say the Spaniards are less
popular than the Italians. Spain is little visited, little studied,
and much less admired than France. I fancy this neglect

[29] ANNUAL NUMBER OF IMMIGRANTS BY NATIONALITIES, 1914–1924*
(Second- and third-class passengers in hundreds of individuals)

	Italians	Spaniards	French	Austrians	Germans	Swiss	British	Russians	Total Immigration.†
1914	361	522	26	21	23	6	13	54	1,153
1915	113	253	13	2	3	3	7	8	453
1916	52	218	8	0.7	1	1	6	4	330
1917	17	125	7	0.3	0.2	0.5	2	3	181
1918	9	92	8	0.1	0.1	0.5	2	2	137
1919	90	208	21	2	20	3	17	1	413
1920	302	407	23	7	48	5	19	4	870
1921	400	401	12	6	41	6	12	3	981
1922	578	433	18	8	65	7	11	7	1,293
1923	920	484	15	22	101	8	9	30	1,951
1924	731	457	12	11	102	6	9	14	1,599

*Resumen estadístico, pp. 8–14 and 16.
†   "   "   p. 32.

comes in part from the Wars of Liberation from Spain, in which all Spanish-American countries participated, wars whose events are kept fresh in tender minds at school, with the Spaniard in the unpleasant rôle of the enemy. The English are put in something of the same shadow in our own schools, as if the function of history were to keep alive the animosities of the past. Brazil had a happier parting from her mother country. When Napoleon came conquering across the Iberian Peninsula, the Portuguese monarch was lucky enough to get away by ship and carry the delights of a royal court to his much-pleased subjects in Brazil. Their sorrow came at the monarch's departure when Napoleon collapsed, and it was assuaged by his leaving his son as emperor. Instead of being liberated the Brazilians were imperialized. As a result of these circumstances Brazil cherishes a most kindly feeling for Portugal and the Portuguese. However, in spite of the close ties between the two countries, the Italians are more numerous than the Portuguese of European birth.[30]

Conclusion

The Italian has not merely an attraction in the New World, but an urge out of Italy in the utter hopelessness of the prospects of the laborer in his native land. This is a fortunate circumstance for the Argentine Republic. If the day ever comes when the Republic actually opens land to deserving Italians, abolishing the present Creole unfulfillment of Creole administrative regulations and the vexatious delays and disattention to the wishes of the poor foreigner on the part of Creole place-holders, no worth-while corner of Argentine land need fail of its harvest. There is no need of advertising, no need of propaganda. "Obras son amores y no muchas palabras" say the ladies of the south, their version of "actions speak louder than words." A change of heart that is a change of deeds will

[30] 558,405 Italians, 433,577 Portuguese (Synopse do recenseamento realizado em 1 de Setembro de 1920: População do Brazil. Direct. Gen. do Estadist., Minist. da Agric., Industria e Commercio, Rio de Janeiro, 1924, p. 16).

be known in numberless villages of Italy with the first returning steamer. What the returned emigrant displays of wealth, what he reports of ownership of land is believed. Thousands of immigrants, hundreds of whom are admirably equipped for the life of the pioneer, are on tiptoe to start as soon as word comes to them in trustworthy ways that by strenuous labor a man may with certainty win land of his own.

APPENDIX

TABLE I—ANNUAL ARGENTINE IMMIGRATION AND EMIGRATION, 1857–1924

For a graph based on this table see, above, Fig. 18

Year	Immigrants	Emigrants	Year	Immigrants	Emigrants
1857	4,951	1,899	1891	28,266	72,380
1858	4,658	2,045	1892	39,973	29,893
1859	4,735	2,375	1893	52,067	26,055
1860	5,656	2,581	1894	54,720	20,586
1861	6,301	3,379	1895	61,226	20,390
1862	6,716	3,502	1896	102,673	20,415
1863	10,408	5,139	1897	72,978	31,192
1864	11,682	7,229	1898	67,130	30,802
1865	11,767	5,743	1899	84,442	38,397
1866	13,696	6,415	1900	84,851	38,334
1867	13,225	6,557	1901	90,127	48,697
1868	25,919	12,302	1902	57,992	44,558
1869	28,958	15,999	1903	75,227	40,610
1870	30,898	16,711	1904	125,567	38,923
1871	15,088	9,318	1905	177,117	42,869
1872	26,218	16,241	1906	252,536	60,124
1873	48,382	30,722	1907	209,103	90,190
1874	40,674	25,966	1908	255,710	85,412
1875	18,332	11,645	1909	231,084	94,644
1876	14,532	9,906	1910	289,640	97,854
1877	14,675	9,209	1911	225,772	120,709
1878	23,624	15,090	1912	323,403	120,260
1879	32,717	25,113	1913	302,047	156,829
1880	26,643	22,555	1914	115,321	178,684
1881	31,431	22,374	1915	45,290	111,459
1882	41,041	8,720	1916	32,990	73,348
1883	52,472	9,510	1917	18,064	50,995
1884	49,623	14,444	1918	13,701	24,075
1885	80,618	14,585	1919	41,299	42,279
1886	65,655	13,907	1920	87,032	57,187
1887	94,608	13,630	1921	98,086	44,638
1888	129,115	16,842	1922	129,263	45,993
1889	218,744	40,649	1923	195,063	46,810
1890	77,815	48,794	1924	159,939	46,105

These figures represent the number of second- and third-class passengers arriving at Buenos Aires from Europe and leaving Buenos Aires for Europe, such being the categories respectively designated immigrants and emigrants in the Argentine official statistics. They are taken from: Resumen estadístico del movimiento migratorio en la República Argentina, años 1857–1924, Direcc. Gen. de Inmigración, Buenos Aires, 1925, pp. 32, 30–31, 52 (except emigrants, 1857–1880, the numbers of which were kindly communicated for this inquiry by Señor Jorge Meneclier, Chief of Immigration Statistics of the Dirección General de Inmigración, Buenos Aires).

There is no record of the numbers coming and going by the land frontiers, but it cannot often pass a thousand a year, to judge from the number of citizens of neighboring countries included at census takings as resident in the Republic.

TABLE II—IMMIGRATION TO THE ARGENTINE BY MONTHS, 1858–1924*
(Second- and third-class passengers in hundreds of individuals)

For a graph of this table for 1893–1924 see, above, Fig. 66

Year	Jan.	Feb.	Mar.	Apr.	May	June	July	Aug.	Sept.	Oct.	Nov.	Dec.	Total for Year
1858	7	4	6	2	4	3	3	4	3	3	3	5	47
1859	5	7	6	2	2	3	5	2	4	3	2	5	47
1860	7	5	4	6	4	3	5	5	4	3	6	5	57
1861	8	5	7	4	3	5	5	5	6	2	5	9	63
1862	6	7	2	7	4	4	5	7	6	6	6	6	67
1863	10	8	9	8	7	7	8	8	7	8	9	16	104
1864	16	16	10	4	6	7	7	8	6	9	6	22	117
1865	15	6	6	9	7	11	13	7	7	10	10	16	118
1866	19	9	10	12	12	9	9	10	11	7	10	21	137
1867	17	10	14	15	11	14	20	14	12	10	15	19	132
1868	34	22	39	31	23	23	15	15	12	22	17	40	259
1869	...	...	...	...	...	...	...	...	...	...	...	...	290
1870	30	28	22	15	24	21	16	13	9	15	24	23	309
1871	25	11	10	16	14	13	7	6	8	10	17	14	151
1872	18	9	9	17	19	29	19	15	10	33	31	53	262
1873	33	32	38	45	38	18	27	25	35	64	63	66	484
1874	59	50	44	29	27	29	25	16	26	32	39	30	407
1875	25	19	14	15	15	9	9	7	9	16	19	25	183
1876	11	13	9	10	13	14	8	6	7	18	23	14	145
1877	11	11	10	13	10	9	8	6	8	17	17	27	147
1878	25	17	18	18	18	10	8	14	14	15	46	34	236
1879	20	20	26	18	23	15	17	18	16	39	56	59	327
1880	24	17	18	18	18	10	10	14	13	35	44	45	266
1881	19	20	24	18	23	15	16	16	19	39	59	47	314
1882	28	20	31	17	25	21	11	27	13	70	77	72	410
1883	63	28	36	39	26	39	21	36	20	74	73	70	525
1884	68	36	36	25	35	20	32	29	42	48	28	96	496
1885	150	91	66	46	65	41	30	25	29	70	87	107	806
1886	70	40	45	42	32	36	34	32	44	88	91	103	657
1887	123	51	37	51	49	55	46	46	68	119	138	202	946
1888	111	102	83	72	82	51	64	71	76	160	184	233	1291
1889	199	203	154	157	163	174	131	154	147	215	294	197	2187
1890	120	94	83	69	66	46	28	43	37	45	79	69	778
1891	38	24	18	17	15	10	15	20	22	28	42	35	283
1892	16	18	15	14	17	20	30	28	41	59	85	55	400
1893	45	30	31	35	29	28	29	36	30	82	85	61	521
1894	48	28	35	29	30	32	30	20	35	76	105	79	547

TABLE II—*Continued*

Year	Jan.	Feb.	Mar.	Apr.	May	June	July	Aug.	Sept.	Oct.	Nov.	Dec.	Total for Year
1895	39	31	33	26	37	28	36	25	52	86	107	111	612
1896	74	49	56	35	48	46	47	51	71	140	230	179	1027
1897	90	72	67	47	44	37	32	35	46	75	99	85	730
1898	43	48	40	36	34	33	33	35	45	91	122	110	671
1899	68	61	56	45	48	41	47	42	78	107	132	120	844
1900	69	56	40	46	45	44	39	44	54	125	145	143	849
1901	79	58	72	50	74	63	39	38	61	119	137	112	901
1902	48	41	36	26	30	34	21	30	37	82	102	94	580
1903	38	33	39	34	35	37	31	36	63	105	169	132	752
1904	79	57	49	56	60	52	47	56	95	184	302	218	1256
1905	97	83	88	73	90	74	82	86	113	244	465	277	1771
1906	226	143	138	151	126	126	87	111	171	390	428	428	2525
1907	193	126	206	127	119	109	81	74	124	250	338	354	2091
1908	161	171	123	128	126	104	98	133	180	390	552	392	2557
1909	168	126	129	139	118	91	98	108	158	344	425	406	2311
1910	169	164	163	152	154	150	110	159	188	340	637	510	2896
1911	268	232	153	135	102	126	103	77	123	214	353	372	2258
1912	205	148	175	156	181	167	145	155	305	508	498	591	3234
1913	301	258	263	160	165	144	119	154	230	378	460	388	3020
1914	188	146	133	94	91	81	68	59	60	71	91	71	1153
1915	48	43	35	36	32	21	20	23	27	51	62	53	453
1916	33	31	23	25	24	20	19	17	20	38	43	37	330
1917	26	19	12	17	10	8	9	8	11	19	18	25	181
1918	15	12	19	16	10	9	8	2	22	2	5	7	137
1919	7	7	28	19	15	29	38	35	41	48	73	74	413
1920	50	85	63	44	49	60	50	63	72	77	149	108	870
1921	86	72	69	72	60	56	47	40	78	116	159	136	981
1922	86	64	68	70	54	48	57	45	121	181	230	268	1293
1923	153	125	156	109	152	114	109	112	136	220	282	253	1951
1924	164	113	132	85	92	80	74	81	109	217	226	227	1599

*Rounded off to the nearest hundred from the following sources:

1858–1870: Rejistro de la República Argentina, 1864–1870, as cited in Georg Hiller: Einwanderung und Einwanderungspolitik in Argentinien, Berlin, 1912, p. 139.

1871–1880: Figures kindly communicated for this inquiry by Señor Jorge Meneclier, Chief of Immigration Statistics of the Dirección General de Inmigración, Buenos Aires.

1881–1924: Resumen estadístico del movimiento migratorio en la República Argentina, años 1857–1924, Direcc. Gen. de Inmigración, Buenos Aires, 1925, pp. 28–29 (1881–1920) and 52 (1921–1924).

All annual totals were taken directly from the annual figures in the Resumen estadístico, p. 32, and, as all figures in the present table are rounded off, do not, for a given year, necessarily tally exactly with the totals of the monthly figures as here given. For the period 1858–1870 no exact concordance between the two sets of totals should be expected, as the monthly figures are taken from one source and the totals from another.

TABLE III—EMIGRATION FROM THE ARGENTINE BY MONTHS, 1881–1924*
(Second- and third-class passengers in hundreds of individuals)

For a graph of this table for 1893–1924 see, above, Fig. 66

Year	Jan.	Feb.	Mar.	Apr.	May	June	July	Aug.	Sept.	Oct.	Nov.	Dec.	Total for Year
1881	10	20	12	19	24	32	20	20	19	21	17	20	224
1882	5	5	10	9	8	7	5	7	8	9	8	6	87
1883	9	6	10	7	8	10	8	9	8	8	8	5	95
1884	8	8	10	16	13	12	10	10	15	15	10	18	144
1885	9	8	9	10	13	12	14	14	11	22	12	12	146
1886	9	7	11	12	9	11	8	7	17	20	14	12	139
1887	8	10	10	13	10	11	11	13	13	11	11	16	136
1888	10	9	11	12	18	17	14	15	10	19	14	18	168
1889	38	39	36	33	34	29	32	37	31	29	34	34	406
1890	18	19	36	38	41	48	43	47	47	68	47	37	488
1891	56	67	70	100	83	71	79	63	48	39	28	19	724
1892	21	30	32	31	48	30	32	23	12	11	14	16	299
1893	15	16	28	46	35	30	26	18	12	12	11	12	261
1894	14	16	26	33	17	17	17	17	14	15	11	8	206
1895	9	12	23	23	19	28	20	22	15	13	10	8	204
1896	8	14	20	21	26	28	22	17	13	13	8	14	204
1897	15	26	45	31	38	34	35	24	20	14	17	13	312
1898	20	27	36	35	37	34	34	25	16	13	18	14	308
1899	17	23	38	79	50	43	40	31	19	16	14	13	384
1900	19	27	39	40	57	48	48	30	24	16	19	17	383
1901	27	55	53	52	60	51	52	36	32	25	22	22	487
1902	28	41	49	56	56	57	46	33	24	19	17	19	446
1903	20	32	48	36	47	64	52	38	23	16	15	15	406
1904	17	25	41	46	58	52	49	32	22	17	17	13	389
1905	17	26	51	50	59	56	50	36	26	20	21	17	429
1906	22	36	62	84	84	84	72	40	35	29	27	26	601
1907	38	72	108	92	110	95	78	59	58	79	55	57	902
1908	34	69	107	105	133	102	86	56	42	39	40	42	854
1909	66	81	110	105	143	133	92	54	44	37	43	39	946
1910	53	73	111	119	102	142	110	74	50	45	51	47	979
1911	90	120	165	170	147	138	109	83	54	45	41	45	1207
1912	56	82	114	134	136	171	138	111	66	67	65	63	1203
1913	89	133	160	160	193	195	176	129	95	85	79	79	1568
1914	122	160	193	200	241	284	258	89	64	68	51	55	1787
1915	69	77	85	81	120	159	140	107	111	76	54	36	1115
1916	45	52	68	60	62	83	58	79	51	53	55	68	733
1917	50	69	60	69	44	55	38	37	30	24	15	19	510
1918	15	17	26	24	20	23	26	20	23	16	10	19	241
1919	4	3	31	53	47	41	48	40	43	42	29	43	423
1920	17	40	39	63	74	84	83	48	57	22	23	21	572
1921	21	30	43	56	53	71	50	33	32	20	19	19	446
1922	20	31	42	53	69	52	65	37	35	22	23	19	460
1923	23	32	50	57	71	53	48	41	22	20	26	23	468
1924	29	34	36	55	76	54	50	35	29	20	27	15	461

*From Resumen estadístico, pp. 30–31 (1881–1920) and 52 (1921–1924).

INDEX